Rethinking the European Unic..

Rethinking World Politics

Series Editor: Professor Michael Cox

In an age of increased academic specialization where more and more books about smaller and smaller topics are becoming the norm, this major new series is designed to provide a forum and stimulus for leading scholars to address big issues in world politics in an accessible but original manner. A key aim is to transcend the intellectual and disciplinary boundaries which have so often served to limit rather than enhance our understanding of the modern world. In the best tradition of engaged scholarship, it aims to provide clear new perspectives to help make sense of a world in flux.

Each book addresses a major issue or event that has had a formative influence on the twentieth-century or the twenty-first-century world which is now emerging. Each makes its own distinctive contribution as well as providing an original but accessible guide to competing lines of interpretation.

Taken as a whole, the series will rethink contemporary international politics in ways that are lively, informed and – above all – provocative.

Rethinking the European Union

Nathaniel Copsey

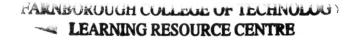

First published 2015 by
PALGRAVE

Palgrave in the UK is an imprint of Macmillan Publishers Limited, registered in England, company number 785998, of 4 Crinan Street, London N1 9XW.

Palgrave in the US is a division of St Martin's Press LLC, 175 Fifth Avenue, New York, NY 10010.

Palgrave is a global academic imprint of the above companies and is represented throughout the world.

Palgrave® and Macmillan® are registered trademarks in the United States, the United Kingdom, Europe and other countries

ISBN: 978-1-137-34167-9   hardback
ISBN: 978-1-137-34166-2   paperback

This book is printed on paper suitable for recycling and made from fully managed and sustained forest sources. Logging, pulping and manufacturing processes are expected to conform to the environmental regulations of the country of origin.

A catalogue record for this book is available from the British Library.

A catalog record for this book is available from the Library of Congress.

Printed in China

To Tatyana

Contents

List of Tables and Figures

Tables

Figures

Foreword

Thinking critically about the European project has never been easy. Indeed, for many years even to raise difficult questions either about its design, coherence or effectiveness almost seemed to cast those who did so into the camp of the no-nothings and the troglodytes. And perhaps for understandable reasons. 'Europe' had after all been one of the great success stories of the late 20th century. It also offered an alternative vision of the West to what many saw as the aggressive image of the United States – a different way of doing international relations no less and one that at the time seemed to appeal to millions of people around the world. It is little wonder that its defenders could write so effusively about it. And how effusively. Thus one leading American predicted with some certainty in 2002 that as the American era faded, which it was bound to do, then the US's place at the head of the international table would be taken, not by a rising China or an emerging Asia (today's favourites), but by the European Union itself. A couple of years on, and another book appeared with the now almost tragic title (and I paraphrase somewhat) that something known as a 'European dream' would slowly but surely – quietly even – eclipse that of America. Another year, and another volume on the same subject. However , this time Europe appeared not in the guise of a dream according to one well known public intellectual, but a serious international player that would one day be running the 21st century.

How cruel the world can be! And how wrong some of those earlier predictions about Europe's future turned out to be – sadly. But as Nat Copsey shows in this challenging volume, the roots of what he calls Europe's 'existential crisis' can be traced back a very long time, certainly long before the so-called 'Euro crisis' engulfed countries as far apart as Ireland and Greece while doing so much damage to the wider European project. The current economic crisis has not caused the damage alone but has rather 'exposed' some pre-existing 'flaws' in the EU's basic economic architecture. Moreover, in dealing with these problems the EU has altered 'quite profoundly' and will no doubt continue to do so in the future. But on one issue we should all be clear, he warns: the challenges facing the European Union in the wake of its most 'testing crisis in 60 years' are profound. Indeed, they are so profound – as others like George Soros have argued – that it is not beyond the bounds of possibility for the project to 'disintegrate in its entirety'. Whether or not this happens or not we can only wait and see. Nothing is certain. But clearly difficult and testing times lie ahead. It is one of the many virtues of this fine volume that it explains just how testing and difficult those times are going to be.

Professor Michael Cox
LSE IDEAS

Acknowledgements

First of all, my thanks are due to the series editor, Michael Cox, and my publisher, Steven Kennedy, whose idea it was to produce a volume on the European Union in the 'Rethinking World Politics' series. For providing extensive constructive feedback on the project, including reading the complete draft more than once, I am deeply grateful to Richard Connolly, Tim Haughton and Darina Malová. For their insightful observations on both the manuscript as a whole and individual chapters I would like to thank Graham Avery, Vlado Bilčík, Michael Cox, Paul Copeland, Anneliese Dodds, John Gaffney, Simon Green, Dermot Hodson, Christian Lequesne, Alan Mayhew, Anand Menon, Willie Paterson, Karolina Pomorska, Carolyn Rowe, Jean-Marc Trouille, Loukas Tsoukalis, Ed Turner, Uwe Wunderlich, and the two anonymous referees. All remaining errors are, of course, my own.

This book took many months to write and is also the product of more than a decade spent reflecting on the nature of the politics, policy and political economy of the European integration project. Many friends and colleagues not already mentioned have influenced my thinking about the EU, including Derek Averre, Simon Bulmer, David Harley, Saskia and Joachim Hermann, Christophe Hillion, Jörg Monar, Peter Rodford, Adam Steinhouse, Mariusz Sielski, Aleks Szczerbiak and, of course, all the contributors to the Journal of Common Market Studies Annual Review whose combined intellectual efforts since 2008 constitute the most complete picture of the European Union at a time of existential crisis. For insights on the big picture of European integration viewed from the policy world within the EU, its member states and its neighbours, I would like to thank Malcolm Harbour, Volodymyr Mialkovskyi, Mirja Peterson and Emma Reynolds, as well as colleagues in the European institutions who prefer to remain anonymous.

I am also grateful to the participants at the Journal of Common Market Studies Annual Review lecture and seminar that took place at Comenius University in May 2013 for their helpful comments on some of the ideas presented in this manuscript, notably Gerda Falkner, Attila Ágh and Leszek Jesień, as well as to colleagues at Comenius University not mentioned above, including Zsolt Gál, Erik Láštic and Marek Rybář.

Institutionally, I would like to thank Aston University and my colleagues in the Aston Centre for Europe and the Politics and International Relations group, particularly Simon Green, for encouragement, moral and intellectual support, and for providing the six-month period of study leave that allowed me to write the bulk of this book. My students at Aston University in Birmingham, the Institut d'Etudes Politiques in Rennes and the European Studies Institute of MGIMO in Moscow all helped form and shape my thinking on the EU and the effects of Eurozone crisis on it. Anne-Claire Marangoni provided diligent, wide-ranging and invaluable research assistance.

Lastly and most importantly, I would like to thank my partner Tatyana Güveli for her unconditional support and encouragement without which this book would not have been written.

Introduction

The Eurozone crisis and the response to it provide an ideal opportunity to rethink the European Union (EU) and European integration more broadly. After the European sovereign debt crisis began in 2009, hard on the heels of the worldwide financial crisis that began in 2007 and the Great Recession of 2008–10, there followed a steadily growing stream of comment about what the EU should do to address its predicament (Aglietta and Brand, 2013; Beck, 2013; Giddens, 2014; Goulard, 2013; Goulard and Monti, 2012; Habermas, 2012; Heisbourg, 2013; Herzog, 2013; Piris, 2011; Streeck, 2013). Surprise and alarm were expressed about the extent of the assault on both the positivist *idea* of Europe as the most effective means of responding to social, economic and political challenges and the normative *ideal* of Europe as the world's most advanced, effective and exciting experiment in international cooperation. As a result, there began a serious discussion of what the choices for Europe were or should be. The aim of this book is to contribute to this debate by examining the effects of the Eurozone crisis on the EU and the integration project more broadly. In doing so, it follows a bold tradition in treating Europe as a 'whole rather than the sum of its components' (Outhwaite, 2008, p. 2; see also *inter alia* Beck and Grande, 2004; Crouch, 1999; Delanty and Rumford, 2005, Delanty, 2006; Therborn, 1995).

No one should underestimate the gravity of the challenges facing the EU in the wake of its most testing crisis. Just because it would be exceptionally hard to unravel European integration does not make it impossible for the project to disintegrate in its entirety. European integration is a social experiment; an innovative, *sui generis* system of supranational government that is qualitatively different from anything that has been tried until now in human history. However, social experiments can fail, as witnesses to the Central and Eastern European revolutions of 1989 can testify. In the spring of 1988, the monolithic institutions, policies and ideologies underpinning one-party rule in the Eastern half of the European continent – democratic centralism, Marxism-Leninism, censorship,

1

the planned economy, the Brezhnev doctrine and so on – appeared unassailable. A few years later all were gone. Of course, such analogies have their limits. The EU is ruled with the consent of its people by politicians who have been democratically elected in competitive elections. Unlike the Communist world, it is wealthy, and remained in aggregate the largest economy in the world in the 2010s, even if the durability of its prosperity was less certain than before. The EU of the 2010s is also a more deeply integrated space than the vanished world of European Communism: the EU has its own currency in the Euro, open borders and a very high level of movement of people as well as goods between states. But history has shown that social experiments do fail and few foresee their impending demise. In January 2013, in what could be a sign of the times, the British Prime Minister, David Cameron, promised a referendum on whether the UK should leave the EU if his party was returned with a parliamentary majority in the 2015 General Election (Copsey and Haughton, 2014).

Although the Eurozone crisis served to focus minds on Europe's shortcomings, its underlying social, economic and political problems had been mounting for several decades. Since European birth rates began to drop in the 1970s, it was clear that Europe would face a day of reckoning for public spending and the welfare state as a result of societal ageing in the 21st century. Unemployment remained stubbornly high across much of Europe between the late 1970s and the 2010s and the twin challenges of growing inequality and social exclusion had also been on the rise (Piketty, 2014). Whilst the macroeconomic picture varied from member state to member state, in much the same way that the fortunes of Arizona, Mississippi or Vermont in the United States vary considerably, a clear trend was discernible. What is most striking here perhaps is how little success both national governments and the EU had had in tackling these negative long-term trends. For example, French President, Jacques Chirac, pledged to make the reduction of unemployment the priority in the first year of his twelve-year Presidency in 1995. Almost twenty years later, François Hollande also cited job creation as his top priority for 2014. French Presidents come and go, but unemployment and other serious social challenges remain, in France and in the rest of Europe too. Indeed, in many cases they have worsened over the past 20 years. Across much of Europe in the 2010s, governments appeared incapable of action on painful structural reform, not least because the balance of evidence suggested that its effects were mixed. Together with many of those who elected them, Europe's leaders were complicit in what amounted to a collective denial of the sheer scale of the challenges that would result from the ageing, low-growth, high-unemployment and high-inequality society that Europe had become.

Thus it is not simply the Eurozone crisis, its effects and the remedies that have been proposed to resolve it that serve as a rationale for this book. It is also motivated by a desire to look both beyond and behind Europe's existential crisis in order to trace holistically the state of the EU in the 2010s after more than half a century of integration. Other attempts to do this pre-date the crisis (Menon, 2008) and, therefore, an updated perspective is required. My reasoning for this deep and broad approach is as follows. The Eurozone crisis exposed some major flaws in the EU's economic architecture to which EU policy-makers responded with an incomplete yet important overhaul of that same architecture (Hodson, 2011). Whether the package of reforms will succeed is a moot point at the time of writing (2014) and time will tell. However, it is safe to assume that little consideration was given to the legitimation of such far-reaching changes to economic governance, fiscal policy, fiscal solidarity, common debt insurance and so on. European Council President, Van Rompuy's *Towards a Genuine Economic and Monetary Union* report merely observed that 'strong mechanisms for legitimate and accountable joint decision making will be needed' (Van Rompuy, 2012, p. 6), without indicating what these will be. There was only a vague statement that there would be 'involvement of European and national parliaments' (p. 7).

At the time of the Maastricht treaty negotiations in 1991–92, EU policy-makers gambled by building a monetary union with a decentralized approach to economic policy-making (Hodson, 2011). Their gamble was partly about economics and doubts about whether a one-size-fits-all interest rate would work for all Eurozone economies. It was also partly about politics. Yet responding to questions about what to do in terms of harmonizing fiscal policy or implementing fiscal solidarity would in turn have required some serious and demanding questions be answered about the legitimation of EU policy-making, questions that the member states were simply not prepared to address at that time. By the mid-2010s it was clear that the EU had altered quite profoundly as a result of the Eurozone crisis. This reopened a Pandora's box of awkward, exceptionally hard-to-answer questions, primarily about the legitimacy of EU decision making, but also relating to the myriad sensitive issues that lay behind this central question of legitimacy. These include the degree of solidarity between the citizens of 28 member states (necessary to provide popular approval for a budgetary union or Eurobonds), the extent to which a shared European identity could be said to exist in the 2010s (arguably a condition for solidarity), and the sustainability of a European integration project that for over half a century had been more or less exclusively market-based and in consequence did not require much attention to be paid to questions of legitimacy, solidarity and identity.

Continuing in this scene-setting vein, it is appropriate to begin with three very brief remarks on the nature of the Eurozone crisis, the response to it and its effects. The first observation is that the principal effect of the Eurozone crisis was to exacerbate – and perhaps even to exaggerate – pre-existing, long-standing and deep-rooted issues that cut across Europe's social, political and economic spheres. Prior to the Great Recession of 2007–09, such issues as drooping rates of economic growth, the ageing society or declining European competitiveness *vis-à-vis* the new entrants into the world economy were at the heart of elite debates on the EU. Since the crisis, these discussions have begun to spread, slowly, across the rest of European society. The explanation for this probably lies in the fact that the kinds of challenges that previously featured in elite-level discourse (for example, *Sapir Report* (Aghion *et al.*, 2003)) were viewed either as simply risks (that by definition might be avoided, somehow) or as bleak prognoses (that by definition lay somewhere in the future). By the mid-2010s, in the aftermath of near state bankruptcy in Southern Europe, sky-high unemployment (25–30% in Greece and Spain (Eurostat, 2013e) and plummeting living standards (for example, down by 13% in the UK (Institute of Fiscal Studies, 2012), 22% in Latvia, and at least 16% in Greece (European Commission, Economic and Financial Affairs, 2013b)), yesterday's gloomy predictions had become today's thoroughly disagreeable reality.

Unsurprisingly, Europeans were deeply dissatisfied both with the effects of the crisis and with the lacklustre reaction of their political leaders. In 2013, in only four EU member states did a majority of the public approve of the actions of the EU's leadership. This was a sharp reduction from 2007, with support falling most in the 15–30 age bracket, traditionally the EU's strongest supporters (Gallup, 2014). Their understandable discontent was manifested in the measureable growth of public dissatisfaction with politics and government in general. 'Anti-system' parties steadily gained favour across Europe. In the European Parliament elections of 2014 they even topped the polls in some member states: France's Front National took 24.9% of the vote, ahead of the mainstream opposition UMP on 20.8% and streets ahead of the socialist government's 14.0%. In Britain, the United Kingdom Independence Party (UKIP) also took first place with 27.5% of the popular vote. Similarly strong results were recorded by, *inter alia*, the Danish People's Party, Beppe Grillo's Five Star Movement in Italy, Syriza and Golden Dawn in Greece (for full results, see European Parliament, 2014). For all the panic and excitement caused by the 2014 results, it should be underlined that, because of low turnout, support for radical anti-EU parties still amounted to only one in ten voters in both the UK and France. Moreover, the results themselves were rather typical of European elections, which voters tend to use as an opportunity to punish their rulers. In the wake of the most serious economic crisis since the 1930s, it was no surprise that voters were angry. Most people do not distinguish between the failures of the EU and the shortcomings of national governments. Of course, it is clearly in the interests of national governments to encourage the electorate to blame Brussels, which many national politicians do. Predictably, this prompted both British Prime Minister Cameron and French President Hollande to insist, sternly, the morning after the elections in May 2014 that Brussels must change (BBC, 2014a, 2014b). All the same, the diverse doctrines of Euroscepticism had by then ceased to be a minority faith. Anti-EU sentiments were being expressed not only by a wider swathe of public opinion but also by the political mainstream as established parties jumped on the populist bandwagon.

My second point is that, despite the package of reforms aimed at shoring up the single currency, comparatively little had been done by the mid-2010s to rescue both the EU and government in Europe more generally from what I would characterize as a kind of existential crisis. A prime example of the seriousness of the situation was underlined by the apparent powerlessness of the EU's collective leadership. After the onset of the Great Recession and the Eurozone crisis, the process of dealing with the numerous financial and economic emergencies in Ireland, Portugal, Greece and Cyprus consumed more or less the entire energy of the European Council as the collective leadership of the EU. Prior to the crisis, the heads of state and government met on average four times a year. In 2008 and 2009, this increased to eight meetings (including Eurozone Summits), rising further to 11 meetings in 2010 alone. The Eurozone crisis dominated the European agenda, yet seemingly could not adequately or satisfactorily be resolved. Worse still, as a result of the crisis's dominance of the European agenda, more or less all the long-standing structural political and economic problems – ageing societies, competitiveness, industrial decline and so on – that faced the EU were ignored. Ultimately, much time and effort were squandered to little effect. What the evidence of the European Council's attempts to resolve the Eurozone crisis appears to prove is that the Union as it was constituted in the 2010s was institutionally not entirely fit for purpose, or at least not entirely fit for crisis.

Despite claims that the governor of the European Central Bank (ECB), 'Super Mario' Draghi, saved the Euro from the risk of immediate breakup with his promise on 26 July 2012 to do 'whatever it takes', in reality rather little of importance to the Eurozone crisis had changed. It is true that the ECB had given itself the right to purchase (indirectly) the government debt of Eurozone countries that got into trouble. It is also the case that new rules and regulations for governing the Euro (such as a Banking Union) and addressing some of the imbalances across the Eurozone and the EU economy (through the European Semester) that were at the heart of the sovereign debt crisis had been drawn up and were beginning to be implemented. But it is also true that no serious attempt was made to unpick economically, socially and politically the underlying causes of the EU's malaise, with a view to a holistic understanding of what might need to be done to remedy them. This book attempts to fill this gap, which is an essential task given that the roots of the Eurozone's troubles lie far deeper than the Euro itself.

My third contention in setting the scene for this book is that the Great Recession and the Eurozone crisis weakened Europe and the EU even more than is commonly recognized. As a result, the political, economic and social choices for Europe had changed by the 2010s. Such an assumption requires examination and interrogation. This is achieved by answering the questions that lie at the heart of this book: Did the Eurozone crisis affect the EU and the European integration project fundamentally, and, if so, how? As was noted above, the Eurozone crisis exposed stark, pre-existing weaknesses that had been building up for a long time. Thus, to understand fully the damage wrought by the Eurozone crisis, it is first necessary to get a detailed picture of the state of the EU and the European integration project on the eve of the crisis in 2007. Europe 'the Union' and Europe 'the project' are grouped together here with good reason. The two advanced together from the 1950s to the 2010s, and this resulted in the creation of what can best be understood as a 'polity-in-the-making' (see also Shaw, 2000). The use of this term to describe the EU is, in my view, less bold than it seems. Schmidt went even further, hinting that the term 'state' might be more appropriate given that 'there is no other word that does justice to the growing power and developing sovereignty – however contingent – of the EU' (2006, pp. 10–14). In essence this book is about the EU as a polity-in-the-making at a time of profound economic crisis. (It should be emphasized here that describing the EU as a 'polity-in-the-making' is not meant to imply the eventual construction of a complete polity.)

These three points of departure have established that a synthetic, analytical review of the European integration project over a long time frame is required in order to uncover the roots of the crisis of European integration in the 2010s. Fortunately, more than half a century of scholarly research into the European integration process provides an extensive literature on which to draw. Building on Newton's observation to Hooke that 'if I have seen further it is by standing on the shoulders of giants' (Newton, 1676), this work advances by synthesizing some of the vast wealth of EU studies literature and, where possible, shedding some new light on existing theoretical controversies, rather than engaging in building new theories. Other scholars have pointed to the way in which historical–institutional developments have shaped the evolution of the EU (Geddes, 2013; Outhwaite, 2008), but no similar attempt has been made to assess the impact of the Eurozone crisis on the Union through the lens of these underlying trends. All academics are, to an extent, synthesizers because new research builds on the foundations of what has been done before. This work is merely more direct in naming its approach.

In carrying out this synthetic and analytical review, a number of broad and crosscutting arguments are put forward. The first is that the Great Recession and the Eurozone's woes produced, or perhaps revealed, an underlying existential crisis for the EU that was four-fold in nature. In the first place, it was a crisis of who identified with the EU. Secondly, and closely linked to this crisis of identity, came a crisis of popular legitimacy. Thirdly, the bitter fall-out from the Eurozone crisis evokes the contested nature of solidarity within the EU. And the seeming inadequacy of the Old Continent's response to the changes brought about by globalization since the 1970s, which dramatically accelerated after 2007, suggests the fourth theme of sustainability. This is the lens through which the twin crises of European capitalism and Europe's place in the 21st century world will be examined. In sum, these elements jointly constitute an existential or systemic European integration crisis of the first order.

What is missing is an explanation of why all of this should be so. Thus far it has been argued that Europe's travails in the 2010s had been both a long time in the making (and long foreseen), that the response to the Eurozone crisis was inadequate and that the crisis weakened the EU far more than is commonly recognized. The EU of the 2010s was stuck in the mire, knew that it was stuck in the mire, and yet was unable to pull itself free. Given Europe's remarkable material and immaterial wealth, its great reserves, broad stock of human and intellectual capital and so on, this state of affairs appears truly puzzling. Thus, if the primary aim of this book is to investigate and describe the effects of the Great Recession and Eurozone crisis on Europe, then the secondary aim must be to explain why the crisis appeared to be so intractable. The most obvious place for a political scientist to search for explanations lies in the numerous choices and actions taken by Europe's political leadership in the 60 years between the foundation of the European integration project in the 1950s and the 2010s. Political and policy decisions often have far-reaching and unintended as well as intended consequences, and the institutions they may establish develop their own ways of functioning. Europe is no exception to this rule. By the 2010s, its institutions and its rules appeared to be locked in place and difficult to change, as was demonstrated by the experience between 2001 and 2009 of trying to make changes to the European rule-book through the abandoned Constitution and the Lisbon Treaty that replaced it. Negotiations between the EU's various political actors and institutions took place against the backdrop and histories of countless precedents and informal gentlemen's agreements as well as formal rules. Seemingly separate issues became tied together – continuing support for the Common Agricultural Policy and the British budgetary rebate, for example – in a way that looks eccentric and illogical to the uninformed outsider. In other words, the principle of 'path dependence', most commonly associated with the approach and insights offered by historical institutionalism, applies. Such institutional processes may become self-reinforcing; the further along a given path one advances, the harder it becomes to turn back (Geddes, 2013; see also Pierson, 1995; and on the related 'new institutionalism' see, for example, Evans *et al.*, 1985; March and Olsen, 1989; North, 1990).

This book argues that such problems of path dependence, and of the inefficiencies, vested interests and even pathologies to which path dependence may lead, are more common in the EU than elsewhere. This is in great part due to the profusion of political players from 28 member states with influence, powers of delay, powers of veto, varying interests, differing ideological viewpoints and so on. This does not mean that the system would be impossible to reform and adapt to changing circumstances, but it does mean that it would be harder to make changes. The political system of the EU in the 2010s was not particularly supple, as might be expected as the sheer volume of path-dependent decisions (and non-decisions) rose and the number of political players had grown over the years. (On the so-called 'joint decision trap', see Scharpf, 1988, 1994.) In seeking explanations for the true roots of Europe's existential crisis, two seem to be of particular importance to this book. The first is that the crisis was one of incomplete institutional transformations that had become locked in and led to the twin problems of market failure and government failure that became so apparent in the wake of the Great Recession and Eurozone crisis. At the European level, it was unfinished or incomplete institution-building that lay behind the crisis. At the member state level, the crisis was more closely linked to building national institutions on half-dug or even rotten foundations. A second path dependence-based explanation relates to the intellectual underpinnings or ideology on which the decisions taken by political leaders are based. Between the Treaty of Rome in 1957 and the Eurozone crisis, European integration was rooted in a policy of progressively lifting barriers to free trade and competition between member states, and protecting the rights of consumers in the process. This book argues that the EU in the mid-2010s was experiencing the crisis of a system that had simply reached its limits, as exposed by the Eurozone crisis. Market-based European integration was no longer sufficient as an ideological underpinning to drive the EU forwards. The farrago over the Services Directive a few years before the Eurozone crisis is but one example of its inadequacy. In the absence of an alternative, the European integration process ground to a halt, and it even appeared possible in the 2010s that it might begin to unravel.

The Structure of the Book

The notion of a polity-in-the-making provides the rationale for the structure of this book as a synthetic and analytical review of the EU at a time of existential crisis while also seeking to explain its seeming intractability. Chapter 1 continues to set the scene with an overview of the Great Recession and the Eurozone crisis that followed: their origins, consequences and broad effects on the EU. The review begins with the crisis precisely because its dramatic and terrible effects served so vividly to demonstrate the pathologies born of institutional and ideological path dependence. Following an overview of the origins of the Eurozone crisis, these pathologies are interrogated in more detail when the chapter turns to an exposé of its institutional nature. Chapter 1 concludes with an examination of how the crisis profoundly shook public support across

Europe for the integration project, and sets the scene for an exploration of the EU as a polity-in-the-making in the thralls of an existential crisis. Characterizing the EU as a polity-in-the-making requires an investigation of how far the progress towards a 'fully-fledged' polity has advanced. In this vein, since a polity requires a *demos* or citizenry, Chapter 2 looks at the theme of European identity. It asks how the European integration project has changed what it means to be European over the long term and as a result of the crisis and for whom. By arguing on the balance of available evidence that perceptions have only changed for the elite, the creation of 'two Europes' is proposed.

Since a polity-in-the-making requires the consent and acceptance of those it governs, Chapter 3 turns to the question of legitimacy. This is all the more pertinent in the context of the record low levels of support for European integration that are presented in Chapter 2. Chapter 3 finds that the problems of Europe's 'democratic deficit' were long-standing, although far less severe than its most vociferous critics would have it, and that democratic shortcomings were as apparent at the member state level as at the EU level. It further argues that the EU is democratic, legitimate and accountable in the majority of its traditional regulatory work. However, the need for a thorough and coordinated response to the Eurozone crisis exposed a serious flaw in EU democracy because saving the Euro required a tough programme of austerity measures which had not been popularly approved. Thus the EU reached the limits of what it had the legitimacy to do without the democratic approval of voters.

Chapter 4 interrogates the theme of solidarity in the EU, what it means and the extent to which Habermas's 'solidarity between strangers' extends to mutual transfers of resources. Solidarity is a concept that appeals to European elites and Chapter 4 argues that the benefits of European integration in the 2010s were concentrated in the hands of the richest 10%. Interestingly, this top decile partly coincided with those who identified themselves as being 'European'. Yet this deep and increasing concentration of wealth in the hands of fewer and fewer people undermined the notion of fairness as a guiding value supporting the European model of capitalism. This further serves to underline the central argument that market-based European integration was no longer sufficient as an ideological underpinning to drive the EU forwards.

A polity-in-the-making should be durable and, for that reason, Chapters 5 and 6 examine the sustainability of the EU, or rather the European integration project, in two dimensions. This raises a highly pertinent question in the context of the Eurozone crisis that at times threatened to pull the Union apart. Sustainability is understood in Chapter 5 in relation to the durability of the EU's economic model and the sustainability of Europe's place in a globalized world is addressed in Chapter 6.

Chapter 4 finds evidence to suggest that the European model of capitalism had only been partially successful in its aim of promoting inclusive prosperity for quite some time. Yet it does not argue that it was European capitalism, with its emphasis on social protection and regulation, that was to blame for Europe's lacklustre performance. The real challenge for Europe was labour market participation. The chapter argues that the best way to create jobs would be through an intelligent liberalization of the services sector to release its enormous potential for wealth creation. Services remained the unfinished business of Europe's Single Market, although as Chapter 5 emphasizes, the liberalization of this area was far from being a variety of 'low hanging fruit' available to policy-makers in search of growth and job creation. An effective liberalization would probably need to be accompanied by deregulation of the nationally-regulated European labour market with a reduction of non-wage costs as a percentage of labour costs. Such reforms would be likely to encounter widespread resistance in many quarters, not least because Europe's cherished welfare states were supported to a significant extent by such non-wage costs. The liberalization of services and the deregulation of labour markets serve as prime examples of the ways that path dependence at the national level led to reform deadlock and high levels of unemployment, illustrating Europe's twin problems of market failure and government failure.

Chapter 6 argues that the rise of new global players in the 21st century meant that Europe could no longer afford the luxury of so much squabbling between countries that held generally similar views about the kind of world governance structures that European foreign policy was designed to build. It finds that, in the absence of a grand strategy on foreign policy, the whole of the EU as a global actor amounted to less than the sum of its 28 member states. The rationale for promoting Europe internationally in the 2010s was that it offered Europe's *peoples* the distinct possibility that the polity in which they lived would remain relevant, influential and a powerful force in world politics. On the other hand, a failure to cooperate meant the certainty of irrelevance in world politics for both the peoples and all the *member states* of the EU, when measured against the emerging titans of the 21st century. It is this question of relevance versus irrelevance that remained by far the strongest argument in favour of the European integration project in the 2010s.

Although the logic for the choice of these four approaches – identity, legitimacy, solidarity and sustainability – that determine the substantive structure of this book is derived from the concept of a polity-in-the-making, they have always formed the backdrop to European integration. Collectively, they can help us to understand where the EU has succeeded and where it has failed, and in turn they are essential elements of the wider process of stock-taking at a time of existential crisis.

Chapter 7 moves away from these themes and is aimed more squarely at an academic readership, interrogating the implications for European integration theory and the notion of a European project that is market-based. It also suggests a number of new avenues for research into European integration. In conclusion, this book reflects on what the arguments about the nature of European integration between the 1950s and the Eurozone crisis can tell us about how the choices for Europe needed to be rethought in the 21st century.

1

The Great Recession, the Eurozone Crisis and European Integration

In the years after 2007, the European Union (EU) underwent a deep and drawn-out economic, social and political crisis. The Great Recession, the Eurozone Crisis and the politics of rigour and austerity plunged half the Eurozone into an exceptionally deep and long-lasting slump. Member-state governments teetered on the edge of bankruptcy. Jobs evaporated. Demonstrations were staged against tax and pension reforms – both real and proposed – and violent protests made against the austere conditions imposed by the bailouts. The morale of business and households sank whilst governments were blown away by the crisis or submitted themselves to the perceived diktat of bond rating agencies. The financial crisis that triggered the Great Recession originated in the United States and rapidly turned into a global economic shock as a result of the highly integrated nature of the world financial system. This financial crisis exposed the European continent's many pre-existing internal weaknesses – most notably high levels of debt in the private and/or public sectors in many member states and the build-up of imbalances (De Grauwe, 2013; Piris, 2012) – all of which served to aggravate the contamination effect.

At the time of writing in the 2010s, several years after the twin crises of the Great Recession and the Eurozone crisis had struck, almost 27 million Europeans, or 11% of the workforce, remained out of work (Eurostat, 2013d). Stark new fault lines had emerged in a European society whose cohesion had already been weakened by 30 years of widening inequalities. Europe's crisis-era divisions fell between younger and older

Europeans; between those who lived in the euphemistically-styled 'programme countries' that were in receipt of international bailouts to keep their governments running and elsewhere; between the employed and the ever-growing numbers of unemployed; between the relatively rich, stable and insulated North and the increasingly precarious, unstable and fragile South. This crisis thus pitched Europeans against Europeans (Le Boucher, 2013). Commentators in the early 2010s forecast that the younger generations of Europeans – those aged under 35 – were likely to live less prosperous, secure and comfortable lives than their baby boomer parents (Willetts, 2010). This was a development that would scarcely have been thought possible on the eve of the Great Recession in 2007 and such gloomy predictions did not escape public attention. In 2013, on aggregate, only 26% of Europeans believed their children would be materially better off than them in adulthood, with a mere 9% of the French, 14% of Italians and 17% of Britons seeing a brighter economic future for their children (Pew, 2013b).

By the mid-2010s, in some countries more than half of all would-be entrants to the labour market were out of work. Europeans living in the programme countries of Greece and Ireland saw GDP fall by around 20% between 2007 and 2012 as the private sector closed up shop, and salaries, pensions and welfare payments were slashed following the imposition of 'austerity' packages (World Bank, 2013b). The rate for casual labour slumped to €2 per hour in Spain (Watkins, 2013). In Portugal, as elsewhere, the young and more than half of the unemployed were not entitled to unemployment benefits. Across Southern Europe, it became more common for multiple generations to survive on a single salary or pension. In Ireland the young migrated once more. These sharp falls in living standards, together with the external, non-democratic imposition of draconian cuts in government spending, were the price of remaining in the Eurozone. In the south of Europe, the dividing line of the 2010s was not between the 'haves' and the 'have-nots', so much as between the 'haves' and the 'hope-nots', locked in their struggle for survival in a progressively bleaker economic and political climate. Worst of all, the great trial of the Eurozone and of European integration seemed little nearer to an end in the mid-2010s than it had done in 2008 or 2009.

Europe's economic troubles and political woes transformed it into an exporter of instability and disorder to the rest of the world for the first time since 1945. In 2011, the disintegration of the Eurozone and its consequences were identified by the United States as a 'Tier I' security threat, alongside, say, Iran's possible acquisition of nuclear weapons or a North Korean strike on South Korea (Council on Foreign Relations, 2011). By the mid-2010s, a disorderly Greek or Cypriot exit from the Euro seemed less likely, but the overall crisis in the Eurozone and the rest of Europe was scarcely any closer to resolution. Yet it would be misleading to present the problems of the 2010s as evenly spread across the EU. Unemployment was as much as 25–30% of the working population in Greece or Spain, but it was a more reasonable 5.3% in the Netherlands, 5.5% in Germany and 4.3% in Austria in 2012 (Eurostat, 2012). These new dividing lines between Europeans after more than half a century of integration were hugely troubling.

Taken together, these trends amounted to Europe's first true existential crisis – a crisis of confidence of the first order. Earlier generations of political scientists and historians termed De Gaulle's 'Empty Chair' fiasco of the 1960s a crisis. (The General instructed French representatives to stop attending meetings of the Council of Ministers, thus blocking all decision-making in a system based on unanimity between all members.) Similarly, Mrs Thatcher's insistent 'I want my money back' demand in the 1980s was described as a European integration crisis of the first order (Dinan, 2005, Jones et al., 2012). In retrospect, these incidents were mere spats; bitter and acrimonious, but ultimately trivial in that they neither pushed millions of Europeans out of work, nor brought down governments, nor fostered the rapid growth of extremist political parties. Nor indeed did they threaten the continued existence of the entire European integration project. Progress towards convergence of living standards between Southern and Northern member states was stopped by the Eurozone crisis; indeed it reversed, particularly in those countries that seemed to have travelled so far in so short a time, such as Greece, Spain, Portugal, Italy and Ireland. As will be argued throughout this chapter, it may be no coincidence that the crisis should be overwhelmingly concentrated in those countries that had jumped furthest and fastest in economic and social terms since the 1980s. Indeed it provides a clue as to the true nature of Europe's catastrophe, which may best be understood as a crisis of unfinished institution-building (especially at the national level), or a parable about the risks of building on half-dug, or worse, rotten institutional foundations.

The structure of the rest of this chapter is as follows. It first considers the global causes of the Eurozone crisis, as an aftershock of the worldwide (if primarily developed world) Great Recession of 2008–10. Secondly, it revisits the faults in Eurozone governance that the crisis exposed, before moving on to the institutional crisis of the Eurozone and then the political crisis of the Eurozone. Following this, it characterizes the Eurozone crisis as being one of incomplete institutional transformation at the EU and national levels. The chapter concludes by reiterating what the connections between the Eurozone crisis and European integration are more broadly, returning to the themes of identity, legitimacy, solidarity and sustainability that form the basis of the rest of this book on the post-Eurozone crisis EU.

The Global Causes of the Eurozone Crisis

Europe's great crisis of integration did not begin on the European continent, even if most European banks and many households were just as exposed to the problems of excessive debt in 2007 as in the United States (Connolly, 2012; Herzog, 2013). Indeed they could not fail to be, given Europe's sheer dominance of the global banking industry that is illustrated in Chapter 6. Yet the Great Recession became an unmistakeably *European* crisis in nature since it was at precisely the point that the rest of the world began to emerge hesitantly from the deep global recession that the Eurozone crisis began in earnest, with the first Greek government request for an international bailout in 2010. In simple terms, the Eurozone or European sovereign debt crisis was precipitated by the fallout from the deep global recession, which generated a cyclical need on the part of European governments to borrow money in response to falling tax revenues and rising welfare payments during 2008–10. Increased government borrowing was a completely normal pattern of behaviour in response to an external economic shock triggering a slow-down or fall in GDP, all the more so because the severity of the slump was far greater than any other recession of the post-1945 period.

This worldwide Great Recession, which was experienced in both advanced and emerging economies, was the deepest economic reversal since the Great Depression of the 1930s that followed the Wall Street crash of 1929 which lowered national income by more than a quarter and increased unemployment to 25% of the workforce in the United States – and contributed decisively to Hitler's coming to power in Germany (Galbraith, 1973). In common with the Great Depression of 1929–33 and the Long Recession of 1873–79, the Great Recession of 2008–10 had its origins in a banking crisis. In this case, it began in the United States and spread outwards across a world economy composed of many other countries that were just as vulnerable through the high stocks of debt built up

(Aglietta and Brand, 2013), and which had become increasingly global-ized and interlinked over the course of the previous 35 years. It has been argued (Glyn, 2006; Stiglitz, 2009) that these imbalances and debts had built up as a result of collective naivety about the efficacy of light-touch regulation of the financial services sector, with insufficient oversight, insufficient recognition of systemic risks and the skewed incentives that resulted from a bonus-driven culture of remuneration.

When the crunch came, America's banking crisis was triggered by an increasing suspicion, which proved to be accurate, that many of the mortgage-backed financial derivatives for sale on the market were far riskier than commonly supposed. (A financial derivative is a financial instrument which derives its value from the value of the underlying en-tities, such as assets, indices or interest rates, and has no intrinsic value in itself.) Such mortgage-backed financial derivatives were in fact based, at least partly, on so-called sub-prime mortgage loans (i.e. loans to bor-rowers with poor credit ratings – and a lower chance of paying back the money they had borrowed), which were then divided into smaller parcels, mixed with loans to individuals and organizations with better credit ratings, repackaged and sold on. As a consequence of this practice, the US – and indeed global – banking sector became contaminated with bad loans, a situation that became even worse as US house prices began to fall in 2007 and 2008. This made it much harder for banks repossess-ing the homes of those who could no longer afford to pay their mort-gages to sell them on and recoup their investment – thus beginning the downwards spiral of the globalized banking and financial services sector, which then dragged the 'real' economy along with it. The first signs of trouble were on 9 August 2007 when BNP Paribas announced that it was ceasing activity in three hedge funds specializing in US mortgage debt. Inter-bank lending seized up as bankers began to question what the true value of the trillions of dollars' worth of US mortgage-backed derivatives might be, resulting in a liquidity crisis (Elliott, 2011; BBC News, 2007).

Given that much of the world was as exposed as the US, over the fol-lowing year, the crisis spread across the global banking industry, prompt-ing government intervention. The Bank of England stepped in first to provide liquidity (i.e. emergency cash to allow the bank to pay its depos-itors) to the Northern Rock in September 2007 (following the first run on a British bank since the collapse of Overend, Gurney & Co. in 1866) (Larsen and Giles, 2007), before the British government became obliged to nationalize it in February 2008. For the first year of the financial crisis, it appeared that governments across the world would not allow banks to fail, with the US stepping in to find a buyer for Bear Sterns in 2008 and the Federal Deposit Insurance Corporation taking control of IndyMac in July of that year. Matters changed on 15 September 2008 when the gigantic Lehman Brothers – the fourth largest bank in America – filed for Chapter 11 bankruptcy protection, triggering a sudden, dramatic loss of business confidence, a stock market crash and a deep worldwide recession.

It was this global slump, when it spread to Europe over 2008–10, that blew holes in government accounts across the EU. Prior to the Great Recession, many of the soon-to-be hard-hit European countries had been running fairly balanced *government* budgets (European Commission, Economic and Financial Affairs, 2013a) (as was the case in Ireland, Spain, Italy or Portugal) and/or had low aggregate levels of national government debt (such as in the UK or Ireland) – even if the private sector debt of households and businesses looked unsustainably high, leaving them exposed to a credit crunch when debts had to be rolled over (European Commission, Economic and Financial Affairs, 2013b). In the pre-Euro era, such as in the early 1980s or 1990s, the need for greater government borrowing during a slump would have been met by issuing and selling more government bonds in a national currency. *In extremis*, those bonds might even be bought directly by a central bank in order to keep the cost of borrowing relatively low, through quantitative easing (colloquially known as 'printing money'); managing the national debt was, after all, what central banks were created to do (Broz, 1998).

The countries of the Eurozone, however, were effectively borrowing money in a foreign currency not under the control of their national central bank, but under the control of the European Central Bank (ECB) in Frankfurt, which was not authorized to intervene by directly buying the sovereign debt of the Eurozone countries. Thus the Eurozone countries had (and have) no buyer of last resort for their government bonds, which is tantamount to removing the cast-iron guarantee that the debt obligations of the governments that issue them will always be honoured in full. The result of this for countries such as Greece, Ireland or Portugal was that the interest payments demanded by the markets on their government bonds rose sharply, topping 12% for Portugal and Ireland, and nearing 30% for Greece (Bloomberg Markets, 2013). Government borrowing at this level of interest payments is unsustainable, especially when the aggregate national debt is large, has short to medium-term redemption dates (less than 10 years) and therefore needs to be rolled over regularly. This explains why Greece, then Ireland, Portugal and Cyprus got into trouble and had to call in international financial assistance to bail them out of trouble in the form of the troika, composed of the International Monetary Fund (IMF), the European Commission and the European Central Bank (see Tables 1.1 and 1.2). The condition imposed by the troika for lending money was that the national debt be first stabilized and made sustainable. This would usually mean that the government in receipt of aid cut its borrowing requirement so that a primary surplus (i.e. before interest payments on debt) was achieved and, ideally, underwent a default or payment holiday on some debt so that the total sum was reduced to a realistic level.

The additional complexity in the Eurozone crisis was that the outstanding debt of governments in the programme countries was owned by banks elsewhere in the Eurozone, notably in those countries running current account surpluses on their international trade and investments, such as Germany, the Netherlands, Austria or Finland (BBC News, 2011a). If the sovereign debts of the peripheral countries were to be

Table 1.1   EU/IMF programme countries: cumulative disbursements
(billion Euros)

	Greece			Ireland			Portugal		
	2011	2012	2013	2011	2012	2013	2011	2012	2013
Total help	71.2	54.1	37.3	38.1	19.0	10.2	38.1	25.0	10.0
EU	53.6	39.4	27.1	25.6	12.7	6.6	25.4	16.7	6.7
IMF	17.6	14.7	10.2	12.5	6.3	3.6	12.7	8.3	3.3

Source: Data from OECD, 2011: 46.

Table 1.2   Second wave programme countries: cumulative disbursements
(billion Euros)

	Cyprus	Spain	
	2013	2012	2013
Total help	10	39.468	41.333
EU (ESM)	9		
IMF	1		

Source: Data from European Stability Mechanism, 2013.

defaulted on, this would in turn put the banks of other Eurozone members (and others) at risk, requiring the governments of those states to step in and provide more capital to save these peripheral countries, thus undermining the strength of their own public balance sheets and increasing the need for more government borrowing. A strict no-bailout clause (Article 125, Treaty of Lisbon) made it illegal for one Eurozone member state to assume the debts of another, even though by doing so, they might simply be acting to prevent a bank run in their own member state. All this meant that the 'sovereign' debt of one member state was less 'sovereign' than met the eye, in that the consequences of defaulting on governmental obligations would have catastrophic effects on the banking sectors of the rest of the Eurozone (and indeed the rest of the world). Yet the no-bailout clause and the stubborn insistence that the debts of one member of a currency union must never be borne by the others meant that the financial assistance that was provided by the troika international institutions had to be provided in such a way that the profligate borrower, not the rapacious lender, should bear the overwhelming brunt of the adjustment needed to honour their debt obligations. In other words, there would be no write-off of the debts of the peripheral countries. Instead they would have to put their houses in order, reduce public spending and increase taxes (in the middle of a profound recession) and continue to pay the interest due to their creditors. In the absence of Drachmas, Escudos or Irish Punts, they would not be able to devalue their non-existent national currencies in order to reduce at a stroke the value of all outstanding debts denominated in those currencies. Nor could these governments stoke the fires of inflation, and through steady price rises, inflate away the true value of their obligations. The only realistic option remaining, short of leaving the euro, was to hunker down, follow the instruction of the troika to impose the austerity needed to produce a balanced budget, come what may, and hope for the best. This was the approach targeted on the unfortunate 'programme countries'. For those countries not participating in the programme, but running into difficulty all the same – essentially Italy and Spain, both of which were probably too big to save through external financial assistance anyway – the fear of being driven into the clutches of 'the programme' prompted them to carry out their own austerity measures. In essence, the imposition of austerity in the middle of an already severe economic depression is what caused the economic collapse of Europe's unfortunate southern periphery after 2010. Figure 1.1 illustrates the economic difficulties of the programme countries compared to other economies in the EU. Why

21

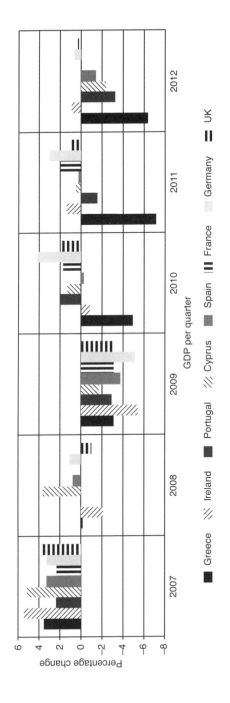

Figure 1.1 Comparative GDP growth rates since the Eurozone crisis

Source: Data from World Bank, 2014b.

did this happen? Much of the answer lies in the governance structure of the Eurozone.

Raising the Stakes Too Far, Too Fast: Design Faults in Eurozone Government

The creation of the Euro in 1999 raised beyond measure the potential for economic, and therefore political, contagion, were one of its members to fall victim to a serious crisis without giving the Eurozone as a whole the means to remedy and repair such a crisis. As De Grauwe (2013) noted, Europe's political leaders neither understood the necessary economic conditions for a successful monetary union, nor did they recognize its inherent fragility. There are three necessary conditions for an Optimal Currency Area: a common economic cycle, flexible goods and labour markets, and a budgetary union (see De Grauwe, 2013; Kenen, 1969; McKinnon, 1963; Mundell, 1961). Despite an abundance of analysis indicating that these conditions were not being met by many countries in the planned Eurozone, Europe's leaders ploughed on regardless. Moreover, at Maastricht they devised convergence criteria for membership of the single currency that had more to do with assuaging German fears about free-riding by profligate Southern European governments than ensuring the viability and endurance of the monetary union. After the single currency came into operation, Europe's financial leaders and central bankers assured themselves that the institutions of the Eurozone were up to the job of running a single currency on the basis of what De Grauwe (2006) termed the 'Brussels-Frankfurt consensus'. According to this doctrine, the Euro would be safe and robust, provided that there were in place flexible national labour markets, balanced national budgets, and a firm price-stabilizing monetary policy from the ECB which in turn would negate the need for the ECB to be concerned with financial stability (De Grauwe, 2013). Furthermore, in the event of a crisis, a strict no-bailout clause was actually written into the terms of the Euro (Marsh, 2009). This was a masterstroke on the part of the Euro's architects. With no possibility of a bailout, it would surely be impossible for the Eurozone's members to get themselves into serious trouble.

In retrospect, this element of the institutional design appears to be akin to an ocean liner setting sail with no lifeboats in order to ensure that its crew take all the necessary safety precautions. The idea that there could be a serious crisis on the scale of that of the 1930s was simply not entertained – the science of economics had come too far. Indeed in the UK, Britain's long-term Labour Chancellor and short-term Prime Minister, Gordon Brown, made such frequent reference to the idea that there would be no return to 'boom and bust' under a Labour government as to prompt speculation that he was claiming to have abolished the business cycle through the appliance of advanced economic theory (Briscoe and Fray, 2010). Rather, the talk was more about how the Euro might respond to more modest sounding 'asymmetric shocks' (Delors Report, 1989). The possibility of a near economic and financial meltdown such as that experienced across Europe and beyond in September 2008 was simply not considered. Over time, the received wisdom of the day anticipated that the member countries of the Euro would gradually complete the economic convergence that they had begun through participation in the Single Market. The single currency was designed, on the insistence of the Germans, to be a 21st-century version of the redoubtable Deutschemark and the European banking system was modelled on the disciplinarian Bundesbank (Dyson, 2000). Thus it was therefore tacitly assumed, or hoped at any rate – particularly in Berlin – that the economies of the rest of the Eurozone would inevitably converge with that of the anchor, Germany. This did not happen and as a result, the fall-out of the economic shock to the weakest Eurozone member states during the Great Recession and Eurozone crisis brought the single currency and the European integration project closer to collapse than anyone thought possible. The paradox of the Euro is that this project, that was designed to integrate Europe so deeply as to make a reversal impossible, actually did more than anything else to destroy the trust that had been painfully established between Europeans over the previous 60 years.

It has often been argued that whilst it was Portugal that was first reported as having violated the Stability and Growth Pact on 24 September 2002 (European Commission, 2002), it was the 2003 decision *not* to launch the excessive deficit procedure against the two largest Eurozone countries France (reported on 2 April 2003) and Germany (reported on 19 November 2002) that undermined the pact's strength and credibility (Council of the EU, 2003). This argument assumes that had the two largest economies in the Eurozone been adequately chastised for their failure to reduce their budget deficit to less than 3% of GDP, then the peripheral Eurozone economies would have heeded the warning. They would have run completely different fiscal policies and restructured their economies before the credit crunch began in 2007. This is simply not credible. The problem of the Euro was more complicated than this particular detail of its design and it relates to all of the substantive themes interrogated in this volume, for the following reasons. First, the institutional and decision-making structures to manage a monetary union effectively at the European level were not yet in place at the onset of the crisis. Second, a shift in the nature of the EU's work from low to high politics had been effected without the necessary institutional changes needed to compensate for this shift, which is connected most evidently to legitimacy, but also to identity and sustainability. Third, a new balance in the relationship between the European centre and the member states of the EU was required to allow for occasional central intervention in the affairs of the member states before a crisis situation was reached, an issue which is linked to questions of sustainability and also solidarity. These three elements will be examined in turn as the institutional crisis, the political crisis and the crisis of incomplete transition.

The Institutional Crisis of the Eurozone

In institutional terms, the most obvious problem of the decentralized governance model of the pre-crisis Eurozone (Hodson, 2011) was the lack of complementary, self-reinforcing structures and organizations that were believed necessary at the European level for the Euro to function as effectively as a 'normal' national currency in a sovereign nation-state would. The EU is, of course, not a sovereign state, and it does not need to become one to save the Euro. However, according to one commentator (Marsh, 2013), what was needed was a complete set of Europe-wide establishments endowed with the necessary powers to manage a currency union. Marsh argued, first, that this would include a European Finance Ministry and Treasury (although he did not state what role this European Finance Ministry would perform) armed with a degree of control over budgets and the overall economic policy of the Eurozone countries, as well as with the power to set and enforce binding rules. In 2010, the European Commission proposed a 'six-pack' of powers to increase its macroeconomic surveillance over the member states in the areas of fiscal policy and macroeconomic imbalances in order to reinforce the Stability and Growth Pact (Council of the EU, 2011a–f). Secondly, Marsh also argued that the ECB needed the power to act as the lender of last resort to both Europe's banks and its governments. Despite serious misgivings about whether it was legal to do so, in 2012 the ECB gave itself the (much contested) ability to buy the bonds of the programme countries in the secondary market under the Outright Monetary Transactions Programme (OMTP), i.e. not directly from the states that issue them (European Central Bank, 2012). Outside of the ECB, Eurozone member states created the European Financial Stability Facility (EFSF) in 2010 as a temporary rescue mechanism to safeguard financial stability in Europe by providing financial assistance to Eurozone member states. The EFSF was transformed into a permanent rescue mechanism, the European Stability Mechanism (ESM), which entered into force in 2012. In the framework of macroeconomic adjustment programmes, the ESM finances the recapitalization of financial institutions indirectly through loans to the member governments. It will be able to recapitalize banks directly once a single supervisory mechanism for Eurozone banks is established. However, with an effective lending capacity of €500 billion, the ESM might not be able to raise the sums required to prevent a financial breakdown at very short notice (Gros and Mayer, 2012). Thirdly, Marsh argued that the proposed Ministry of Finance and Treasury would need modest revenue-raising powers, independent of the member states, ideally through VAT. This would provide it with its own resources to be deployed in the management of the European economy for European interests, as opposed to the narrow national interests of its member states *in extremis* only. In calm periods, there might be no need for any intervention at all, but the power of intervention would be present for deployment in response to economic shocks. Fourthly, Marsh's Ministry of Finance and the Treasury would be able to issue Eurobonds for new, Eurozone-wide government borrowing. These might be used to fund infrastructure projects with trans-European benefits, but for the most part they would be a supplement to the 'own resources' of the Eurozone economic government, to be used mostly in times of crisis, with the debt issued then retired in calmer economic periods. Fifthly, Marsh's envisaged European Central Bank should be given the powers to put in place a full banking union for the Eurozone countries, bringing stability in the long term to the EU. Lastly, for Marsh, new, more comprehensive rules needed to be devised, governing entrance to and exit from the Eurozone, spelling out clearly how non-Eurozone countries could continue to participate in the Single Market and a wider, revived 'European Community', which would also be easier for third countries (i.e. not already members of the EU) to join.

Marsh's plan constituted a wildly ambitious list in the anti-European political climate that prevailed in the 2010s; at the same time however, in Marsh's opinion, it was a barely adequate prescription to save the

Eurozone from its self-imposed stagnation trap. This claim was probably a little exaggerated and others would certainly contest whether quite such wide-reaching reforms were indeed necessary, given that decentralized Eurozone government before the crisis had been less of a disaster than Marsh painted it to be (Hodson, 2011). In the absence of a Eurozone budgetary union, many scholars argued that collectively-guaranteed Eurobonds would be a more pragmatic step towards restoring investors' confidence in the debt issued by the Eurozone's member states (De Grauwe, 2013; De Grauwe and Moesen, 2009). Many problems would have to be overcome for Eurobonds to be issued (Gros, 2012), but at least they would be a step in the right direction. What these points illustrate is that the EU, especially the Eurozone, changed profoundly as a result of the Eurozone crisis. Legitimating decisions about the kinds of far-reaching reforms needed – fiscal cooperation, collectively-backed Eurobonds – received much less attention, not least because it seemed in the 2010s that no European leader had a clear idea about how best this might be achieved.

A secondary, but equally serious, fault in the EU's institutional design revealed by the Eurozone crisis was that its decision-making structures simply could not cope with a genuine emergency. Policy-makers in Brussels were accustomed to working slowly and deliberatively towards a compromise on which all parties could agree. This model of decision-making had been handed down with incremental modifications from the early days of European integration when the stakes were much lower and concerned with issues such as the guaranteed price of wheat in a given year. It was an ideal system for agreeing upon the regulations and directives that governed issues including the Single Market, or even modifications to justice matters and home affairs. In other words, it was perfect for reconciling competing interests in fair weather. But what the consensual culture of decision-making in Brussels emphatically could not do was to take prompt and decisive action in a crisis, action that not only charted a clear course back to safety, but could also stem a mounting loss of confidence and general panic. Worse still, the model of decision making in lengthy all-night meetings of the Council of the EU, from which officials and politicians emerged bleary eyed at 5am, faced increasing challenges as member state governments in national capitals refused to honour the deals hammered out by their representatives in Brussels (Falkner, 2013).

There was almost no chance in the mid-2010s that the institutional changes suggested by Marsh, or the Eurobonds approach advocated by

De Grauwe and others, to make the Eurozone function properly would be put in place – even though the alternative if no action was taken would be continued economic stagnation, decline, uncertainty and human misery in the hardest hit countries of the Eurozone. Europe's politicians decided that 'more Europe' should not be the answer to the Eurozone's woes. In the words of the Dutch Foreign Minister Frans Timmermans, speaking in 2013, the time of an 'ever closer union is behind us' (Government of the Netherlands News, 2013). More importantly, no one knew what a realistic plan for 'more Europe' should really look like, still less how it could be legitimated by an increasingly sceptical European public. Europe's politicians in their national capitals seemed keen during the Eurozone crisis to point the finger of blame at the Euro, at the European institutions, or at the governments of other member states– or indeed at anyone apart from themselves – to account for what had gone wrong. What the member states governments did not consider was that it was they themselves (or more accurately their predecessors at Maastricht) who had not equipped the Eurozone with the powers and institutions to function. Moreover, these same governments acting in the European Council seemed to be supremely lacklustre both in understanding the true nature of the crisis (De Grauwe, 2013) and in fixing it.

In the words of a polemical, if insightful, French commentator and politician, national governments in Europe, like spoilt children, seemed to want contradictory objectives: the benefits of the European integration without the need to share more sovereignty; competitiveness without painful reforms; and a strong EU with weak institutions (Goulard, 2013). The reactions of national governments to the crisis appeared also to be the best illustration of the fact that the member states were in denial about the profound, cross-cutting nature of the crisis and the scale of the political, economic and social changes that would be needed to resolve it. At the same time, European institutions that could not fight back and speak up for themselves were a tempting target of blame for nostalgic, backwards-looking national politicians, who imagined that there was a solution to be found in a return to a pre-Euro past (Furet, 1997, quoted in Goulard, 2013).

In the absence of new Europe-wide establishments to manage the government of the Euro, the alternative was continued and decentralized policy-making in the Eurozone, albeit with greater policy coordination between member state governments. This, in essence, was what the European Commission and other member states, led by Germany, were trying to do in the form of the six-pack of reforms, the Fiscal Compact, the European Semester and so on (Rehn, 2011). Yet the main thrust of all these policies was targeted at reducing government borrowing and reducing or eliminating current account deficits – following the German or Dutch model. In these aims, the policies achieved their aims by the mid-2010s at the cost of a dramatic reduction in domestic demand and sky-rocketing unemployment (see Tables 1.3, 1.4 and 1.5).

On aggregate, by 2012 the Eurozone and the EU as a whole were running quite substantial current account surpluses, the former shifting from a deficit of €86 billion in 2008 to a surplus of €228 billion by 2012. In Spain, the current account deficit shrank from minus €144 billion to minus €15 billion euros in the same time period. In comparison, China had been running a large, if declining, surplus, and the United States a very large, if also declining, deficit.

An export-based economic development policy would be highly appropriate for an undeveloped industrializing country, but anachronistic – and even damaging – for the EU as the largest and richest economy in the world. What was even more worrying about the post-crisis prescription for the Eurozone was that insufficient attention was paid to the *national* institutional structures, policies and political cultures that predisposed the peripheral Eurozone countries to get into trouble during the Euro's first decade from 1999 to 2008. A more appropriate approach to repairing the Eurozone would have been something akin to the conditionality policy that the EU applies to would-be member states, which was developed in the late 1990s and 2000s for Central and Eastern Europe. Such a reform agenda would encourage a more holistic assessment of the challenges that each state was facing and the structural reforms required. Moreover, the EU could also provide some incentives for restructuring member state governments in the form of financial aid to compensate for painful reform. This approach would perhaps have been more likely to yield long-term, lasting results in the Eurozone. Without such an approach, which would also have required the member states to leave their position of burying their heads in the sand and hoping that something would turn up, the institutional crisis was unlikely to be resolved. This in turn led to a political crisis.

The Political Crisis of the Eurozone

In political terms, the problem of the Euro was that it shifted the realm of European politics away from the low politics of regulatory policy into

Table 1.3 General government deficit/surplus, defined as the net borrowing/lending position (€, million)

Area	2007	2008	2009	2010	2011	2012
EU-28			−810 811	−803 471	−565 254	−510 002
EU-27	−111 795	−303 999	−808 443	−800 647	−561 798	−507 828
Eurozone (17)	−60 550	−196 737	−566 895	−569 127	−392 045	−350 146
Eurozone (16)	−60 933	−196 259	−566 621	−569 153	−392 225	−350 105
Germany	5 760	−1 860	−73 730	−104 150	−22 020	2 380
Ireland	296	−13 309	−22 170	−48 389	−21 358	−13 511
Greece	−14 475	−22 880	−36 166	−23 715	−19 869	−17 414
Spain	20 748	−49 113	−116 429	−100 508	−100 072	−109 572
Netherlands	1 048	3 073	−32 074	−30 109	−26 010	−24 323
Portugal	−5 333	−6 236	−17 114	−16 982	−7 398	−10 641

Source: Data from Eurostat, 2013g.

Table 1.4 Current accounts in selected member states (current US$, million)

Member states	2007	2008	2009	2010	2011	2012
Germany	248 783	226 272	199 476	207 725	223 324	238 453
Spain	-144 540	-154 529	-69 775	-62 498	-55 066	-15 142
Greece	-44587.3	-51 313	-35 913	-30 274	-28 583	-8 625
Portugal	-23 517	-31 906	-25 652	-24 186	-16 761	-3 365
Ireland	-13 850	-15 297	-5 001	2 319	2 514	10 346
Netherlands	52 526	38 036	41 575	60 963	84 590	77 929

Source: Data from World Bank, 2013d.

Table 1.5 Current account balances (current US$, million)

	2007	2008	2009	2010	2011	2012
Eurozone	33 070	-86 643	35 612	73 050	93 429	228 430
EU	-87 680	-174 572	10 610	10 847	78 144	161 217
China	353 183	420 569	243 257	237 810	136 097	193 139
US	-713 352	-681 341	-381 638	-449 477	-457 729	-440 423

Source: Data from World Bank, 2013d.

the high politics of monetary policy without a commensurate move into the realm of fiscal policy. This included the joint regulation of the financial and banking sectors, which remained decentralized (Hodson, 2011), relying instead on a looser stability and growth pact to provide a degree of macroeconomic policy coordination. With the surrender of monetary policy to the ECB from 1999, one of the realms of high politics had already passed to the supranational level of control (Piodi, 2012). Although this attracted a certain amount of attention at the time because it represented a pooling of what had until then been regarded as a core competence of the nation-state, in reality rather little had changed. In the first place, the central banks of most member states had already taken a technocratic turn away from democratic politics in handing control of monetary policy and the setting of interest rates to central bankers in order to prevent politically-motivated loosening of the credit strings in the run-up to an election. In the second place, most EU member states had effectively passed control of interest rates over to the precursor of the European Central Bank, the Bundesbank. Prior to the launch of the Eurozone, whenever the Bundesbank changed interest rates, the other central banks would follow suit in what was an altogether less *communautaire* means of policy coordination. Ironically, in seeking to escape from German economic domination of Europe via the mighty Deutschemark and the Bundesbank (described by David Marsh with only a little exaggeration as the 'bank that rules Europe', 1992), all the Eurozone's members did was to create an alternative mechanism for Germany's (involuntary) de facto domination – with the notable difference that this time there was no escape from what the British Foreign Secretary William Hague described as a 'burning building with no exits' (Blitz, 2011).

The shift in the high politics of European monetary policy from national to EU competence might well have proven rather uninteresting were it not for the financial crisis. As was noted in the previous section, the financial crisis became a more generalized economic crisis and a crisis of jobs and living standards, both of which lie at the heart of democratic politics and election campaigns. Technocratic politics could not address a crisis of this sort, particularly when there was no common fiscal policy. Even worse, a technocratic solution to a European problem, such as the sovereign debt crises, meant that tax increases, spending cuts and austerity had to be imposed from outside, often against severe public opposition. From the technocratic perspective, the solutions proffered might have been optimal; however, if the policies were to fail there was no one to take the blame or to be dismissed from office (Benn and Worcester,

1991). Were policies to fail, the technocrats would simply prescribe new measures. Even from a purely rational standpoint, such a way of doing business is inefficient. One can hardly expect a government and civil service to implement enthusiastically measures that have been forced upon them, and which they may believe to be unlikely to succeed – which in turn will result in politicians (not technocrats) losing office.

In theory, democracy prevails in Eurozone decision-making because the Eurogroup and the European Council, that handled most of the Eurozone crisis, however badly, are composed of elected politicians. Where this assumption falls down is in looking at who decides. Where surplus countries were pitted against deficit countries coming cap-in-hand to them, it was ultimately the surplus countries – Germany and its Northern European counterparts – who decided, as was the case when the German Bundestag voted to approve a Greek bailout on 30 November 2012 (Wiesmann, 2012). The basic democratic fault here was that Angela Merkel was not running for re-election in Greece, and therefore could not be held responsible by the Greek people for the decisions that her government had taken, although they were the ones that would be affected by them. The demands that were made of Greece, Cyprus, Portugal and Ireland – where public sector salaries fell by up to 50% in cash terms for those still in employment (Alderman, 2012) – to save bondholders and banks were argued to be reminiscent of the demands for war reparations made on Weimar Germany in that the conditions were imposed from outside with scant regard for the impact on the people of those states being asked to pay.

In summarizing the political dilemma in which Europe found itself in the wake of the Eurozone crisis, it must be concluded that neither the architecture of the EU nor that of the single currency gave adequate consideration to the *common European interest*. This in essence would have been the best means of resolving the conflicts and competing interests of people living in the different countries of the Eurozone. The apparent selfishness, short-sightedness and denial of reality on the part of Europe's member state governments, that perpetuated the Eurozone crisis, was born of an inability to see beyond the national borders, which was natural enough given that they were elected by national electorates. Yet the situation became intolerable when national politicians were making decisions that would affect the lives of electorates whom they would never have to face at the ballot box – a hugely dangerous precedent. The government of the Eurozone during the crisis violated the fundamental principle of democracy: that legitimate decisions about our lives can only be made by those whom we have elected to do so, and whom we may vote out of office at the next opportunity.

These institutional and political crises explain why European integration found itself at a crossroads in the wake of the Eurozone crisis. Three basic choices could be said to exist for Europe at that juncture, but none of them provided an obvious, neutral, let alone 'win-win' option. The first choice would have been to continue with the politics of denial by pretending that somehow the economics of austerity would eventually work. All countries would then converge on the German economic cycle and Europe's problems of debt and structural economic weakness could be cured, without far-reaching institutional reforms, and without the Northern European countries having to bear any of the costs. The risk here was an obvious one: the misery wrought by austerity would become too much and a country would leave the Euro in a disorderly fashion, provoking the kind of civil disorder that had been known to unseat democratic governments and replace them with military rule in historical precedent. This would have made the crisis as it unveiled between 2009 and 2012 appear to be a mere bagatelle. The second choice would be to accept that the Euro as it was designed did not work, but that the political will to create the institutions that would fix it did not exist, and therefore the honest, forward-looking approach would be to give up the Euro and return to the EU of the 1980s and 1990s. The costs would be high, but the retreat to the past could be planned and sequenced in such a way as to minimize uncertainty. The downside to this would be that the reborn Deutschemark, Guilder and Schilling would be likely to appreciate by something like 100% against the new Peseta, Lira and Drachma, and, of course, there would be a return to all the old problems of fluctuating exchange rates that the Euro was designed to fix. There was also a risk in this second scenario of collateral damage, in that some countries might be tempted to quit the EU altogether. The third option would have been to look again at what was needed to save Europe and the Euro – and then to do whatever was necessary, either by agreeing to issue Eurobonds or to create something similar, if not identical, to the institutions and structures of Eurozone and European economic government that were outlined in the discussion on the institutional crisis (pp. 24–6). This last option would also involve putting into place a programme of economic reform aimed at restoring competitiveness (an internal devaluation) to be carried out by the member state governments, akin to the conditionality policy that is applied to would-be EU member states. This would be the hardest path of all.

Until the 2010s, the choice for 'more Europe' would have been the obvious solution to troubles in the Eurozone, following the functionalist logic of the Monnet method by which incomplete European integration in one area prompts spillover effects by necessitating further integration in other areas. The Common Market prompted the doctrine of the Supremacy of EU law and later the Single Market, Qualified Majority Voting, the Single Currency and so on. Similarly, free movement of persons led to the creation of the Schengen area and the extension of EU powers into migration and asylum. This was how European integration worked for 50 years. That it no longer functioned in this manner in the wake of the Eurozone crisis prompts us to enquire as to what had changed. The answer lies in the observation made at the outset of this chapter that it was precisely those countries of the EU that had jumped fastest and furthest forwards economically and socially in the short period since the 1980s – Spain, Greece and Portugal – that had suffered most during the crisis. Older member states that had had the highest living standards, the strongest institutions and the most advanced economies for a long time (Germany, France, Denmark, Belgium, the UK, Sweden or the Netherlands) also emerged *relatively* well from the crisis. The newest member states from central Europe, admittedly not for the most part Eurozone members when the crisis struck, also fared relatively well during the crisis (although the crisis in the small and open Baltic economies was severe indeed). Those countries that performed tolerably well during the crisis were those either with the oldest and strongest institutions of government (the older member states minus Italy with its long-running problem of institutional weakness and stagnation) or those that had undergone a painful, yet effective restructuring of governmental institutions under the watchful eye of the EU in the 1990s and early 2000s (the central Europeans). Those who had performed badly had undergone a less rigorous process of institutional adjustment and reform (Spain and Portugal) or almost no European integration-prompted process of reform (Italy and Greece). Ireland, it is true, entered the 'programme' with all its negative consequences, but appeared to flourish. The central argument of this chapter is that it was an incomplete process of transition and reform, at both the EU-level and the national level in some member states that led to the Eurozone crisis and the subsequent existential crisis of European integration. Although this book is primarily about Europe as a whole, as opposed to its individual 28 member states, it would be obstinate to the point of stupidity to ignore their idiosyncrasies and differences entirely.

Therefore the next part of this chapter examines Europe's incomplete transformation both as a Europe-wide and as a national phenomenon.

The Real Crisis: Institutions and Europe's Incomplete Transition

Although it was not universally accepted in 1999, the launch of the Euro that year brought the EU much further along the road towards a federal polity through a massive increase in the member states' level of exposure to economic risk. This reality remained hidden for the first decade of the Euro's existence when, to all intents and purposes, nothing very much appeared to have changed for the national economies of the Eurozone. The only exception was the cost of borrowing for households, businesses and governments, which fell dramatically. Cheap money as we now know, and as might have been predicted in 1999, caused a long expansionary credit bubble in the Southern Eurozone that burst after the collapse of Lehman Brothers in 2008. The limited centralized government of the Eurozone in the first decade of the single currency's existence focused (through the Stability and Growth Pact) on monitoring the growth in government borrowing and debt. A little less attention was paid to the considerable expansion of private sector debt and the build-up of imbalances, about which the Commission issued regular warnings that were essentially ignored (European Commission, Economic and Financial Affairs, 2013b). Yet when the Eurozone's banks needed to be rescued by the governments of the countries to which they nominally belonged, the excessive private sector debt that had been built up effectively became public debt. Where debt becomes unsustainable, debtors, theoretically including the governments of sovereign states, have the option of bankruptcy. Having taken one look at the effects on the world economy of the collapse of one systemic bank, Lehman Brothers, the Eurozone countries were in no mood to allow an entire country to fail with all the consequent effects that this would entail. Since the possibility of default on one Eurozone member's public debt was too awful for the others to contemplate, regardless of the rules of the Eurozone, the other members were forced to intervene and bail out the countries that got into trouble. The nature of these bailouts is frequently misunderstood – in Germany at the height of the crisis the public perception was akin to waggon loads of Euros being carted off from the deepest vaults of the Bundesbank to support luxurious profligacy in the Southern member states. However, they did constitute an unplanned and undesired transfer of funds in the form of interest-bearing, preferential loans from one member state to another. And as with all loans, there was a genuine risk that the loans would not be repaid. Thus the Euro had created the *de facto*, if not *de jure*, sharing of risk that exists in a federal-style union. This is the quintessence of Europe's crisis of transition that explains its origins, its protracted nature and unfortunately why it seemed unlikely to be resolved promptly.

Europe's crisis of transition was much wider than the Euro; in fact, the role of the single currency in the crisis was limited to casting the spotlight on deeper problems that had been in existence for a very long time and which touched on many dimensions of European integration. Simply put, the European political system as it was set up on the eve of the Eurozone crisis was woefully inadequate for the task of governing Europe, and in the mid-2010s there appeared to be no obvious means of fixing it. The EU, in the wake of the crisis, was an incomplete union in that its member states had not endowed it with the powers to make it work properly. And to reiterate, its member states were in denial that fundamental change was needed to correct the problems (even if at the EU level Van Rompuy (2012) had begun to address this, much of what he argued fell on deaf ears). Even in the post-Lisbon Treaty era, the European structures that were in place – the institutions, the nature of the relationship between member states, rules governing elections to the European Parliament and so on – were designed for a completely different, far more modest international organization. They were not appropriate for the quasi-federal, or con-federal, polity-in-the-making that had resulted from the risks and responsibilities of governing the single currency.

An additional problem which was highlighted by the crisis was that, to outside appearances, Europe is fiendishly complicated. It takes a Master's degree in European politics or European administration to understand how the EU works (from the legal doctrines of direct effect and supremacy to the intricacies of the co-decision procedure and from the committee system to its actual policies, to say nothing of the politics of the relationship between the numerous actors in this multi-level system). The same is, of course, true of a nation-state, with two obvious differences. In the first place, many people think they understand more about the functioning of their own nation-state than perhaps they do; and whether they actually do or not is less important than the fact that they think they do. In the second place, nation-states usually (but not always, Belgium is an exception) do not have to vault over the same hurdles that the EU does in winning public approval for their activities and their continued existence. Such approval is more automatic because political life in the average European nation-state is both more institutionalized and thus more accepted as 'normal'. Europe's crisis in the wake of the Eurozone's woes was a systemic one, which had been instigated when the Treaty of Maastricht set the Union along the road to a single currency whilst ignoring the kind of political system that was necessary for it to work properly. Broadly speaking, there are three systemic areas that must be addressed if Europe is to end its crisis and complete the process of transition.

First amongst the elements lacking in Europe's polity-in-the-making are the central, European-level structures for the effective management of the single currency and for steering the European economy as a whole. Some of these functions are covered by the Treaty on Stability, Coordination and Governance in the Economic and Monetary Union, also known as the 'Fiscal Compact'. This treaty not only introduced additional rules for convergence in economic policy targets between its signatories, but also brought in the novel principle of sanctions. This took the form of fines to be levied by the European Court of Justice on member states of up to 0.1% of the guilty party's GDP (Article 8.2, Treaty on Stability, Coordination and Governance in the Economic and Monetary Union). Although some of the other innovations required would be covered by the Eurozone Banking Union that was agreed in 2014, these changes in themselves appeared insufficient to act as an early warning system for economic storms lying ahead and for dealing decisively with a crisis in its early stages. The inadequacy of such a light-touch approach can only be grasped by reference to the other two governance shortcomings that plagued the EU.

The second component in dealing effectively with the Eurozone crisis are strong institutions at the member-state level. This also received some attention in the public debate about the future of Europe, although both the popular diagnosis and the prescription to deal with it differed from the analysis offered in this book. It has already been noted that the member states that got into the most trouble in the Great Recession and the Eurozone crisis were those that had made the greatest socioeconomic strides forward since the early-1980s: Greece, Spain, Portugal and Ireland. Tellingly, these were also countries that had experienced only a light form of institution-transforming conditionality (or none at all in the case of Greece) before joining the EU. Conditionality simply means that a would-be entrant should be ready to cope with the serious demands that membership will bring economically, politically, socially and institutionally (European Commission, 2013c; European Council,

1993; Sedelmeier and Schimmelfenning, 2005; Mayhew, 1998) – which in itself is a very tall order. Concretely, the terms of membership amount to a strong, fair and well-functioning legal system, a public realm as free of corruption as possible, a rigorous democracy and an economy fit to compete with the most highly-developed and productive member states of the EU. These conditions amount to better-equipped member states that will continue their socio-economic and political development in a sustainable fashion, gradually converging with the standards that pertain in the rest of the Union. Tellingly, although the crisis also hit some of the 12 new member states that joined in 2004 and 2007 very hard indeed – notably Latvia, Lithuania, Estonia and Bulgaria – many others were affected to a lesser extent. For example, Slovakia's Eurozone membership actually shielded it from the worst of the post-2008 devaluations of the central European currencies (Connolly, 2013; Hodson, 2013); and Poland continued to enjoy a domestic boom on the back of higher consumption and infrastructural development funded in part by the EU. Indeed, Poland escaped unscathed from the Great Recession – a truly remarkable achievement unique in Europe (Cienski, 2013).

Economically, in the wake of the Eurozone crisis the weakest Southern member states of the Eurozone had exhausted the limits of two outdated growth models. The first growth model was based on competing in low- to mid-technology industries. The second growth model was based on a credit-fuelled construction and consumption boom that ended in 2008–09. The peripheral member states of the Eurozone needed to find a new niche in the world economy. Institutionally and politically it was also now clear that the Eurozone's periphery needed to complete the transition that began in the 1970s and 1980s. What was needed on the part of the EU was the power to impose binding constraints on its member states after their accession to the EU. For that conditionality to work, the EU must have something to offer countries in return for their transformation. This implied additional resources at the centre of the EU and brings us to the next element that is missing in Europe's incomplete union.

Europe's third missing piece of the con-federal or federal jigsaw puzzle related to the transformation of European politics towards greater legitimacy for EU decisions and more solidarity between Europeans. Yet public support for European integration was at an all-time low in most of the Union's member states in the mid-2010s (Pew, 2013b), falling from 60% to 45% of those polled between 2012 and 2013, as illustrated in Table 1.6. The economic crisis had transformed itself into a confidence crisis in the EU. In France, support fell from 60% to 41% (two percentage points lower than in the UK). German support for the EU fell from

68% to 60% and in Greece, an already low 37% dropped to 33% over the same timeframe.

Paradoxically, the bailouts were almost as unpopular in the countries that were in receipt of them as in the countries that were underwriting them through interest-bearing loans. The discontent stemmed from the fact that the single currency was effectively 'mis-sold' to the peoples of Europe because they were not made aware of the risks that it carried. In the case of the Germans, even if they were aware of these risks, they were not given the chance to have their say and an opportunity to reject the Euro. The absence of solidarity in the wake of the Eurozone crisis was partly a reflection of this past trickery. (Deception would be too strong a word since it implies that the Prime Ministers and Presidents of the EU's member states knew fully what they had signed up to in the Maastricht Treaty – they did not; see Marsh, 2013, p. 43). However, it was partly a reflection of the lack of 'solidarity between strangers' to which attention will be drawn in Chapter 2. Unless solidarity could be woven into Europe's political culture, the politics of the single currency and with it, the EU, seemed unlikely to work.

Yet as Marsh argues, 'crises breed egotism amongst governments and peoples, not solidarity' (2013, p. 6). This egotism was buttressed or justified by the highly dubious idea that somehow 'the pain felt by the peripheral states is overwhelmingly their own fault ... [having been living] beyond their means' (Marsh, 2013, p. 8). This might be described as the

Table 1.6   Waning popularity of the EU

	2007 %	2009 %	2010 %	2011 %	2012 %	2013 %	2007–13 change
Spain	80	77	77	72	60	46	–34
France	62	62	64	63	60	41	–21
Italy	78	–	–	–	59	58	–20
Czech. Rep.	54	–	–	–	34	38	–16
Poland	83	77	81	74	69	68	–15
Britain	52	50	49	51	45	43	–9
Germany	68	65	62	66	68	60	–8
Greece	–	–	–	–	37	33	–

Source: Data from Pew, 2013b.

tabloid *Bild-Zeitung* view of the crisis: the feckless, immoral southerners spend beyond their means and expect the good, earnest and hard-working northerners to bail them out. The natural concomitant of this is never mentioned: that the Northern European surplus countries were living too much within their means and not consuming enough. Difficult as it may be to appreciate, every balance sheet has two sides. The trade surplus on German exports meant that the Germans were not, for example, importing enough Italian white goods, wines or shoes, or buying sufficient feta cheese or taking enough holidays in Greece. The savings that built up in German bank accounts had to be productively lent out in order to generate the profits that would allow interest payments to be paid to depositors. And where better to lend than to another Eurozone country with an appetite for borrowing? Thus, although a surplus is an easier problem to tackle than a deficit, in that it requires improvements in the standard of living rather than cutbacks, in aggregate saving excessively is less of a virtue than it seems. The institutional, societal and cultural factors that drive some Northern Europeans to such paranoid parsimony are as important as those that drive the debtor countries towards reckless consumption. Balance is key.

What might be termed the 'financial morality' of the Eurozone crisis was highly selective in the principles on which it operated. This was perhaps not altogether unsurprising in a largely post-Christian European society. Nonetheless, the moralizing and lecturing of politicians in some Northern European creditor states to those whom they perceived as feckless southerners was one of the least appealing aspects of the crisis of solidarity that the Eurozone's travails had produced. The Christian proverb perhaps most appropriate to this political sourness that has followed the bailouts of the 'programme countries' is that of the prodigal son (King James Bible, 1611, Luke 15: 11–32).

Finding a resolution to Europe's current political and economic deadlock in the wake of the Eurozone crisis seemed likely to require an enormous effort, both cognitive and emotional, on the part of Europe's politicians and its peoples. What this would amount to, if European integration were to work in the long-term, could be summarized in two simple statements. First, for everyone living in the EU: its peoples, its politicians, Europe and the EU needed to become 'us', not 'them'. This would entail an end to the politics of denial. Second, for the peoples of Europe, the institutions in Brussels, Frankfurt, Luxembourg and Strasbourg needed to become 'our government' as much as that in their national capital. Thus it is not just the structures, institutions and policies of the EU that needed to catch up with the realities of a high-risk currency union, but also the EU's politics – particularly its popular politics.

For the politicians and officials of Europe, nearly all of whom were – and are – attached to one or another of the member states, a quantitative and qualitative leap was needed in the way that the continent's political, social and economic dilemmas were perceived. The kind of government that the EU needed could only work if the principal actors had some basic idea of the European interest. Understanding the bigger picture is perhaps harder for the 21st-century generation of European politicians to appreciate than it was for their parents and grandparents. The strategic case for European integration was more obvious to those who had experienced two world wars, experienced or presided over the end of the European empires and lived with the daily threat of nuclear Armageddon. The experience of these struggles for survival brought a depth of consideration and understanding – and with it the clear vision that the case for Europe was always about the fundamental choice between the distinct possibility of continued political and economic strength and the certainty of weakness and irrelevance.

At the level of national institutions in the economically weakest member states of the old EU-15, in the wake of the Eurozone crisis there was a need for an on-going programme of profound reform. To an extent, this was forced upon the institutions of Greece and Portugal, for example, by the Troika. Moreover, reform efforts were catalyzed in Spain and even Italy by the desire to avoid at all costs the need for a bailout – which in any case might simply not have been affordable – and the humiliation of joining the 'programme countries'. Yet this approach was inadequate and it may also have been damaging. Externally-imposed reform agendas are undemocratic. In practical terms, precisely because they are external, they may miss those parts of the state that are in most need of reform. Some of the changes that were necessary in the weakest countries of the Eurozone are fundamental in nature, and relate, for example, to the ability or inability of the state to enforce court rulings (Falkner, 2013). What was needed was more of the spirit of the Central Europeans in the 1990s: a supply of reform from Brussels that is matched by demand for assistance with reforms from the troubled countries of the Eurozone themselves. In other words, there should be a desire and willingness to change, rather than a sulky acceptance of the need for reform to avoid disaster which is likely to result in extensive slippage of reform momentum as soon as the external pressure is relaxed. In order to succeed, social, economic and political reform of national institutions in the EU must be driven by demand at the national level.

To draw a metaphor, at the outset of the 21st century, Europe's politicians behaved like the second-generation owners of a family business: 'Europa S.A.' –is still a world-leading manufacturer, but one that is increasingly uncertain of its future. Set up in the austere conditions of the late 1940s, the firm had to fight for survival in the early years, before undergoing a dramatic expansion in the 1960s. Following a difficult merger in the 1970s with Britannia Plc., a former market leader fallen on hard times, the company underwent a profound transformation between the mid-1980s and mid-1990s. Control of the world-beating firm was handed to a second generation at the turn of the century, but the new owners did not appreciate how much hard work had been involved in setting up the business. In the 2010s, politicians, all the more so in the old democracies to be found in the north western parts of the European continent – paraphrasing Wilde – demand to know the price of European integration, but appear to have no sense of its value (Wilde, 1892).

Conclusions

In retrospect, the decision to create the Euro was as over-ambitious as its potential economic and political consequences were inadequately understood. The generation of politicians and officials who negotiated the Maastricht Treaty at the beginning of the 1990s were perhaps partly to blame. They were operating in the warm afterglow of the West's resounding victory in the Cold War which would now permit the reunification of Europe. As the veteran Dutch central banker André Szasz believed, 'not one of the politicians who signed the Maastricht treaty knew what they were doing' (Marsh, 2013, p. 43). Yet it is too easy to be wise in hindsight. First of all, no one present around the negotiating table in Maastricht could have predicted the extraordinary changes to the world economy that would take place in just 20 years, catapulting China towards the front rank of the world's economic powers, and at the same time robbing some of the Southern European countries of their competitive production niche in the globalized economy. Moreover, the attraction of the European model was at a near all-time high in the early 1990s. Europe's economy had surged forwards over the previous few years in the drive towards the completion of the Single Market, expanding at its fastest rate since the first oil crisis of 1973. Politically, European liberal democracy, combined with a relatively generous ensuring and enabling welfare state, was providing a more prosperous and safer life for the peoples of Western Europe. In a short time, these benefits would be shared with the Central and Eastern Europeans, just as Helmut Kohl in 1990 had promised East Germans 'blooming landscapes' within a few years (Kohl, 1990).

Previous ambitious plans for European integration had been dismissed as foolhardy, a step too far and likely to produce chaos. European integration history, however, tells us that previous drives for deeper integration had created sufficiently 'more Europe' for the schemes to work through the process of spill-over, a sequence of actively targeted events. On the face of it, spill-overs have been created by the Euro in the form of the treaties establishing the European Stability Mechanism or the Fiscal Compact, but no one can truly claim that the Euro is the resounding success and the catalyst for deeper European political, social and economic integration that some of its creators (Kohl and Mitterrand at least, if not Major) hoped it would be. Certainly, the Euro appeared in the 2010s to have been a success for Germany, those member states economically compatible with Germany and the *Modell Deutschland* approach to productivity, cost control and growth. But more obviously, what the Eurozone crisis did was to pit the Eurozone's creditor members against its debtor member countries (Marsh, 2013). In doing so, it weakened legitimating public support, not only for the further European integration that was urgently needed if the currency union were to be made sustainable, but also for the EU as it was then conceived. Thus in the 2010s, the Euro must be considered a near-failure. Over the 60 years from 1950–2010, European integration moved forwards in great bounds, rather like a free runner jumping from building to building, often succeeding against the odds and to the surprise of the spectators. Yet at the time of writing in the mid-2010s, the free runner was clinging to the ledge of his targeted building with his fingers slipping very slowly away.

The old model of European integration was broken by the Eurozone crisis. It had been exhausted because the limits of market-based integration had been reached. Nonetheless, the EU's member states seemed to be in denial about what this implied. The situation in Europe in the 2010s recalled that of 1989 in Eastern Europe (Goulard, 2013, p. 129), although the analogy ends there since the EU can hardly be compared to a one-party Communist state doing its best to manage the absurdities of the planned economy. More of the same, however, was clearly no longer enough.

The serious risks to the future of market-based European integration in the mid-2010s stemmed from the frustration, sense of impotence and even outrage amongst Europe's populations and governments who no longer felt 'in control of their own destiny' (Marsh, 2013, p. 5). European politics appeared increasingly detached from their lives, creating a palpable sense of growing anger about what appeared to be a lack of democratic control and legitimacy in the governance of the EU. Unfortunately, the new, progressively more intricate structures of Eurozone governance that emerged in the wake of the crisis and were supposed to correct the Euro's ills seemed less democratic than anything imagined previously, with national budgets subjected to the control of unelected officials and fines for the recalcitrant. Europe needed a democratic 'Big-Bang' to allow for the direct elections of the politicians who would manage the Euro and some form of European economic government. Unfortunately, the mood in the member states was precisely the opposite of what was needed, and was summed up in the assessment of the Dutch foreign minister Frans Timmermanns that the age of ever-closer union was over. Democracy is about choices and Europe – for all its weaknesses and failings – was still rich enough to have options available to it.

This opening analysis has set the scene for the argument that will be developed in subsequent chapters. It illustrates that the drawn-out and, at times, seemingly intractable Eurozone crisis focused public opinions and governments alike on the economic dimension of European integration, which in turn pointed to a political and social crisis. This was starkly depicted in the low levels of Europeans' faith in the fairness of their economic system in 2013, with 77% of Europeans expressing the sentiment that the 'current economic system favours the wealthy', a figure that rose to 95% and 89% in crisis-hit Greece and Spain. Even in supposedly liberal Britain, some 72% of respondents believed that the gap between rich and poor had increased (Pew, 2013). On aggregate, some 60% of Europeans believed that the rich–poor gap is 'a very big problem'. These figures were supported by the economic focus of Europeans' worries. Between September 2006 and May 2013, the economic situation in general and unemployment in particular were at the forefront of popular concern. Public perceptions about the economy as the number one problem rose from 6% to 36% in Britain between 2007 and 2011; from 9% to 65% in Spain; and from 39% to 72% in Greece (Eurobarometer, 2006–13). A similar story was told for unemployment, which rose to being the joint most important public policy dilemma (together with the general health of the economy) in Britain from 8% to 38% between 2007 and 2011;

from 19% to 79% in Spain over the same period; and from 51% to 66% in France. Only in Germany did this figure fall: from 70% in 2006 to 18% in 2011.

These economic worries, combined with the intensity and duration of the crisis that the EU underwent, triggered reactive posturing towards the Union. Most Europeans were profoundly concerned about the state of their economies: only 1% of the Greeks, 3% of the Italians, 4% of the Spanish and 9% of the French thought that economic conditions were good (Pew, 2013). In every member state (barring Malta) economic matters were considered to be the main issue countries were facing in the mid-2010s (Eurobarometer, No. 79). Consequently, EU citizens adopted a more materialistic approach to integration, anxious of the economic benefits – or lack thereof – of integration. One of the perverse effects of the economic crisis was to increase the mobility of people within the EU, from recession-hit countries to relatively better employment conditions. In the UK for instance, the number of EU immigrants increased by 25 000 or 16% over the year, because of a surge in economic migration from Spain, Portugal, Italy and Greece (Warrell, 2013). In the context of the British government's efforts to restrict migrants from outside the EU, the strain that rising economic immigration placed on public services was a major concern for the voters. An 'us versus them' dialectic, within the EU itself, appeared to be increasingly influential over attitudes towards the EU (Fligstein, 2008). Chapters 2 to 6 chart both continuity and change in the EU at a time of existential crisis, with a focus on the themes of identity, legitimacy, solidarity and sustainability that were presented in the introduction as being vital to understanding the true nature of the fallout from the Eurozone crisis. In doing so, it sets the scene for a fuller understanding of the choices for Europe in the 2010s.

2

European Identity

European identity is a highly complicated matter; it has always been easier to determine what Europe is not, rather than what it is. Clearly, Europe is not a nation-state with a neatly delineated national identity, a set of familiar national myths and a common language, but neither are the terms Europe and European simply figures of speech. The European integration project in the 2010s was only half a century old and a European identity, a European culture or a European society takes time to come into existence (Outhwaite, 2008). Identity matters because it is at the heart of any community, political or otherwise, and is a powerful instrument of political mobilization. It naturally follows that members of a polity share some sense of being part of it, a sense of 'we-ness' as opposed to an 'other' group for a number of reasons (Barth, 1969; Bellamy and Castiglione, 2013). First, a common identity is necessary for a political community to succeed and be sustainable, whilst secondly, it is also essential in legitimizing redistributive and other social policy initiatives (Outhwaite, 2008). These two elements are as true for the EU as a polity-in-the-making as it is for a nation-state. In addition, in the case of Europe specifically, the existence of a common identity is also a springboard for the development of globalized political structures and 'cosmopolitan democracy' (Held, 1995). The 1993 Copenhagen criteria define the common ground on which the Union is to be built: the rule of law, respect for human rights, liberal democracy and the market economy. They form a set of constitutive norms which accession candidates have to comply with before entering membership negotiations (article 49 Treaty on the European Union), but they miss the cultural meaning of Europe (Risse, 2010). At the national level, identities have been constructed on the basis of a collective narrative, a common history – even a common culture. For instance, the collective identity of the French Fifth

Republic refers back to the French revolution, the *Déclaration des Droits de l'Homme et du Citoyen* and the trio of Republican values (liberty, equality and fraternity – although sharp eyed readers will note that equality was a later addition). The idea of Europe may also refer to the various European ways of life, understood and adopted as such in other parts of the world – for example, food, wine and films (Outhwaite, 2008), or indeed to a model of industrial relations (Crouch, 1993).

At the EU level, the process of identity construction along this classical model has proved controversial. The construction of the 'House of European History' to celebrate Europe's collective memory triggered opposition (Waterfield, 2009a). References to a common European history or a shared cultural and religious heritage were also debated during the negotiation of the Constitutional Treaty (2004) and the Lisbon Treaty (2007). The Union aimed to be perceived as the embodiment and actualization of a number of values and principles and to project this identity outwardly through its external policy towards third countries. As Outhwaite says, 'social and cultural forms ... are warmed up [in Europe] and (re-)exported to other regions of the globe, where they develop in ways which often eclipse their European variants' (2008, p. 13). Yet this outwards-looking identity does not suffice to define what it means to be European internally and that requires, in Ernest Renan's words, a 'daily plebiscite' (Renan, 1882). This in turn begs the questions: What does it mean to be/feel European? and, Who feels European? (Bruter, 2005). The relationship between identity and political community is not a simply one-way process by which the contours of a particular shared identity set the boundaries of the political community that belongs to that identity. The connection is surely two-way, and a sense of belonging to a political community should impact upon an individual's sense of his or her own identity. Thus, if a European political community exists, it should in some way have changed, or made an impression upon, what it means to be European. It is on this issue that this chapter will concentrate.

As will be argued in this chapter, the balance of evidence suggests that the European Union (EU) *has* changed what it means to be European, although only in the eyes of the elite. For most Europeans, an ability to identify with Europe requires three elements: (1) the individual engages in cognitive reflection about what it means to be European; (2) the EU as a subject of politics is salient to the individual; and (3) at the conclusion of this thinking process, the individual recognizes that European integration is of personal benefit. Reflecting cognitively on one's identity is rather unusual. Almost by definition, identity is more of a given than the subject of discussion so the 'identity bar' is set very high indeed, which in turn explains why European identity remains the preserve of the elite.

As a consequence of this, the chapter argues that 'two Europes' have come into being since the early days of European integration: that is two distinct European societies which transcend national barriers in both old and new member states. The first of these is the Europe of a broad 'elite', which comprises about one in five or one in six Europeans. This community shares a common European identity, believes that it benefits directly from European integration and is usually politically Europhile (Fligstein, 2008; Risse, 2010). The second of the two Europes consists of everyone else. This much larger group has either a very weak or non-existent bond to European identity and is not interested in either European politics or the EU. Within this group lie the Eurosceptics, although they do not form a majority since the great mass of the group simply do not care enough about EU politics to take a strong view one way or another. This, in essence, was the composition of the European political community in the 2010s. The question of how to bring these two Europes closer together and to work towards a cohesive European identity is a topical one, rendered even more salient by the economic difficulties faced by the EU in the 2010s (Risse, 2010). How can the groups who control society convince those who have less wealth, income and status that they belong to the same polity and share a common identity (Deutsch, 1966; Habermas, 2009)?

This chapter begins by establishing why a European identity can be said to exist. It then turns to the question of who identifies as a European, and follows this with an investigation into what the determinants of a European identity appear to be. Subsequently, it explores how and why the EU has changed our understanding of what it means to be European in the 21st century, and looks at the effects of European integration on galvanizing other forms of identity into political communities.

Does a European Identity Exist?

There are solid grounds to suggest that a European identity, or a feeling of identity with Europe, does exist. To begin with, 15–20% of Europeans think of themselves as holding not only their own national identity, but also a European one, 'most of the time'. If this figure is added to those who feel European only 'some of the time', then it can be stated that about half of Europe's citizens feel themselves to be European either some or all of the time (Eurobarometer, 1992–2010), and as Figure 2.1 shows, this statistic has been fairly stable over the twenty-year period to 2012.

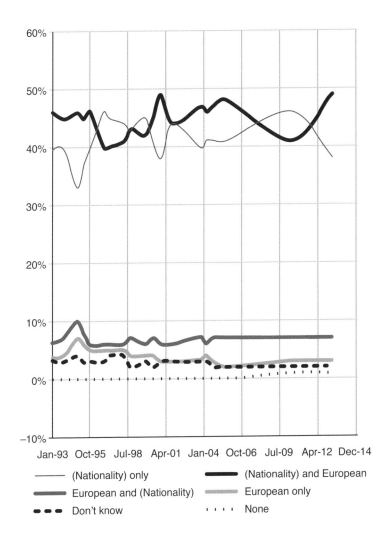

Figure 2.1 European identity

Source: Data from Eurobarometer, 1992–2012.

Unfortunately, matters of identity in Europe are more complicated than this, and the small number of 'don't know' responses reveals that there is more to the picture of European identity than meets the eye. To revisit and invert the Eurobarometer statistics, around 50% of Europe's citizens *never* feel European. If this figure is added to those who feel European only some of the time, we reach a total of about 80% to 85% of Europeans who feel either no connection or a loose connection to Europe. Once again, these figures have been fairly constant over the same 20-year period. Thus the great majority of Europeans do not experience (or perhaps have not yet experienced) feelings of solidarity between themselves and strangers from other European countries. Their attitudes towards European integration therefore, range from the lukewarm and indifferent to the sceptical and even hostile. Looking behind the headline numbers, this segment of public opinion tends to be older, from lower socio-economic groups, less well-educated, suspicious of migration and resolutely anti-cosmopolitan (see Fligstein, 2008). Its members are also very numerous.

Rather than being an imagined community (Anderson, 1983), identity needs to become real (Bruter, 2005; Risse, 2008). Nation-building in member states has crystallized on symbols of identity such as a flag, an anthem, a currency, a language or military conscription. This process has taken decades, even centuries in certain nation-states, and continues to be put at risk by various centrifugal forces such as the rise of regionalist claims (for instance, in Spain, Belgium, the UK and Italy) or, to a lesser extent, by international migration. At the European level, these symbols are at best confusing, at worst simply absent. For instance, although ubiquitous in Europe, the European flag and the European anthem have been abandoned by the Lisbon Treaty. The 'single currency' was common to only 18 out of 28 member states as of 1 January 2014. Moreover, the Euro reveals a dual identity: with one side of the coins and banknotes being common to the Eurozone and the other side designed to be country-specific. In the same line of reasoning, passports juxtapose national and European identity as they have both the inscription of 'EU' and the respective nation-state on their cover. There is no European army and the idea of dying for Europe evokes a distinct air of bathos. Fligstein (2008) also notes the role of media and of a European popular culture in both constructing and revealing the existence of a European identity. The openness of EU borders also perpetually questions the construction of European identity. Immigration into the EU, in particular from groups with seemingly little appetite for integration, calls into question the very ability to forge a common identity and may even provoke the return of more chauvinistic kinds of national or ethnic identities. These reactions bring to the fore the EU's own contradictions: its universal rhetoric *vs.* its exclusiveness, or the borderless internal space *vs.* the perception of this space as a 'fortress Europe'. These tensions are even further exacerbated during times of economic crisis (Warrell, 2013).

Who Identifies as European?

An exploration of the wider picture behind the headline numbers of EU citizens who feel an attachment to Europe all or some of the time reveals an inverted socio-economic situation. Demographically speaking, it is evident that certain features have positive correlations with European identification (Fligstein, 2008; Risse, 2010). For example, in terms of gender, men are more likely to identify themselves as Europeans than women, although at the level of being proud to be European, gender does not seem to be significant. In fact the gender issue may be more about the persistent levels of inequality between men's and women's employment patterns, with men occupying more senior and better-paid positions. Those with white-collar jobs were less likely to identify themselves as holding only their nationality, in comparison to blue-collar workers and the unemployed. Younger people and students were far more likely to feel European, compared to older people and pensioners. Education was a significant indicator for the existence of a European identity; the better educated were more prone to feel European, rather than just their nationality. Being more informed about the EU also appears to have a positive effect on identifying more closely with Europe. In sum therefore, the combination of social position, education, knowledge and interest implies that a sense of European identity is largely a matter of *cognitive mobilization* (see also, Inglehart 1970), rather than a deeper, more emotive attachment.

The existence of an elite European identity is further supported by the evidence put forward by Risse, Bruter and Fligstein. They reveal that there is a thriving European civil society composed not only of the numerous Europe-wide associations of commerce, industry, law, academia, medicine, trade unions and so on, but also of those whose working lives could be said to integrate them into a 'European community' through regular personal contacts with colleagues across the 28 member states (see Bruter, 2005; Fligstein, 2008; Risse, 2010). This mainly professional and managerial elite is the group whose lives have been most transformed in a positive way by European integration. In turn, the permanence of these contacts also validates the idea of a community that is derived from European integration. If collective identity is measured by an awareness or a sensation of sharing something with people we do not personally know – what Habermas referred to as 'solidarity between strangers' – then it is evident that a common European identity of sorts does indeed exist, but it is overwhelmingly concentrated amongst this broad elite group (Habermas, 2009). However, in turn, elites may have a crucial impact on citizens' identity by exposing them to European symbols and conveying a positive message on European integration (Bruter, 2005; Shore, 2000).

Further anecdotal evidence bolsters the case for European identity as a marker of elite status in that the feeling of sharing something intangible becomes most apparent to Europeans when they travel outside their continent, even when visiting a Western country such as the United States. In this context, quite suddenly and, for the most part, unconsciously, the European, particularly if he or she is accustomed to travelling within the EU-28, experiences a feeling of commonality with his or her fellow Europeans because the United States feels distinctly 'foreign' or 'other'. One prosaic explanation for this is that 50 years of shared rule-making meant that many aspects of daily life across the EU-28 had become similar by the 2010s. Yet there is more to this sense of European identity than shared rules on compensation for delayed flights (Your Europe, 2012), or cheaper mobile roaming charges (European Commission, 2013c). The integration project has transformed the lives of many Europeans, often in subtle ways which are more apparent to some social groups than others. In doing so, it has helped to create a particular kind of European identity that higher socio-economic groups feel they can sign up to, at least in part. This is surely a remarkable achievement. However, what is particularly striking is the extent to which the experience of European identity is an elite one. What is also worthy of comment is that experiencing a feeling of European identity is not the same as public support for that country's membership of the EU, as Figure 2.2 illustrates.

Figure 2.2 shows that support for membership of the EU since the early 1970s has varied between about 46–72% of those polled. It shows that support for European integration rises during periods of economic expansion (during the recovery of the mid-1980s around the time of the launch of the Single Market drive, or during the recoveries of the mid-1990s and mid-2000s), falls during recessions (post-Oil crisis in the 1970s, in the early 1980s or early 1990s) and is influenced by one-off

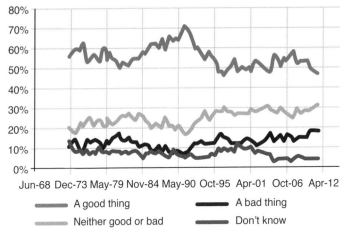

Figure 2.2 Support for membership of the EU (EC)

Source: Data from Eurobarometer, 1973–2011.

exogenous factors such as the Central and Eastern European revolutions of 1989. Overall, a majority of Europeans support their country's membership of the EU. Similar results were obtained in earlier studies that looked at support for 'West European Unification' between 1971 and the mid-1990s (Eurobarometer, 1971–95). These figures need to be contextualized against the extent to which most Europeans thought about European politics from one day to the next – how salient the issue was to them over a similar timeframe. Between the 1970s and the launch of the Single Market in the late 1980s about 75% of Europeans polled had either 'no interest' or 'not much interest' in European politics, a figure which fell to 50–60% thereafter (Eurobarometer, 1971–95). Over the long term, it is possible to conclude that, whilst Europeans might support their particular country's membership of the EU, they did not particularly regard EU membership as being an important issue for them.

Taken collectively therefore, the data appear to point to three things. First, European *identity* is a minority interest that is concentrated in the upper strata of society. Second, *support* for European integration is strong amongst a majority of citizens over time, with peaks and troughs that correspond mostly to the economic climate prevailing at the time of polling. Third, it shows that for most citizens the EU is of rather *limited interest* or salience.

Combining these three factors, a few propositions can be put forward about the nature of European identity and its relationship to the European integration project. On the surface, it would appear that European integration has not affected European identity because feelings of European identity in aggregate have not varied all that much over the twenty-year period for which data are available. Yet this would be too superficial a conclusion to draw, and a deeper analysis points to a more nuanced picture.

On the basis of the public opinion data given above, there appear to be two separate European societies, coexisting along a European identity spectrum with considerable overlap in membership. At one extreme of this spectrum is the European elite, which feels European most of the time and comprises around 15% to 20% of Europeans (between 75 and 100 million people). Those who fall into this category are characterized by their cognitive skills, their level of education, the depth and breadth of their knowledge and their relative prosperity. They are more likely to be politically mobilized and more likely to vote. At the other end of the spectrum is the mass of European public opinion, which never feels European or only sometimes, comprising between 60% and 85% of the population (between 300 and 425 million people). They are characterized by their lower cognitive skills, their basic level of education, their limited level of knowledge of, or interest in, European politics, and their lower-than-mean levels of income. Clearly, there are people with a fuzzy sense of European identity whose opinions come between the two ends of the spectrum.

To unpack further the point, it seems that that the EU has primarily benefited directly Europe's professional and managerial elite. It is true that there are hard-to-discern but significant benefits flowing from the Single Market in terms of greater consumer choice, lower prices and better standards of quality and safety that benefit everyone. Nonetheless, it is professionals and managers who, through their interactions with one another in common European federations and associations, have created a shared European civil society. Questions of identity constitute a field where political, social and religious conflicts are played out between factions: for example, the secular *vs.* the religious, or the liberal *vs.* the reactionary. In the case of the EU, the conflict is between the Europhile and Eurosceptic. This has much in common with conflicts between the cosmopolitan elite, with its strong European identity, and the populist mass, with its weak or non-existent European identity. Euroscepticism also appears to be rooted in a lack of consciousness or a simple lack of awareness about where one's true interests lie. To illustrate this point by anecdote, the ERASMUS student and the international businessman not only have an interest, or perhaps a stake, in European integration, but they are both more likely to be conscious of it. The British, German or Dutch holidaymakers and retirees on the Costa del Sol also share this interest – arguably even more so in the case of the pensioner in need of medical treatment – yet they may also harbour Eurosceptic feelings. In other words, they may not always realize where their interests lie. Why this should be the case is of profound interest and requires immediate explanation.

If the proposition is that there are two European societies when it comes to questions of European identity – the elite and the mass – the immediate question is what determines a citizen's affiliation to one or the other. The evidence suggests that having a strong sense of European identity requires three separate conditions: (1) European politics should be a modestly salient issue for the person in question; (2) he or she should have a cognitive recognition of the benefits brought by European integration, both at the personal and societal level, and (3) he or she should be conscious of these two elements. The elite segment of European society is far more likely to be able to vault over this high 'European identity bar'.

Consciousness of the benefits of integration is particularly important because the process has brought direct material advantages to all Europeans. Even if these benefits are not felt immediately by an individual, it is unlikely to have caused him or her direct harm either. The vast majority of Europeans have indirectly profited, for example, from the improved quality, consumer choice and lower prices brought about by the Single Market (European Commission, 2007), or from the ease of travel within the Schengen area. However, most Europeans are either not conscious of these facts at all, take them for granted, or more prosaically perhaps, never consider them unless they are asked a direct question about whether they think that EU membership is a good or a bad thing. If we accept the proposition that European identity appears to be a matter of cognitive mobilization, then this helps us to explain the apparent paradox of high levels of support for EU membership or the unification of Europe (Figure 2.2) and the much smaller degree to which citizens identify with Europe (Figure 2.1).

It could be stated, therefore, that there is a direct and two-way link between the extent to which 'elite Europe' feels connected to the European integration project and the extent to which they, as a group, feel European. In other words, European identity is both instrumental and formed in contact with other Europeans, but this applies only to a certain cosmopolitan segment of European society (Fligstein, 2008). A key argument of this book is that the notion of the EU as a market-driven, 'instrumental' project with limited emotional pull on its citizens has probably run its course. The EU has sought to legitimize itself by appealing to citizens at a cognitive level. It has succeeded to a great extent in winning over the minds of the elite who were, after all, the principal beneficiaries of 60 years of integration by the 2010s. Yet this focus on education and cognitive decision-making has failed to tap into a deeper, instinctive or emotional level in a way that would allow the EU to connect with the mass of the people. The absence of a deeper attachment on the part of its citizens means that there are no grounds for complacency in thinking that the European integration paradigm, or the elite model of European identity it has created, will endure forever. European history is littered with discarded identities belonging to extinct polities: those of the Soviets (in the 1990s the 'Soviet' identity was the preferred identifier of many older Russian-speaking Ukrainians; for more discussion, see Bassin and Kelly, 2012), Czechoslovaks, Yugoslavs or Ottomans. It is also worthy of comment that what all these societies shared was a cognitive, elite-created identity that failed to mobilize mass opinion at the emotional level.

There are also differences between the mainly Western European EU-15 and the Central European countries that joined in 2004 and 2007. Here, at least for some Central Europeans, identity is both emotional (signalling an end to the misery of Communist-era isolation and post-Communist second-class status as Europeans for those born before 1990) and, for the young and mobile, instrumental. Until the 2004 and 2007 enlargements, intra-European mobility was largely, something from which only elites profited – the 'Eurostars' of Fligstein (2008). Between 2004 and the British census of 2011, around 1.1 million citizens of the new member states moved to the UK and remained. (Inward flows were even higher, but many returned to their own countries; Vargas-Silva, 2013.) For this group especially, and for their fellow citizens who stayed resident in their home country but profited from the unrestricted travel opportunities that EU membership brought, there was a real experience of an enabling, common European identity through citizenship. This experience has increased quite dramatically the number of people who 'feel European'. That said, this aspect of intra-European migration does not undermine the elite–mass dichotomy. What is significant here is less to do with membership of an elite and more with the experience of the practical, personal value that the fruits of European integration bring, which have been appreciated by Central Europeans in all social groups. In 2008, intra-EU migration amounted to around 14.7 million people living in a different member state from the one in which they were born – or around 3% of the European population. The member states with the highest number of inhabitants from other EU countries were the UK (2 million, or 3.1% of the population), Spain (2.8 million or 4% of the population), Germany (3.4 million or 4% of the population) and France (2.1 million or 3% of the population) (Eurostat, 2011b).

In broad terms, the distance between the instrumental and the emotive goes some way towards explaining the separation between elite and mass opinion on the benefits of European integration. This gap was always present, but after the 1990s – as the Maastricht and subsequent referendums showed – it turned into a chasm that seemed to be growing ever wider (Eichenberg and Dalton, 2007). Those who think about Europe and weigh up the pros and cons seriously are more likely to find a great deal in the project that is to their liking since, as Galbraith argued, 'people approve most of what they best understand' (2001, p. 20). Those who do not engage in this cognitive process of reflection, and simply base their view of the EU on instinct, have a higher propensity to be Eurosceptic – they dislike what they do not understand or cannot be bothered to try to understand. This in turn means that, as noted above, cognitive reflection upon European identity is not enough. The EU must also be salient to an individual as a political issue if he or she is to identify with it. And, lastly, citizens need to be consciously aware that EU integration benefits them. In combination, it must be said that these three criteria represent a very high level at which to set the identity bar. The nation-state, which relies on an instinctive, emotional level of identification from its citizens, does not have to meet these stringent and exacting standards. Herein lies the political problem of European identity, which in turn feeds into arguments about the legitimacy of the EU's decision-making procedures, as will be demonstrated in Chapter 3.

What are the Determinants of European Identity?

Determining what makes a European a European is difficult. This chapter is not the place for a lengthy historical overview of the currents of European history, which in any case would only be useful if such an effort would identify what Europeans have in common or what their shared historical memories are. The constitutive elements of a European identity are hard to tie down, but what has come to matter is the interaction between those identities and the EU. Europe is capitalist and remains largely Christian. Since the secularization of politics, and even more so taking pride in the separation of the religious and the political, is a European specificity (Habermas, 2006), there is little sense in pursuing this angle further. The historical memories of Europe *do* matter (Mayer and Palmowski, 2004), but their interpretations differ widely, remain national in character and are therefore no basis for a shared sense of self. Europe has few shared cultural symbols, beyond its flag, an anthem that few would recognize and a passport that not all Europeans hold since they need only identity cards for intra-EU travel. More promisingly, Europe has its currency, the Euro, which unfortunately has become a focus of popular discontent and in any case is not yet used in all European states. Europeans do not share a common language. More Europeans may speak German as their first language than French, English or any other language, but this does not make German the European lingua franca. A great many Europeans – particularly amongst the elite – now speak English or are multilingual, and so the idea of multilingualism could be put forward, but multilingualism is not the preserve of Europeans alone. So what, therefore, could usefully be said to be specifically European?

Mayer and Palmowski (2004), Habermas (2006) and others have suggested potential sources of European identity, a great many of which are based on the notion of shared values. All of these are normative and none are universal, but they form a useful starting point for discussion.

The first is the notion of a common European civilization, which is in some way superior to, or more advanced than, the other civilizations of the world. The term 'civilization' itself is by default normative and notoriously hard to define. Civilization for our purposes is understood to mean culture in its broadest sense, encompassing science, technological accomplishment, the arts and perhaps a particular sense of the aesthetic. Some might understand it to include the means by which society is ordered – democracy, the rule of the law and so on – but these values are shared with the United States and many other developed countries. However, it is the inherent *relativity* of the superiority of European civilization that precludes it from forming the basis of a 21st century European identity. In other words, for European civilization to be superior, other civilizations and cultures must be inferior. This was the attitude that the Europeans carried with them around the world when they began to 'discover' it in the 16th century. In the smug afterglow of the technological and industrial revolution of the 18th and 19th centuries that allowed the Europeans to conquer and rule half the world, this notion of 'being better' than others flourished. In the first half of the 20th century it nourished European fascists, as well as European colonialists who thought they were acting in the interests of the native populations they ruled over. Thus the notion of European civilization as superior to others is by default prejudiced, at best old-fashioned, most definitely out-of-step with the spirit of the times and certainly politically incorrect. Thus, even if this notion is given some credit amongst certain segments of the population, it is unlikely to find universal favour, and is a potentially dangerous approach for those seeking to build a common European identity.

The second proposal is the idea of European-ness being about heterogeneity –'United in diversity' as the EU slogan would have it. Again, this will not work as an underlying source of identity because many countries are as diverse as the EU. A more fundamental drawback is that it is a mere slogan, largely devoid of deeper meaning. The American motto, '*E pluribus unum*' (Out of many one), implies the creation of something distinct and shared. Europe's slogan implies that the Europeans are a diverse set of peoples – and that they remain so, which does not imply that Europe is forging a common bond.

Thirdly, a much more promising notion is that of the uniqueness of the European way of life. Most of Europe at the beginning of the 21st century remains very rich in per-capita terms, so Europeans can afford to live comfortably by world standards. However, the European way of life is not just about money, since the United States and other parts of the developed world are just as wealthy. Moreover, many member states have joined the middle-income bracket of countries since the 1990s, which means that the gap between the West and 'the Rest' is not nearly as large as it once was, and a comfortable way of life is no longer unusual in global terms. The argument of this chapter is that the uniqueness of Europe's way of life rests not so much on its wealth as on its social model – even if wealth is a necessary, though not sufficient, condition for it to exist. The European variant of capitalism (see Chapters 4 and 5) involves the provision of a considerable range of public goods and services, as well as a large-scale system of social protection. Unfortunately, this promising notion of the singularity of Europe's social model falls short when it is noted that the level of spending on the welfare state in EU countries is not significantly greater (26% of GDP) than that in the US (19% of GDP). It is also true that there is a great diversity of social models in the EU (Wincott, 2003), although there appears to be gradual convergence (Schmidt, 2002). Castles identifies a cluster of four European 'families' rather than a single European social model: English-speaking, Nordic, continental Western European and Southern European.

> In 1960, continental Western Europe was the area making much the greatest welfare effort, with little to choose between the English-speaking and Scandinavian countries in the middle of the distribution, and with Southern Europe, Italy excepted in the rearguard. By 1980, however, this clear hierarchy of spending had collapsed into two broader groupings, with the Scandinavian and continental Western European countries spending around a quarter of GDP for social policy purposes and the English-speaking and Southern European countries around 15 per cent. Finally ... hierarchy was restored, but along lines rather different to those of the early post-war era. By 1998, the Scandinavian countries had become outright welfare leaders, with average spending levels of just below 30 per cent of GDP. The countries of continental Western Europe followed close behind, with Southern Europe now somewhat ahead of an English-speaking rearguard. (Castles, 2004, pp. 26–7)

A unifying factor that does help to set Europe apart from other wealthy countries is that *support* both for government intervention (see Chapter 5) and the welfare state appears to be more or less universal in Europe – which does not appear to be true for the United States. Making a rather different point in 2012, Angela Merkel noted that, 'Europe today accounts for just over 7 per cent of the world's population, produces around 25 per cent of global GDP and has to finance 50 per cent of global social spending' (Merkel, quoted by Peel, 2012). Statistically, those who believed that the 'government should redistribute' income amounted to 71% of Belgians, 83% of the French, 69% of Swedes and over 90% of Portuguese and Greeks. Britain and the Netherlands amounted to an almost two-thirds majority in favour of redistribution (Mau and Burkhardt, 2009). The equivalent figure for the United States was barely 50% (Newport, 2013). In other words, the idea that welfare ought to be provided is not the subject of serious political contestation in Europe. The consensus that 'politics and the state should act as a *corrective* to material outcomes' (Habermas, 2006) could form at least part of the basis for a common European identity.

Fourthly, it has been argued that Europe has set itself apart from the rest of the world with its respect for the principle of non-violence at home and abroad (Habermas, 2006). The EU began as a project for the promotion of peace between West European countries. Moreover, all of the EU and nearly all of the European continent is a death penalty-free zone. Even if European states still undertake military operations (around half of the EU participated in the Second Gulf War) and two are nuclear powers, the European public's appetite for foreign adventures seems limited. A nuanced attitude towards the use of force helps to differentiate Europe from, for example, the United States and Russia, even if more generally the world is a much less violent place in terms of wars between states than it was 100 years ago (Pinker, 2012). Here, to an extent, Europe appears to be leading a wider trend through the promotion of peace and non-violence as values.

Peace and non-violence point towards Mayer and Palmowski's fifth point, which is the notion of European identity being based on sharing certain features. Mayer and Palmowski identified these as institutions, rules, policies and politics. *Shared experiences* should be added to the list. These were traditionally the preserve of the elite, but they are also a core part of the formation of many Central Europeans' attitudes to European identity. Here at last is some kind of basis for a shared European identity, since no other group of countries in the world have integrated themselves to the same degree as the EU's member states. Developing Mayer and Palmowski's point further, there are four principal strands to this shared identity, which will be described here.

Common policies form the first strand. The early years of European integration required the creation of a common market and *common policies*; for example, the common external tariff on goods entering the European Community and the Common Agricultural Policy, which was designed to make Europe self-sufficient in food. Since the early 1960s, these shared policies have extended, invisibly for the most part, to many areas of European life. For instance, the products Europeans buy conform to the same, harmonized safety and environmental standards. Occasionally, the harmonization of policies is obvious, for example, in crossing borders within the Schengen area or in making payments in Euros within the Eurozone, but much of what has been harmonized (such as regulations on the construction of pleasure craft, batteries or dentists' drills, to draw three random examples) does not appear to the metaphorical naked eye.

A second strand of these shared attributes concerning Europeans living in EU member states, which once again is not immediately apparent to most Europeans, is the *rulebook*. It is no great exaggeration to state that what made European integration work was the creation of a new legal order. It is not the focus of this book to dwell on how this works, but it meant the creation of a level playing field to ensure that all parties are treated equally. And for that to happen, two things were required. First, EU legislation is always superior to national legislation (known as 'supremacy'). And second, where member states are tardy in putting the necessary secondary legislation in place to meet an EU objective, EU legislation can take effect without secondary legislation (known as 'direct effect'). No other system of international cooperation like this exists in the world. It is truly a 'new legal order'. That said, most EU citizens appear to remain blissfully unaware of this important technical innovation, which limits its scope in the formation of European identity.

A third strand is the common European *polity*. Politicians are elected as representatives to three forums: the European Council (as heads of state and government), the Council of the EU (as the ministers delegated by member state governments) and in the European Parliament (as Members of the European Parliament or MEPs). The primary responsibility of those who sit in the European Council and Council of the EU is not European, but national, politics, and this forms the basis on which they are elected. For that reason, these two parts of the European polity do not provide a basis for a common European identity. However, the European Parliament is composed of representatives whose work is exclusively European politics and policy; they are elected directly to represent European citizens in the policy-making process. Election campaigns for the European Parliament are still usually fought on national, rather than European platforms (see the 'second-order elections' theory in Reif and Schmitt, 1980):

> National elections tend to be focussed on substantive policy issues that increasingly can only be fully addressed at the EU level, such as immigration, food safety, environment, or economic growth, while European Parliamentary elections tend to focus more on general polity issues that can only be resolved by nationally based actors, such as how to reform EU institutions – where, that is, they are concerned with EU issues at all. (Schmidt, 2006, p. 33)

Despite this fact, the European Parliament does form the basis for a European political identity in an attempt to reverse the acknowledgement that 'while the EU has *policy without politics*, the member states end up with *politics without policy* in EU related areas' (emphasis in original, Schmidt, 2006, p. 33). Moreover, after twenty years of incremental change through co-decision, by the 2010s the European Parliament had acquired a substantial policy-making role that was equal to that of the

Council of Ministers' in decision making. However, even though the European Parliament represents substantial theoretical progress in the creation of a European identity through a shared polity, it is hamstrung by the fact that only half of those European citizens eligible to vote bothered to do so in the elections of 2014, 2009, 2004 and 1999. This is a remarkably similar figure to those 50% of Europeans who say that they 'feel European' some or all of the time. However, the parallel in these figures does not mean that the percentage of those who voted in European elections is actually Europhile: anti-European MEPs have been elected in the past and anti-European parties are well represented in the European Parliament. In the 2014 European Parliament elections, Eurosceptics or Europhobic MEPs of left- and right-wing orientation were returned to more than one-third of the seats in the legislature.

Linked to this theme of a shared European way of doing politics is the notion that ideological competition forms the basis for contestation between political parties. Habermas (2006) sees this contraposition as a core part of European democracy. In comparison with the limited ideological differences between the Republican and Democratic parties in the United States, on the surface of things this may be true. Many Western European countries appear to be largely characterized by a Left–Right political split (SPD–CDU in Germany; Parti Socialiste–Gaullist in France; Labour–Conservative in the UK; PP–PSOE in Spain), but this was never the case in all member states. Divisions between Fine Gael and Fianna Fáil in the Irish Republic are less ideological than historical and the political divisions in some new member states are also out of step with the Left–Right dichotomy. For example, the Polish political divide in the 1990s had more to do with attitudes towards its Communist past and in the 2010s was related to social mores (Szczerbiak, 2008). Another important point is that the decline of the industrial working class in Western Europe has shifted ideological contestation towards the centre, at least between the largest political parties (Crouch, 1997; Kirchheimer, 1966). Thus the Labour Party in the UK or the SPD in Germany are less left-wing than in the 1960s and 1970s. Moreover, politics has become more fragmented in some of the old member states, with the more extreme left-wing or right-wing parties entering the political mainstream. Thus, although it could be argued that ideological competition is alive and well, it is neither uniquely European (think of Chile or Australia) nor a feature in all member states.

A final and crucially important point is the idea of shared experiences forging the common European identity. In the nation-state, such shared experiences might result from compulsory schooling on the basis of a single curriculum or military service (Weber, 1976). In the EU, shared experiences tend to be those of the cosmopolitan elite and may stem from collaboration through work in the form of conferences in Brussels or Frankfurt, higher education for the ERASMUS generation of students, holidays in Italy or France, or weekend breaks in Paris or Gdańsk. Another shared experience is migration for work. This has an elite character to it – in the increasing mobility between the different European offices of a given firm – although it is more widespread than just the higher socio-economic groups, as shown by the mass migration experiences of some Central Europeans since 2004.

So what do we know about the determinants of European identity? It is not the same as a national identity. Europeans do not speak the same language, and whilst some of their history, culture and traditions are shared, their interpretations of these differ widely. Two hundred years ago, the same was true for many of Europe's nation-states. It took generations to create a shared German, French, Italian, Slovak or Finnish identity, so perhaps there is no great cause for concern that the European identity is felt by only one European in two. In essence, what the Europeans hold in common are *values* and a *polity-in-the-making* that is governed according to those values. It does not matter particularly that these values are shared with states beyond Europe; indeed if anything, it makes them all the more powerful and legitimate. It also does not matter particularly that the European identity has not been formed in the same way as a national one and is not as deeply rooted, because the European identity is not exclusive, it is held alongside national, regional or local ones.

What is missing from the picture is an emotional attachment to the EU, which goes beyond a pragmatic assessment of whether it delivers benefits or otherwise. This is a point of particular importance, which is at the heart of explaining the limited appeal of European integration beyond Europe's elites and direct beneficiaries. This was not always the case. In the early years of European integration, the emotional part of the case for Europe was provided by the need to prevent another major European war. This persisted into the mid-1990s, and then faded into the background as the generation of political leaders with direct experience of the Second World War left office and was replaced by the baby boomers. By the 2010s, twenty years on from Kohl, Mitterrand and Delors, the idea of another great European conflagration seemed impossible, at least between West European states. The risks to European security were much altered, and centred more on managing economic and demographic shifts than questions of war and peace.

Has the EU Changed What it Means to be European?

The central premise of this chapter is the notion that the European identity can best be understood as combination of a polity-in-the-making, a rulebook, a set of norms and values as well as the facilitation of shared experiences through the right to free movement. It then logically follows that European integration has in some way shifted our ideas about what it means to be European – even if this is only true for some of the population. What, then, is the relationship between multiple identities – community, sub-national, national and European? Also, there is the question of 'what effects different cultural items or forms have on one another' (Outhwaite, 2008, p. 20). Since the 1950s, the idea of a single, shared Western European cultural heritage stretching from antiquity to the present day has retreated. Across much of the European continent, the Christian faith that went hand in hand with this notion of Western civilization has also ceased to play much of a role directly in the lives or worldviews of most Europeans. The societies of all West European countries have undergone profound social and ethnic transformations since the 1950s, particularly in the largest cities which have become cosmopolitan and diverse. The causes of these shifts – migration, materialism, de-industrialization (see Crouch, 2008) and the cultural revolution that started in the 1960s – are not the concern of this book, but to a certain extent, the consequences are. European society in the 2010s is radically different from European society in the 1950s. In addition to being more ethnically diverse, the population has become much older, a trend that would continue over the 21st century. This is not to suggest that European integration has completely replaced historical, cultural and religious markers of identity. My premise is more simple: in the context of the enormous social changes that took place between the 1950s and the early 21st century, a European identity based on uncontested values, a rulebook, a polity-in-the-making and, above all, shared experiences fits the picture of contemporary European society more accurately than historical, ethnic, religious or civilizational notions which were inevitably filtered through national lenses.

Normatively, a narrative of European identity that is based on shared values (however long or short the period of time; Mazower, 1998) and institutions has the value of inclusiveness. More recent arrivals on the European continent who share these values and experiences can become Europeans, or at least feel that they have a share in the European polity. In other words, those who share these values (and live in the continent of Europe) can identify themselves as Europeans. This exchange also provides the logic for EU enlargement: countries wishing to share the institutions and thus the European polity have to share European values. It could be argued – as is claimed in countries such as Russia or Ukraine – that a values-based, rather than historical–cultural notion of European identity is essentially an expropriation of European-ness by the EU. Evidence on the declining sense of European-ness in Russia (White *et al.*, 2008) also appears to suggest that, for countries outside the EU that share Europe's cultural heritage, European identity has become increasingly associated with the EU and its values, not all of which are shared by Russia.

Identities are bound up with the shared representation of a collective self (Checkel and Katzenstein, 2009), which means being certain as to what the group is and who belongs to it. Identity, by its nature can be exclusive. Questions of identity tend to be ignored or addressed in a fairly superficial manner in the official European integration narrative. There are a great many reasons for this, but of particular importance is that the so-called founding fathers of the European project hoped that *national* identities would be neutered in the process of being subsumed into a greater European whole. A shift in the loyalties to Europe could result for ideational reasons (Parsons, 2002), satisfaction with the organization's performance (Haas, 1964), appropriateness (Risse, 2005) or a combination of consequentialism and appropriateness (Easton, 1965). In the context of the post-war period with its immediate memories of pre-war nationalism, there was good reason to hope that this would be the case. Yet, although exposure to European integration has played a role in constructing a European identity since then (see for instance Bruter, 2005), Europe has never really got beneath the skin of a nation. Whilst national identities in some member states have either mutated or simply weakened since the 1950s, they have not done so quite in the way that was foreseen in the aftermath of the Second World War, and this movement has not systematically resulted in an enhanced European identity. European identity cannot be conceptualized in a zero-sum game:

> These two identities are compatible because they are of different order and endowed with different meanings ... attachment to national identity is largely 'cultural', while attachment to a European identity is primarily 'instrumental'... [but] the particular configuration of national identities in each country gives rise to distinct dynamics and historical inertias that have an impact on the emergence and configuration of a European identity. (Ruiz Jiménez *et al.*, 2004, p. 18)

An increasing sense of European identity over time, which is inevitably hard to prove, does not mean a decrease in national or subnational identities (Bruter, 2005). Bruter notes that European and national identities are actually positively correlated. Be it the 'Russian Matruska doll' model – which posits a hierarchy between multiple identities – or the 'marble cake' model – which visualizes the superposition of different identities that influence each other, it is clear that many identify with the notion of being European in addition to their national identity.

As noted already, there is a substantial body of evidence to suggest, on balance, that the EU has in some way changed our understanding of what it means to be European. Whilst the EU has not decisively shaped Europeans' varying and contested views of their historical or cultural identity, it has had the effect of creating an identity for Europe, based on rules, behavioural norms and values. Furthermore, it has transformed the life chances and outcomes of a European elite, which through its shared experiences of working, studying and holidaying within the Union, has adopted a European identity. It could tentatively also be suggested that the EU has in some instances rewritten European history. In central European states during the 1990s and early 2000s the notion of the 'Return to Europe' was widely touted. Although this is a pleasing and memorable slogan, it conceals the fact that some of the states that now constitute the EU-28 had historically never been united with the rest of Europe, except by means of short-lived military conquests by European states. This particular conceit matters less than the fact that 'returning to Europe' has allowed central Europeans to travel freely and work across the EU-28, thus participating fully in the life of a European community.

Conclusions

This chapter has argued that the balance of evidence suggests that European integration had changed what it means to be European by the 2010s, but only for the elite. Moreover, in doing so, what could be termed 'two Europes' had been created. The integration process provided an underpinning of what it means to be European centred on shared values. More prosaically, but just as importantly, it dramatically transformed the life chances of many Europeans, although only a minority of the beneficiaries are aware of this. Crucially, however, the material benefits of integration accrued more to managerial and professional elites, as will be explained in Chapter 3 (Fligstein, 2008; Risse, 2010). Indeed, despite the rising prosperity of the European continent since the immediate post-war period, European integration also corresponded with a period of de-industrialization, particularly since the 1970s, which disproportionately affected non-elite groups (Crouch, 2008). This phenomenon increased intra-member-state (as opposed to intra-European) differences, focusing benefits on a small portion of Europeans and thus sharpening the division between those who had directly benefited from integration and those who had not. Furthermore, the markers of European identity were now more about shared values, shared experiences, shared institutions and a common polity-in-the-making than shared cultural–historical or religious narratives, which tend both to be contested and filtered through national lenses. However, the shared experiences that appear to contribute to European identity formation are primarily (if not exclusively) shared by a narrow, if numerically substantial, European elite.

These identity shifts are indirectly attributable to European integration. They are also part of a global process of increasing migration, increasing materialism and increasing consumerism, not least because European integration has helped to fuel these processes. Yet, identitification with Europe is too complicated, too fluid and too subject to contestation for a single European identity to emerge around anything other than a mixed bag of factors. These elements include the cognitive calculation of the benefits of European integration, shared democratic values, shared experiences and shared institutions. That said, however, the shared experiences of European integration appear to remain the preserve of Europe's elites in the old EU-15 and the preserve of the young and the mobile in the post-2004 member states. European identity formation has proved to be a messy process and one that is difficult to quantify. Yet the same is true for identity formation at the national level, as attested by the examples of Spain, the UK, Cyprus, Latvia, Belgium and others.

Although European integration made the issue of what it means to be European of interest to academics, it is less obvious that the issue matters much to most Europeans. Yet, 50 years into the European integration project, identity had become a serious, if often concealed, issue for European politics and policy-making because of its relevance to other areas. Questions of European identity feed into the other macro themes that are the focus of this book – solidarity, legitimacy and sustainability – and into micro-political issues like the size and focus of the EU's budget or the system of voting in the Council of Ministers. In consequence, questions of identity had transcended the merely sociological, historical or cultural and became matters of great importance to anyone with an interest in contemporary Europe. Disappointingly, however, European mass opinion had failed to become interested in these debates, quite possibly because the linkages to Europeans as individuals are far from obvious.

One explanation is that, despite all that has been achieved, only half of Europeans feel that the European identity is something that belongs to them or something that they share. The bulk of those who did feel themselves to be Europeans tended to come from the higher socio-economic groups and to be better educated. Fligstein and others have established that a belief in European integration as a good thing is most strongly correlated with the managerial and professional elites and the well-educated. These are the groups for whom European integration has transformed both their life chances and their life experiences. It has provided them with opportunities that were simply not open to earlier generations: to study in another country easily, to work abroad, to retire abroad, to open businesses in other member states and so on. It is this elite group that benefits the most from European integration and experiences its value. It comes as no surprise, therefore, that they should be both its most enthusiastic proponents and those who cognitively identify most closely with it.

In considering the attitudes of the non-elite segments of European society, by the 2010s it appeared that European identity had not managed to transcend the rational and reach out to the sensibilities and emotions of most Europeans. Even when it did, it tended to tap into emotions that were more Eurosceptic than pro-European. Emphatically, this was not the case in all member states to the same extent in the 2010s: European integration is associated with freedom, democracy and international acceptance in some member states, mostly those states that have been left- or right-wing authoritarian regimes within living memory (Central and South-Western Europe). But not all member states believed that the EU had brought democracy. Some even thought that it has weakened democracy and freedom, as is the case for many in the UK and Scandinavia. Whatever the picture across individual member states, however, the majority of the data appears to point one way: European integration appeals most to those who have benefited most from it, which in Western Europe at least means the elite. In the newer member states of Central Europe, European integration appeals to a much larger segment of society since it provided the blueprint for successful economic, social and political transformation after 1989. In Central Europe, European integration has brought opportunities in terms of travel, work, social advancement and so on that would have been thought impossible in the 1980s. Yet these feelings still originate in cost–benefit calculations rather than a deeper sense of attachment.

Europe's allusive emotional narrative however, may be less problematic than is commonly supposed. In practical terms, grudging acceptance, rather than a sense of identity, will just about do for the European polity to function – and the EU has this already (see Chapter 3). In other words, the support of an enthusiastic minority backed up by an apathetic majority should be an adequate basis on which the polity can function. Support for the EU – at least before the Eurozone crisis – was strongest among Europeans under 35 years of age. This was arguably because the EU had always been in existence for them, and therefore commanded a measure of the unthinking, automatic self-identification that is one of the hallmarks of the nation-state. It may, therefore, be that the formation of a European identity has time, demography and the steady drip of shared experiences on its side in the long term.

It is worth raising the contextual point in conclusion that it is sensible to avoid the pitfalls of excessive Eurocentrism in the European identity debate. Europe is not the only part of the world where a multiplicity of languages, cultures and histories coexist within a polity and where conflict between member states and the union at the centre of that polity is a perennial feature of the political scene. Europeans would do well to look across the world to other hugely diverse sub-continental states for a degree of inspiration – or perhaps comfort. Perhaps a sense of understanding what it means to be Gujarati, Tamil or Marathi as well as Indian would make a useful contribution to our understanding of European identity (see for instance Marquand, 2011).

Even if the long-term outlook seemed positive in the 2010s, the attractiveness of a shared European identity appeared, as long as the Eurozone crisis continued, to be bound up with the success or failure of the European project as a whole. It could not be otherwise if Europeans' support for the EU is based to some extent on a cost–benefit analysis. European history is littered with discarded identities that failed to deliver security or prosperity – or both. Because European identity is, for the most part, a product of shared experiences and cognitive reflection on the part of a relatively small West European elite supplemented by a larger group of Central Europeans, the EU is highly vulnerable to changes in external circumstances that make it more difficult to deliver concrete, material benefits. For the EU to succeed, it needs its people to identify more closely both with one another and with the wider European project in an emotional as well as a cognitive fashion. It therefore needs to become a completely accepted or 'normal' – as opposed to contested – part of the European political environment: it needs the idea of a Europe without the EU to become unthinkable. This may well happen with the advent of a generation that has no memories of Europe before Schengen, the Euro and the 2004 enlargement. Some new founding myths of European integration, in addition to the old 'war and peace' narrative, would also help greatly in this process. This does not mean that the EU can ignore the key challenge for European policy as the continent emerges from the Great Recession, which is that of making sure that the benefits of European integration are felt more widely. This goes beyond the familiar mantra of the EU as motor of jobs-and-growth and touches upon the issue of fairness, how the fruits of Europe's continued prosperity are shared. It is to this vital issue of European solidarity, and its prerequisite of legitimacy, that we turn in Chapter 3.

3

Legitimacy: Democracy, Accountability and Credibility

Questions of legitimacy are always at the forefront of debate about the European Union (EU). All kinds of polity are obliged to legitimize their manner of government by one means or another. In contemporary liberal democratic nation-states, legitimacy is rooted in the competitive principle that voters choose the political party they wish to represent them in government through regular elections conducted under universal suffrage. In non-democratic states, attempts can be made to legitimize military or one-party rule as the only means of ensuring external security or preventing internal violence and disorder. Central and Eastern Europe's former ruling Communist parties derived their self-proclaimed legitimacy from claims about the optimal means of achieving a socialist society, or protection from potentially belligerent neighbours. Since the EU is not a nation-state, it does not elect a single government. Decisions are made jointly by the elected representatives of national governments in the Council of the EU, and by directly elected Members of the European Parliament (MEPs). The legitimacy of this arrangement is constantly called into question (Beetham and Lord, 1998; Bolleyer and Reh, 2011; Follesdal, 2006; Hix, 2008; Lord, 2004; Mair, 2013; Majone, 1998, 2009; Moravcsik, 2002; Scharpf, 1991, 2002; Schmidt, 2013) because the EU is a *supranational* body with the power to make *binding* decisions about what will happen in the member states. These decisions may be enforced by courts which have powers to oblige both *states* and *citizens* to observe commonly agreed rules. There is an argument that the link between the voter and the decision making of European institutions is stretched so far that the Union's technocratic system of politics cannot be said to conform to the highest standards of democratic legitimacy. In the words of Joseph Weiler, the pre-eminent legal scholar of the EU:

> a system that enjoys formal legitimacy may not necessarily enjoy social legitimacy ... democracy can be measured by the closeness, responsiveness, representativeness, and accountability of the governors to the governed. (1999, p. 81)

Precisely what standards constitute democratic legitimacy in a supranational polity is one of the most contentious issues in the study and practice of EU politics. This question is also open to various interpretations depending on the political organization of member states – on a spectrum from unitary states to decentralized and regional states – and the impact that Europeanization has had on the structures of their polities (Schmidt, 2006).

Comparing legitimacy at European and national levels is a fascinating area of study. This stems partly from the fact that the EU is the most advanced intergovernmental and supranational polity in the world, and partly because, for a polity to function and be legitimate, the people who live in its framework must give their consent to its activities. In a national or regional political system, this consent stems from the fact that the attachment formed between citizen and state is so engrained that the electorate seldom has cause to reflect upon it at all. Occasionally, there is a problem in the electoral system that leads to an unusual outcome, as was the case in the United States after the election of President George W. Bush in 2000. His opponent, Al Gore, won half a million more votes nationwide while Bush's electoral college victory in Florida, which brought him to the Presidency was delivered by 537 votes, well within a possible margin of error (Shafer, 2002). Such cases are all the more notorious for their rarity. Mostly, for the citizens of a nation-state, their government simply *is*; in political terms, its existence and right to govern is a given. Therefore, it is very unusual for a national government's legitimacy to be called into serious question. Political oppositions contest a government's actions but not its legitimacy, hence the nomenclature 'Her Majesty's Most Loyal Opposition' that is used in the Westminster parliamentary system. The EU remains subject to on-going contestation about both whether it is needed and whether it enjoys the legitimacy to govern. For some the issue is clear-cut, as Karlheinz Neunreither put it, there is 'no chance of a possible EU democracy, because there is no European people, no demos. No demos, no democracy – quite simple' (2000, p. 148; see also Dahl, 1989). To suggest that the EU is completely undemocratic because a Europe-wide demos is either non-existent or, as I would suggest, nascent seems an exaggeration. Yet the very fact that this perception is so widespread means that questions of what constitutes democratic legitimacy in a supranational polity are highly pertinent in the EU and form an integral part of its politics and its interaction with its citizens.

Legitimacy was not always so salient in EU politics, between the 1960s and the 1980s it was assumed that there existed a 'permissive consensus' between rulers and their citizens about the merits of European integration (Lindberg and Scheingold, 1970). This is no longer the case and legitimacy has come increasingly to the fore since the Maastricht referendums of the early 1990s. That further European integration is subject to serious political contestation was most vividly illustrated by the failure of the Constitutional treaty to win approval in referendums in France and the Netherlands in 2005 (Hurrelmann, 2007). Legitimacy is a fundamentally important concern centred on the extent to which Europeans feel that community institutions have the necessary democratically-given right to govern them. This chapter examines the issue by asking three basic questions:

- Is the EU democratic?
- Is the EU accountable?
- Is it perceived by the peoples of Europe to be democratic and accountable? In other words, does the EU enjoy the confidence of its citizens, and, if not, why not?

Legitimacy and credibility matter enormously in any democratic system and the EU has not been unquestionably endowed with these two attributes since the Maastricht Treaty of the early 1990s. The Eurozone crisis has further served to undermine the popular legitimacy of the EU, as Figure 3.1 demonstrates starkly.

Although support for European integration went into free-fall during the Eurozone crisis, arguments about the EU's democratic deficit did not begin with the financial crisis and the Great Recession. This chapter's central argument is that the democratic deficit is both uneven in nature and spread diffusely across the different levels of government in the contemporary EU. The causes are just as much related to globalization as to European integration (Mair, 2013; Majone, 2009). Moreover, as

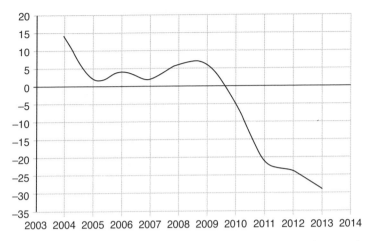

Figure 3.1   Level of net support in the EU for the EU (difference between the proportion that trusts the EU and the proportion that does not trust it)

Source: Data from Eurobarometer 2003–13, author's own calculations.

many scholars have noted (Mair, 2013; Majone, 2009; Scharpf, 1999), Europe's democratic deficit is by no means limited to the EU level of government; it is also to be found operating at the member-state level (Schmidt, 2006). In some areas of its activity, the EU is not only both fundamentally democratic and accountable, but can justifiably deem itself a highly effective international organization. In other areas, almost the opposite is true. Matters are not at all clear-cut when it comes to democratic accountability in the EU. This chapter argues that the EU remains democratic, legitimate and accountable in its traditional areas of activity, primarily the politics of regulation. This view has been roundly contested by Fritz Scharpf, who argued long before the Eurozone crisis that it was precisely the shift of regulatory powers to the European level (combined with globalization) that had deprived democratic governments at the member-state level of many of their 'problem-solving capabilities' (1999). Too much European integration was negative in nature (i.e. removing the member states' regulatory powers to act in certain areas), and had too few positive effects (i.e. bringing in Europe-wide regulation to counteract problems of market failure). For Scharpf, the EU prevented national governments from implementing the kinds of regulatory policies that could help address serious problems such as high levels of unemployment or what he saw as the steady erosion of the tax basis of national welfare states (1999). This point was contested by Giandomenico Majone (2009) who argued that the opposite was true: the toolkit available to national policy-makers is enhanced by participation in the EU.

My argument is that, while acknowledging the imperfections in the EU system of democratic accountability, it should not be assumed that the EU as it stands represents the end-point for democratic development in a supranational organization. As Peter Mair (2013) argued, it is quite possible that a European demos of sorts may gradually emerge through socialization. Chapter 2 presented evidence to suggest that this might already be happening – at least for the upper strata of European society. But the primary focus of this chapter relates to the EU as it is, before moving on to the normative question of the EU as it should be. It is well-known that, at the member-state level, the EU has played a vital role in *enhancing* the quality of democratic government at the national level by, for example, helping to protect citizens from their own governments (see Majone, 2009; and, *inter alia*, European Court Case 152/84, M.H. Marshall *vs*. Southampton and South-West Hampshire Area Health Authority (Teaching)). It also provided a counterweight to majoritarian politics by giving a voice to those who were under-represented at national level, such as foreign economic interests. These long-standing achievements need to be offset against the case that is made by the most forthright advocates of the EU's democratic deficit. Other defenders of the EU model have argued that the EU rode to the 'rescue' of member states unable to fulfil their citizens' needs (Milward, 1992) – a point with which Jean Monnet would have fully concurred. Some would carry the argument even further and claim that the EU acts as a form of corrective to the problems of short-termism that are inherent in democratic systems that are governed by the needs of the electoral cycle (Zakaria, 1997). For all of these observations, it cannot be denied that the crisis of democratic legitimacy in the EU is real and growing. This growth may partly be explained by two important changes which support the arguments in favour of the EU as a counterweight to help balance (and improve) national democratic systems. First, the EU only works effectively as a counterweight when national democratic systems are functioning properly. Second, the EU can only be an effective counterweight to national democratic systems when its own functions are limited. Both of these two conditions had eroded significantly by the mid-2010s.

This chapter will examine the arguments for and against the democratic deficit in turn. Given that my approach is normative as well as positive, it also offers three basic prescriptions on how to improve matters.

First of all, the EU needs to change its approach to political contestation, building upon the seminal arguments put forward by distinguished scholars elsewhere (see, for example, Follesdal, 2006; Hix, 2008). My justification in making this proposition is that the era of an exclusively technocratic or regulatory EU is passing, as the Eurozone crisis threw into sharp relief the limitations to the EU's current way of operating. The notion of an exclusively market-based model of European integration has had its day. Others would question this assertion, including Majone (2009) and Weingast (1995). Indeed, Majone suggests that the opposite is true – a federal EU would have to limit itself to 'market-preserving federalism' – before suggesting that the EU would work better as a 'model confederation' than a 'failed federation' (Majone, 1999, pp. 220–1). A second prescription, and one that builds on the all-important notion of political contestation, is that the EU needs to put into place a 'loyal opposition'. This point is derived from Mair's (2013) observation that the third milestone along the road to democracy that was articulated by Dahl (1966) – the right to opposition – does not truly exist in the EU. Since European integration has traditionally been subject to a high degree of political consensus in most mainstream political parties, the legitimate business of opposition has been left to Eurosceptic, even Europhobic, political parties who are, for the most part, opposed to the European integration project *tout court*. This is simply unacceptable in a mature political system – however consensual its political culture. The third prescription builds on Majone's (2005) argument that to democratize the EU it is primarily necessary to improve 'the quality of democracy at the national and subnational level' (p. 195) which will in turn allow citizens to reclaim participation in decisions that had 'previously been abandoned to executive prerogative' (p. 201). Going beyond this, it could be suggested that, in order to made serious inroads into reducing the democratic deficit in the EU, the Union needs powers of post-accession conditionality to facilitate the renewal and reform of those national institutions that are no longer fit for purpose. Vivien Schmidt (2006) has also strongly argued that institutional strength or weakness in Europe depends on the degree to which national institutional structures are able to dovetail with the EU-level apparatuses of governance (see also Rosamond, 2008). In the longer term, such strengthened (or better-fitting) institutions might also help guide the political cultures of their member states in a positive direction. Thus the optimal role for the EU is to underpin and support effective democratic government at the national and subnational levels in the 28 member states.

Complaints about the democratic deficit have been growing since the signing and ratification of the Maastricht Treaty on EU (TEU) in the early 1990s. Prior to this, however, the democratic deficit was the cause of relatively little controversy. Principled opponents to European integration existed in the UK, for example, both on the left (Gaitskell) and the right (Powell), but their concerns related as much to parliamentary sovereignty and claims of cultural difference as anything else. In the pre-Maastricht era, the EU mostly dealt in the currency of low politics (the removal of barriers to trade, harmonization and the regulation of the Single Market) whilst delivering the loftiest of political aims in the form of peace and prosperity. High political aims were delivered by low political means. Success was assured by always choosing what Jean Monnet famously referred to as 'the path of least resistance' (1978, p. 338). Integration in the era from the 1960s to the 1990s was largely a 'win-win' path, creating opportunities, wealth and an improved quality of life for most Europeans with relatively few, usually short-lived, negative consequences. Importantly, whilst not everybody shared equally in the fruits of European integration, relatively few were losers in the process. Moreover, because European integration was centred almost exclusively on affairs of low politics, the material and social gains seemed almost to spring from nowhere, to be appreciated by Europeans like manna from the heavens.

The creation of the Euro caused a sudden shift in the distinction between high and low politics when monetary policy joined the catalogue of EU competences, in this case exercised by the European Central Bank. Monetary policy, together with fiscal policy (which emphatically is not the responsibility of the EU), is one of the two basic tools of macroeconomic policy by means of which governments seek to control the economy. Given its influence on the cost of credit, employment, economic growth and the cost of living, monetary policy has a deep political impact. This being said, the shift in control of monetary policy might have proven rather uninteresting were it not for the financial crisis of 2007 and the Great Recession that followed. The crisis was as unpredicted (with some notable exceptions, e.g. Feldstein, 1997) as it was severe and prolonged, challenging the economic orthodoxies that had prevailed in Western liberal democracies for a generation. It is unfair to blame governments, the EU, international organizations or even economists for their failure to foresee the outbreak of the crisis. Policy-making, like all forms of future planning, must be rooted in a series of assumptions about the way in which the world operates. Unfortunately, these assumptions are not as fixed as social scientists would like them to be. The future is by definition uncertain and perfect information about what is to come conspicuous in its absence. Those who put their faith in complex mathematical models to map all possible human reactions to different scenarios were disappointed, and were provided with a reminder that it is unreasonable to expect omniscience from fallible human minds.

The financial crisis began as a more generalized economic slump followed by a crisis of jobs and living standards, both of which lie at the heart of democratic politics and election campaigns because they require governments to make hard choices that will have a real impact on people's lives. To make matters worse, the design of the Euro was flawed in that it Europeanized only one aspect of macroeconomic policy-making: monetary policy. Taxes, spending and most of the other means by which states attempt to steer the economy remained in the hands of national governments. This was akin to asking someone to drive a car, but only giving him control of the gear stick and clutch, with the steering wheel, brakes and accelerator controlled by a co-driver (see also Tsoukalis, 2011). The EU had introduced guidelines on macroeconomic policy management (the Stability and Growth Pact or SGP), but these were not enforced. Returning to the analogy, this was a bit like insisting that the co-drivers of the car attend an annual refresher course in motoring skills and neglecting to penalize them for not turning up. As a result of this imbalance in the levels of macroeconomic policy-making, the economic crisis became a sovereign debt crisis, the effects of which are investigated more fully in Chapters 1 and 6.

Although the democratic deficit was already the subject of considerable lively academic debate (Beetham and Lord, 1998; Bolleyer and Reh, 2011; Follesdal, 2006; Hix, 2008; Lord, 2004; Mair, 2013; Majone, 1998, 2009; Moravcsik, 2002; Scharpf, 1991, 2001; Schmidt, 2013), it was the economic and sovereign debt crisis that exposed the weaknesses of the EU's policy-making model to the general public at large. This is what transported Euroscepticism to the political mainstream of European politics, although as noted above, the basis for opposition to the 'democratic deficit' was already well-established. Technocratic politics could not address the Eurozone crisis, particularly when there was no common fiscal policy. Even worse, a technocratic solution to the European problem of sovereign debt crises meant that tax increases, spending cuts and austerity had to be imposed from outside, effectively by other member states, often against tooth-and-nail public opposition. This kind of macroeconomic authoritarianism was completely undemocratic

(Tsoukalis, 2011). The net result was that the Euro blew a hole in the EU's legitimacy, credibility and accountability. Even if the crisis of legitimacy relates exclusively to the high politics of the Eurozone crisis, its consequence was to undermine the claims of democratic accountability by the European integration project as a whole. Moreover, whilst the shortcomings of the EU's democratic system had been apparent to many observers for some time (Scharpf, 1999), most were uncertain what could be done about it (Bellamy and Warleigh, 2001) – with a few exceptions (Hix, 2008). This was precisely why those who believed deeply in the merits of European integration were terrified of the political fallout that would follow a disorderly collapse of the Eurozone. As German Chancellor, Angela Merkel, warned at the height of the crisis: 'the euro is much, much more than a currency ... the euro is the guarantee of a united Europe. If the euro fails, then Europe fails' (Spiegel, 2011). Merkel's fear, which was shared by many other European leaders, stemmed from a concern that, were the Eurosceptics to take the upper-hand, it would be hard to say where the unravelling of European integration might end.

Having begun to address the Achilles heel of the EU's democratic legitimacy and accountability, this chapter returns to the basic questions raised at the outset, building on the discussion of the Eurozone crisis in Chapter 1. This part focuses on those areas of EU activity that are not connected to the high politics of the Euro. First, it analyzes whether the EU is democratic and accountable through an investigation into how the Union's decision-making processes operate. Second, it asks whether the EU is perceived as being democratic and accountable by the peoples of Europe, which deals in essence with the credibility of the Union.

Is the EU Democratic and Accountable?

The academic and political debate on matters of legitimacy and accountability between the Maastricht referendums of 1992 and the sovereign debt crisis of the 2010s covered a great deal of ground on the issue of whether there was a 'democratic deficit' in the EU. For those who argued that there was such a deficit, the corollary was an investigation into what might be done to remedy matters. The solutions usually involved an increase in the powers of the European Parliament, sometimes included the notion of holding direct, popular elections to certain key positions and occasionally mooted a change in the organization of European political parties. The debate was both intellectually rigorous and hard-fought, engaging many of the most eminent scholars of European integration (Follesdal, 2006; Hix, 2008; Majone, 1998; Moravcsik, 2008; Weiler, 1999). Since this section of the chapter looks at the overall democratic credentials of the EU in the pre-Euro crisis period, there is no need to re-explore how the EU operates or the extent to which its legitimacy, accountability and credibility stand up to scrutiny. The investigation synthesizes the arguments put forward by leading scholars of European integration, with a few modest additions of my own.

It is a remarkable, and perhaps unique, feature of European politics that an institution that is composed exclusively of democratic countries which have chosen to join it and is governed by the rule of law should be so widely regarded as an affront to democratic principles. The EU is neither a liberal state nor a totalitarian dictatorship, it is a third type of polity: 'one with affinities to the historical empires in Europe and elsewhere but fundamentally different in its democratic structure' (Outhwaite, 2008, p. 3). As one would expect within a democratic institution, all political decisions within the EU are taken by elected politicians or the representatives of elected national governments. This was always the case, even before the introduction of a directly-elected European Parliament in 1979 because the Council of Ministers is composed of ministers from the elected, democratic national governments of the member states. In common with a nation-state, the politicians who sit on the Council of Ministers are served by a civil service: the European Commission. This is not elected – but neither are the civil services of the member states. The laws enacted by elected politicians are upheld and enforced by an independent (non-elected) judiciary in the form of the European Court of Justice. These are the simple, unequivocal facts that could be advanced by those seeking to defend the EU from attacks on its democratic credentials.

It is the now-dominant supranational mode of decision-making in the EU system that is the source of much discontent on the part of member states and the European public. This is an important point. With few exceptions, most EU decisions are made in accordance with the 'ordinary legislative procedure' that consists of a joint decision on the basis of Qualified Majority Voting (QMV) in the Council of the EU (the Council of Ministers) together with the passage of the legislation through the European Parliament. This means that a member state cannot usually block legislation if it is acting alone and in consequence it may find itself having to adopt legislation to which it has not consented. The system is designed to prevent legislative deadlock. Some might see it as undemocratic, particularly if they consider democratic legitimacy to be vested uniquely with nation-states (see Neunreither, 2000). Others would respond that the European Parliament is elected by all EU citizens, and that its members usually vote along ideological or party political, not national, lines. This mode of politics looks rather normal, even 'routine' and it is under these circumstances that the EU works best (Olsen, 2007). Furthermore, it could be posited that the essence of democracy consists of understanding that one might not always win the battle. The argument could fairly be made either way.

Why then should the EU be viewed by its critics as a technocratic monstrosity, an 'encroaching superstate' intent on stifling public participation (Moravcsik, 2008), or a 'gentle monster' (Enzensberger, 2011)? The answer lies in differing understandings of what a democratic system should look like. The normative 'should' is important here because our understanding of normal is, by definition, based on what already exists and is familiar to us. Again we are reminded of Galbraith's dictum that we favour most what we understand best (Galbraith, 2001). This close bond in our mind's eye between what we regard as normal and what is familiar is of exceptional importance. When it comes to assessing 'normality', the EU has no truly comparable international organizations that can be used as benchmark against which its democratic standards can be measured. After all, many international institutions do not require their members to be democratic. In order to join the United Nations, a state need only be sovereign and 'peace-loving', but not democratic:

> If the Security Council recommends the applicant State for membership, the General Assembly shall consider whether the applicant is a peace-loving State and is able and willing to carry out the obligations contained in the Charter. (UN, Rule 136)

In any case, no other international organization is as deeply integrated as the EU with its supranational powers and wide scope of responsibilities. In consequence, when we think of a democracy or a democratic system, we think of a nation-state. Here we come back to Neunreither's (2000) argument that there can be no democracy without a demos. At first glance, this appears to be an insurmountable problem for the EU (this issue is discussed in more detail in Chapter 7). Yet at the same time, we know that there exist what Almond (1960) and Lijphart (1977) referred to as consociational, consensual, even 'working' democracies that are multi-ethnic or multi-cultural in nature. These are states, such as Belgium or Switzerland, that function adequately and democratically despite the diverse linguistic and cultural nature of their inhabitants. Democratic systems can also be made to flourish in situations where the two sides have a history of bitter and recent antagonism, as is the case for Northern Ireland (Mair, 2013). The logical conclusion is that unconventional nation-states, polities or state-like bodies can also be fully democratic. Given that the EU is not a nation-state and that it is unique in so many ways, it is essential to define what standards of democracy and accountability are appropriate before the question of whether or not it is democratic can be answered. In doing so, this chapter first draws on the work of Majone (1998) and others who argued *against* the notion of an insurmountable democratic deficit.

Majone reasoned that there are broadly four categories of standards by which legitimacy and accountability in the EU could be measured. First, there are standards based on an analogy between the EU and its institutions and a nation-state and its national institutions. If these standards are adhered to, then the European Parliament should have the powers of a national parliament, which of necessity would remove the role of the Commission in initiating legislation.

Second, there are standards based on the majoritarian or 'winner-takes-all' Westminster model of parliamentary sovereignty. In this model, the directly-elected European Parliament should be the sole repository of legitimacy. It would follow that whoever wins a parliamentary majority could run a kind of 'elected dictatorship' until the following election, when an obliging electorate could extend this term and a disobliging electorate could throw the government out.

Third, there are standards derived from the democratic legitimacy of the member states. These standards appear to be on fairly safe ground since they form the classic paradigm for legitimating an international organization. In this model, the EU's member states have delegated authority to the EU in certain areas, are free to leave the organization when they choose (which is how the British state came to accept EU supremacy through the first two *Factortame* rulings of 1990 and 1991) and submit to supranational powers only because they have freely decided to do so. National veto rights are crucial here because they preserve the legitimacy of member states' decisions.

Fourth, and here the Majone model has been somewhat adapted, there is the 'legitimation through doing' model (the output-legitimacy of Scharpf, 1999), in which an organization provides certain public benefits to citizens (prosperity, peace or public goods) and receives public approval and legitimacy in exchange. Of course this legitimacy lasts only so long as these benefits continue to be provided. In simple terms, this is how most authoritarian states that fall short of out-and-out totalitarianism function including (e.g. China, Cuba, central Asian states, Russia or the Arab monarchies of the Gulf). For Majone, the public benefit in the EU was social policy. He argued that this was a potential means by which the EU could legitimate itself, given that the creation of welfare states had helped to secure democratic legitimacy for the nation-state in the 20th century.

What these four approaches share in common is their inadequacy, on an individual basis, for assessing the legitimacy of the EU. Yet an assessment of each of the models in turn shows that some of them have something to offer. Thus by synthesizing what is valuable in each of these models, we can put together a means by which the democratic legitimacy of the EU could be judged.

The first model – needing institutions analogous to national ones – would appear to be a blueprint for a federal European state along a German or American model. There is no demand for this, either from the member states or from public opinion. Here again, one might also ask why the EU, as an original and bold experiment, should be obliged to emulate a pre-existing model of a federal nation-state.

The second, majoritarian model does not suit the EU's structure of large and small member states and of differences in ideologies, languages, culture and so on. In any case, it is not widely practised around the world and has no system for separation of powers or checks and balances. It is also out of step with the consensual decision-making culture of the EU.

The third means of legitimating the EU, through the democratic credentials of its member states, is much more promising, and was regarded as quite sufficient during much of the history of European integration. Member states appointed the EU to act as their agent, primarily in reducing non-tariff barriers or in setting agricultural quotas, and the competences of the EU expanded in order to meet this mandate. A body of European case law grew up in parallel to protect individuals against the short-term practical interest of their member states, which in turn could be said to have provided a popular legitimacy. The problem with this approach is that not all powers are suitable for delegation to a classic international organization modelled like the European Community of the 1970s and 1980s. A secondary criticism is that international organizations that evolve substantially may turn into something very different from the organization to which national parliaments originally delegated their powers. Therefore this means of legitimation is also insufficient for the contemporary EU.

The final kind of legitimacy – *output* legitimacy – is provided 'by doing', or by achieving useful ends which would otherwise not be possible. This source of legitimacy is absolutely essential and at the same time inadequate and flawed. It is essential because, if the EU were entirely ineffective, it could not claim any legitimacy. It is flawed because it leaves the EU hostage to fortune should it, even temporarily or for reasons beyond its control, struggle to provide particular public benefits. That this is the favoured means of achieving legitimacy in authoritarian states also does little to recommend it. Moreover, as has been argued in Chapter 2, what the EU lacks is an instinctive, automatic legitimacy that can only come from *input* legitimacy.

Critics of the relevance of the input model of democratic legitimation for the EU abound. One of the most respected, Fritz Scharpf (1999), was adamant that 'all the important preconditions' for a common political space in the EU were lacking. For this reason and others, he argued that the EU would not become in the 'foreseeable future … a democratic polity' (1999, p. 200). In common with Neunreither (2000), Scharpf (1999, 2001) pointed to the lack of a common European identity as precluding the creation of a European demos, despite the claims of Weiler (1999) that this was not necessary and the claims of Habermas (1996, 2012) that values could be used as a substitute. In a completely different vein, Ulrich Beck and Edgar Grande argue that the whole approach to understanding democratic legitimacy in Europe by reference to nation-states is wrong. In their view, political scientists completely misconstrue the EU by attempting to perceive its true nature through the 'outdated political and scientific framework of the nation, whereas the realities which are producing Europeanization represent *the* historical counter-example to the political and social ontology of the nation-state' (Beck and Grande, 2004, p. 2, italics in original).

Yet it was not simply the perceived democratic deficit at the European level of decision making to which Scharpf (1999) and others objected. Nor was it merely the fact that the EU was 'an elite-led process which has largely been unexplained and certainly under-advocated to the average citizen' (Bellamy and Warleigh, 2001, p. 9) that caused so much consternation. The arguments advanced by other proponents of the democratic deficit were more wide-ranging, more subtle and, arguably, more devastating. Mair (2013) developed Scharpf's earlier (1999) argument that the

EU had deprived the nation-state of too much of its toolkit in socio-economic policy-making by adding that European integration had also reduced the size of the policy space and limited the capacities of nationally elected parliaments. More radically, he went so far as to posit that the EU was deliberately designed by European elites precisely to avoid the constraints of representative democracy or to make policy-making 'safe from democracy'. Although theoretically the European voter has the chance to take part in the political process twice, at the national and at the European level, in practice he or she does neither. Moreover, electing the European Parliament actually serves to undermine the democratic process further because voters are so uninterested in the elections, and turn out to vote in such small numbers. By way of contextualization, Mair makes the point that these challenges to democratic accountability are not limited to the EU, or even to Europe, but are being faced by mature representative democracies around the world. As a result, in the EU, voters use the 'European issue' as a 'hammer to beat the establishment' for its perceived failings. If we follow Mair's argument a little further, the EU is an institution both deliberately designed to take the democracy out of policy-making, and a convenient Aunt Sally for disgruntled voters to take out their frustrations on.

Mair's notion of the EU as a political system that has been made 'safe from democracy' is an interesting one. In a post-deferential age, voters could be presumed less likely to accept short-term painful measures that political leaders tell them will be good for them and good for society in the longer term. Unpopular policies may be necessary but the electoral cycle prevents political parties in government from taking them, for fear of the consequences at the ballot box. Therefore, as Fareed Zakaria (1997) and Philip Pettit (2001) have argued, too much democracy may indeed be a bad thing. This is not to argue in favour of some kind of benign authoritarianism, but merely to point out that it is important to strike a balance between legitimate representation of interests and mere populism in the 'bread and circuses' tradition. For these reasons, a European level of government with a weather eye on the needs of the future, as well as the popular demands of the present, can even be a useful corrective to the short-termism that is inherent in a democratic system by compensating for some of the shortcomings deriving from the electoral cycle.

This chapter argues that the means by which the EU legitimates itself is a fusion of different models – input-oriented, output-oriented and compensatory – which could be said to function in the following way. Primarily, the EU is legitimated by its member states, which have freely delegated *limited* powers to it and have consented to the creation of a new legal order, a common currency, open borders and supranational government in certain, clearly-defined areas and under strict conditions. In the second place, the EU is legitimated by virtue of the fact that all its decision-makers are elected (or at least nominated by elected politicians), either in the form of MEPs, who sit in the European Parliament, or national governments, which are represented in the Council of Ministers. Those who defend this model most rigorously argue that democratizing 'Europe after the model of the nation-state ... [would] not increase but undermine the capacity of the Euro-polity to allocate rights and claims in a "nation-blind" manner' (Offe and Preuss, 2006, pp. 197–8). In other words, the EU needs to act as a referee. In the third place, the EU enjoys a degree of 'legitimacy by doing' through the provision of public goods and benefits, demanded by voters, which a member state would not be able to provide acting alone. European integration, as Chapter 4 will show, has increased the welfare of all the European peoples (even if some groups of individuals have profited rather more than others). To these three sources of legitimacy should be added three points on the accountability of the EU.

Accountability in the EU is ensured through a careful system of checks and balances. This is best demonstrated by the formidable set of obstacles that must be overcome for legislation to come into force. The EU's legislative system usually involves the surmounting of five hurdles: (1) the elected European Council must agree by consensus on a work plan for a given period; (2) the technocratic European Commission must decide by majority that a particular piece of legislation may be put forward for consideration; (3) the elected Council of Ministers must agree on the basis of consensus for that piece of legislation to proceed (Hayes-Renshaw *et al.*, 2006); (4) the elected European Parliament must agree by absolute majority for the legislation to pass; and (5) elected national parliaments or technocratic national civil services must then agree on how to transpose that legislation into national law and implement it.

Throughout this process, which contains more opportunities for discussion, deliberation, amendment and even veto than national legislative procedures, there are countless openings for concerned parties to lobby the Commission, the Parliament or national civil servants working in their Permanent Representations in Brussels. As a result, given the diverse range of actors involved in the process and the fact that a good part of the deliberation takes place in public, the EU legislative procedure is much more transparent than most national systems and, often, far more open to dialogue with social partners and concerned parties. Indeed, such participation from outside is actively welcomed. As Mair (2013), acknowledges, this consultative aspect of EU policy-making acts as a useful corrective to national systems. For instance, public consultations are one of the instruments widely used by the European Commission in the preparation of legislative proposals. This method does not only aim at improving the transparency of and the public involvement in decision-making. Its objective is also to enhance the quality of the policy output by collecting expertise, assessing the situation from different perspectives and informing the discussion of policy options (OECD, 2013a). Public consultations may consist of different exercises such as online surveys, public conferences and meetings with stakeholders to gather outsiders' views on a specific issue. The Commission then qualitatively assesses the results of the consultation, publicizes them and feeds them into the possible drafting of a proposal – the summary of a public consultation for instance, informs debates within the Commission and is included in the documents accompanying the proposal (Marangoni, 2013). The Commission and its administrative Directorate-Generals (DGs) emphasize the participative character of public consultations as an instrument of decision-making. The communication and design of the web pages dedicated to this is telling. As an exercise in direct democracy, consultations constitute an opportunity 'to give [one's] opinion on EU policies and influence their direction' and to make one's voice heard (see for instance European Commission, 2013f and European Commission, DG Trade, 2013a). Public consultations contribute to the 'throughput legitimacy', which is in turn expected to enhance the legitimacy of EU legislation (Schmidt, 2013). Finally, the mandate of the EU, in common with the resources at its disposal, is severely limited and in practice it is exceptionally hard for mission creep to occur. What the EU may or may not do has always been laid out by treaty. Thus, for those who believe that government must be limited for it to be both democratic and accountable, the EU here is surely a paragon of restraint.

Focusing on the issue of democratic accountability, the EU can only comply with this requirement if those who govern are answerable for their actions to the people they govern. This means that the possibility must exist for those who make or shape political decisions to be voted out of office by the people whose interests they ostensibly represent. Here the EU struggles. Although every individual who participates in the formal process of making decisions in the EU is either elected or the representative of an elected national government, voters cannot remove the government of other member states from office. Yet this does not mean that national elections do not count. Indeed, national elections matter a great deal in the EU's political calendar since changes at the member-state level can seriously affect the stakes on the table in the Brussels game. For this reason, all the EU's decision-makers, be they Presidents, Prime Ministers, Ministers, MEPs or national politicians, are focused on opinion polls and forthcoming elections in other member states as well as their own. European politics involves an almost excessive focus on upcoming polls since in a Union of 28 member states there will nearly always be an important election coming up in a member state. Finally, it should be noted that the European Commission as a whole can resign or be dismissed should it lose public confidence – as indeed happened in 1999 when the entire Santer Commission resigned following the publication of a report alleging 'fraud, mismanagement and nepotism' (House of Commons, 1999).

In concluding this segment, it would be remiss not to address those parts of the European government machine that are appointed by democratically elected politicians, but not themselves elected. These key European actors include the European Central Bank, the European Court of Justice and the European Commission. Importantly, the Commission alone has the right to make formal legislative proposals since its role is to act above politics in the common interest of Europe as a whole – something elected politicians with particular constituencies to please would struggle to do. To this list should also be added the 32 European regulatory agencies (from medicines to frontier control to food safety) that are tasked with providing specific services, information and expertise. It can be convincingly argued that there is nothing unusual in the fact that these agencies are not elected.

Central bankers, senior civil servants and the upper ranks of the judiciary are not usually elected since the effective and unbiased performance of their functions necessitates a measure of insulation from popular pressure. The decision to separate technocratic decision-makers from day-to-day political concerns in this way is, of course, a normative one. Before the late 1990s, for example, interest-rate setting in the UK and France was performed by elected finance ministers acting in concert with the governors of the Bank of England and the Banque de France, respectively. The predictable consequence was that finance ministers tended to loosen monetary policy and thus credit conditions in the build-up to an election in the hopes of creating a mini-boom and a feel-good factor. As a result of this practice, normal practice shifted so that operational independence in control of monetary policy along the lines of the Bundesbank in Germany prior to the launch of European Economic and Monetary Union was seen as the best means of controlling inflation (see Marsh, 1992). The case of central banking illustrates that, counter-intuitively, in particular circumstances elected decision-makers will not only fail to make optimal decisions, but are actually less accountable in the long term than technocrats, since politics is dictated by the electoral cycle. In common with best practice (although this is contested, see McNamara, 2002) in liberal democracies therefore, the EU system delegates specific decisions to technocratic experts, who have been appointed by democratically elected politicians. Thus, although the EU decision-making system may be original and different from that of a nation-state, it nonetheless is entitled to claim both legitimacy and democratic accountability because decisions are ultimately taken by elected leaders and, most importantly, because it acts as a necessary *corrective* to the failings of electorally-driven representative democracies.

Is the EU a Credible Democratic System in the Eyes of its Voters?

This chapter argues that the credibility of the EU rests on four pillars: whether voters perceive it as legitimate and trustworthy, the degree to which voters accept its policy agenda, the level of implicit or explicit voter acceptance of its ideological worldview, and the degree to which voters believe that it is a permanent feature of the political landscape. Well-designed, well-functioning democratic systems should surely be durable. It is hard to see why anyone should take seriously a democratic system that appears constantly at risk of being swept away. As this chapter shows, since 2010 the Eurozone crisis has had a serious negative effect on the first of these pillars of credibility (Figure 3.2).

Although scholars tend to speak about the EU's historical 'permissive consensus' (Lindberg and Scheingold, 1970), in which voters broadly endorsed the politics and policies of the EU, in practice this amounted to citizens not taking much of an interest in what was going on. This may also be true of governments. A perhaps apocryphal tale is that General de Gaulle did not read the Rome Treaty until 1963 because until that time he had been completely preoccupied with the Algerian crisis. When he did read it, he was appalled. Permissive consensus faded a little after Maastricht as the EU acquired critics, particularly amongst parties operating on the fringe of politics in several member states. Nonetheless, for

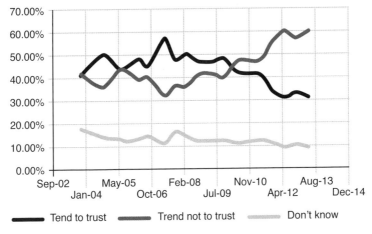

Figure 3.2 Trust in the EU (EU-wide, %)

Source: Data from Eurobarometers, 2003–2013.

the most part Eurosceptic political parties failed to gain serious traction. Until the Great Recession, public opinion remained largely in favour of EU integration in most member states. Even in states where European integration was not automatically seen in a positive light, the sceptics remained a minority, with a maximum of 20–25% of voters taking either a 'hard' or a 'soft' Eurosceptic stance and an equal number who were highly enthusiastic about the EU. The great majority of voters were not particularly interested one way or another (Eurobarometers, 1971–2008). Since the financial crisis, this permissive consensus has shifted, with many previously indifferent voters now adopting more Eurosceptic attitudes. Across the member states, the percentage of voters expressing stronger or milder Eurosceptic attitudes rose: from around 30% to 50% in the UK, 25% to 35% in Sweden, 12% to 25% in Germany, 17% to 27% in France and from about 15% to 30% across the whole EU (Eurobarometer, 2008–13).

As the data show, in those member states of the Eurozone that were subject to 'special measures' – the 'programme countries' – as a result of the sovereign debt crisis trust in the EU has plummeted. Those who do not trust the EU in 2013 had risen to 80% of the population in Greece, 61% in Italy, 71% in Portugal, 83% in Cyprus and 75% in Spain. The turnaround is all the more dramatic when set against the figures for those who trusted the EU before the crisis, which amounted to 60–75% of those polled in all those countries. Thus support for the EU was more or less inverted in the programme countries between 2008 and 2013.

A similar, if less dramatic, story can be told for public opinion of the solvent 'creditor' countries of the Eurozone, not subject to 'special measures' but labouring under the belief that somehow they were personally paying for the mistakes of the programme countries. Opposition to the EU rose to 61% in Austria (from 50%), 54% in Finland (from 40%) and 61% in Germany (from 40%) over the same 2008–13 timeframe (Eurobarometer, 2008–13).

All of the above indicates a very significant shift in the perceived credibility of the EU in the great majority of member states – creditor and debtor alike – after the outbreak of the sovereign debt crisis. Much of this increased Euroscepticism appeared to be in direct response to a perceived lack of democratic choice. Many disillusioned voters in the debtor member states did not believe that they had chosen or voted for austerity. In turn, public opinion in some quarters of the creditor countries did not believe that they had voted for a 'transfer union'.

Although the data appear to point to a weakening of public trust in the European integration project overall, this is perhaps a little simplistic. A more nuanced view is that the Eurozone crisis appeared to be causing a significant shift in the politics of Euroscepticism and Euro-enthusiasm. The previous model of a permissive consensus vs. 'hard' or 'soft' Euroscepticism needs considerable rethinking (Taggart and Szczerbiak, 2004). The full spectrum of attitudes towards the EU might include the following five camps.

At the negative extreme lie the 'diehard Eurosceptics', who might better be termed 'Europhobics', including parties such as France's Front National or the United Kingdom Independence Party (UKIP). In essence, this group simply rejects all the arguments for the EU's democratic legitimacy in their entirety. For them, the EU is an aberration. Their fervent hope is that the EU and European integration will come to an end and their particular nation-state can return to a pre-lapsarian era of national sovereignty with an ethnic and cultural homogeneity that EU membership appears to threaten. Much of their politics is emotive rather than reasoned. It appeals in particular to older and poorer voters who are pessimistic about the future, worried about multiculturalism and concerned about rising levels of migration. This group of voters is not going to be converted to the cause of European integration. It has increased in numbers since the onset of the Euro crisis. The British case is exemplified by a group of 30 Conservative MPs for whom the EU would not be acceptable even if every regulation were rewritten and 'the other member states agreed to pay the Queen's weight in gold in annual tribute' (*The Economist*, 2013).

The camp of 'principled, hard Eurosceptics' bases its criticisms of the EU on reasoned judgement. A significant number of this group were probably in favour of European integration in the form of removal of barriers to trade, but worry that the EU has gone too far and cannot be redeemed except through a fundamental re-design, the scrapping of certain projects, such as the Euro, and the repatriation of certain powers to the member states. This group includes the Polish Law and Justice party, Czech Presidents Václav Klaus and Miloš Zeman, and many in the UK Conservative Party. It should come as no surprise that they have formed a group in the European Parliament.

In the centre of the debate lie two groups. The first could be termed 'grudging pragmatists' who accept the need for the EU, primarily because it would be more trouble than it is worth to unwind it and, on the face of it, it continues to perform useful functions. Yet this group, which includes Italy's Lega Nord, does not believe in further integration for its own sake, although it would reluctantly consent to it if absolutely necessary.

On the positive side of the centre lies the second group: the 'Europhiles'. Their views reflect the previously prevailing orthodoxy that European integration is a good thing in itself. This group includes Christian Democrats in Germany and the mainstream of the centre-right and centre-left in France. Here, as in many member states, they remain the majority, but they are far less unassailable than before. Countering the decline in their support in the heartlands of European integration are representatives of the new member states, which are pragmatic in their approach but generally in favour of 'more Europe'. The Europhiles remain most common in the new member states as well as Germany.

At the far end of the Euro-enthusiast camp lie the federalists. This group has become an increasingly endangered species, albeit with a few isolated pockets remaining in parts of Belgium and Luxembourg. It is more or less extinct in the Netherlands. The Eurozone crisis has done more to erode support for this grouping than to enhance it.

Underlying these shifts in attitudes towards the EU is the fact that what it means to be Europhile or Eurosceptic has shifted considerably since the 1990s, and dramatically since the start of the Eurozone crisis. This has implied movement in the constituencies where European integration previously had its strongest appeal. The old market-driven, economically liberal integration model was highly attractive to those on the centre-right of the political spectrum – the UK Conservative party of Macmillan, Heath and Thatcher, *whilst in office*, was perceived as 'the party of Europe'. It was also attractive to political parties in sovereignty-sensitive countries because the gains of European integration benefited the constituencies of the centre-right (commerce, industry and farming), but did not seem to involve the surrender of too much national control. Moreover, where national control was ceded in favour of QMV, it was in the cause of reducing barriers to economic competition within the single market.

Since the onset of the sovereign debt crisis, the EU has lost support amongst some of its core constituencies, notably on the centre-right. From the Treaty of Rome onwards, the European integration project has been ideologically founded on an economically liberal worldview, leaving social protection to the member states. The notion of a 'social Europe' was mooted in the 1980s by Jacques Delors, but it failed to make much headway because of starkly different opinions between the member states about whether or not this was a matter for the EU (Delors, 2013). Economic liberalism was an appropriate ideology for an international organization whose central purpose was creating and regulating a common market that became a single market. Economic liberalism is a woefully insufficient ideology for today's EU that includes a single currency zone at its core because it forces pre-Keynesian policy solutions (i.e. wage cuts, austerity, liquidation of assets) on democratic societies from the outside. European integration will not work if its people perceive Europe to be an authoritarian policeman of liberal economic policies that protect the integrity of the world financial system at the expense of Europe's weakest nations.

The European integration project has outgrown the market-driven, economically liberal model on which it was founded. The old worldview appealed primarily to the centre-right, although it found supporters in all centrist political parties and, by the 1990s, also in the mainstream centre-left as part of a broader policy mix that included support for European social models and other social democratic policies. A key part of centre-left support for European integration was that national governments retained control of social policies, which helped to insulate those who would lose out from the short-term negative effects of European integration. The sovereign debt crisis fatally undermined this model for the simple reason that those member states of the Eurozone that were placed under 'special measures' lost control of the means by which losers in the process of economic liberalization could be compensated.

A final problem for the EU in its quest for credibility is the degree to which the Union has become accepted as a 'permanent' feature of European democracy, which I argue must be a core element of its legitimacy and credibility. As Juan Linz and Alfred Stepan argued, the key feature of a consolidated democracy is the extent to which democracy has become 'the only game in town' (1996). Of course the EU is not the only game in town and it does not seek to be since it shares responsibility for government with the member states. What is important, however, is the extent to which voters believe that the EU is as permanent as the process of democratic government at the member-state level. On-going contestation of the legitimacy of the EU system is unhelpful because it distracts attention from the business of policy-making and policy implementation. In this question of perceived 'permanence', the disconnection between what the technocratic European Commission believes and what European voters believe is most evident. The official answer put forward by the European Commission and other institutions to the question of why so many European voters feel disconnected from, or hostile towards, the EU is that they simply do not understand it properly. (For this reason, Commissioner Wallström launched the so-called Plan D for 'democracy, dialogue and debate' in 2005 in an attempt to (re)connect voters to the EU, see EurActiv, 2005). In other words, if people had perfect knowledge of the system, they would love it. This explanation seems to ignore the fact that most voters have a hazy knowledge of the detail of how democracy functions in their own member states. It seems that they accept the system because (for the most part) it has been around in a similar form for a long time – it is the 'normal' form of democratic government – and because there is patently no alternative. For the EU to become 'normal', it needs to be accepted as permanent – and vice versa. The successful resolution of the Eurozone crisis will be a vital part of this process.

Conclusion

Despite the lively debate about what some see as the EU's democratic deficit, this chapter argued that in much of its work the EU remains highly democratic, legitimate and accountable. Those who remain unconvinced by these arguments should note that member states may democratically decide to leave the EU if they decide that the conditions of membership have become overbearing – this procedure is formally provided for in Article 50 of the Lisbon Treaty. Until the onset of the Eurozone crisis, the democratic deficit was more the concern of academics than European voters, even if it was beginning to creep towards the political spotlight. The need for a thorough and coordinated response to the Eurozone crisis exposed a serious flaw in EU democracy. It required a tough programme of austerity measures to save the Euro, and these had not been popularly approved. The EU had reached the limits of what it had the legitimacy to do without the democratic approval of voters. The chapter proposed three solutions to resolve these issues. First, what is needed is political contestation and a choice between competing political programmes. Some argue that such contestation would lead to US-style deadlock, but this is not a necessary consequence. The referendums that now prevail in European democracy on big-picture issues are no substitute for true political contestation between different policies, ideas and ideologies. Second, there is a case for the formation of a 'loyal opposition' within the EU political system. This is complicated by the obvious absence of 'government benches' within the European Parliament, but it does mean that, at the very least, the EU needs to distinguish between its critical friends and its avowed enemies. Treating all Eurosceptics as traitors to the cause of European integration gives the impression of political immaturity. It also plays into the hands of the EU's most fervent Europhobic opponents. Lastly, the EU needs to focus more on the means by which it can enhance the quality of democratic representation at the member-state level. In other words, European integration should enrich rather than constrain the political powers and policy scope of member-state governments (Majone, 2009).

This chapter identified several explanations for the problems of the EU's democratic deficit. In the first place, the EU is a path-dependent organization with its roots in post-war reconciliation between historical enemies. The need for consensus was sacrosanct in such an environment, as was the absolute necessity of setting clear boundaries to what could be discussed and what could not. Notably, mentioning the Second World War in any context other than that of reconciliation was a taboo that was not broken by a senior European politician for 50 years. (That occasion came when Polish President Kaczyński alluded to what the population of Poland might have been were it not for the German invasion and extermination of much of the pre-war population.) Such an environment does not foster frank political debate, at least not in public. In the second place, there was a broad consensus between the member states that integration was to be market-based. This gave European integration an economically liberal flavour, albeit one tempered by a belief in the social market economy or welfare capitalism (see Chapter 4). In the third place, a consensual political approach was necessitated by the diversity of the Union in all aspects: linguistic, cultural, economic and geographical. The potential for conflict in such a system was enormous, as was the need to protect small and weak member states from large and powerful neighbours. A final element to be added to this mix was the risk of causing offence to negotiating partners either through different cultural norms, or simply as a result of working in a multi-lingual environment with massive potential for misunderstandings. All these factors combined to produce an agreeable, collegiate and altogether gentlemanly atmosphere in which disagreements could be smoothed over within a culture of consensus and package deals.

In such a culture of consensus, offering real choices to voters was exceptionally difficult. This explains why there appears to be so little political competition between ideas in EU democracy. The net result of this is that the peoples of the EU are not offered real and complex choices by their representatives. It also accounts for the strange rebirth of that populist, clumsy and downright undemocratic tool so beloved of dictators like Napoleon – the referendum – as a means of engaging the European public in political debate. Crudely, this means that the European voter has not been offered a choice between policy X, Y or Z or between a number of competing manifestos, but simply a choice between X, Y and Z in its totality or not at all. This would not need to happen if the EU had, within the parliaments of its member states and European Parliament, something approximating a competent and *loyal* opposition. The increasingly common practice of returning to voters time after time with the same question until they get the answer right merely serves to confirm the fact that a series of referendums is no way to govern a serious liberal democracy. Contestation is exciting. Making real choices about issues that will affect them galvanizes voters and invigorates democratic practice. It is the failure of the EU's politicians to offer real choices that has led to so much apathy on the part of European voters towards the European integration project. Worse still, it has left too much of the debate on European integration in some member states to the fanatics. As the brief survey into the changing politics of Euroscepticism showed, the extremists have begun to shape the European integration debate in ways that would have been unthinkable just a decade ago. We consider some of these normative choices for Europe in the Conclusion.

A thoroughgoing and long-lasting response to Europe's economic and political crisis means that a new pact needs to be forged between the member states and between the European electorate as a whole. This new deal for Europe is far too complex and important to be put to a referendum where a package is presented to voters – as to spectators in the Colosseum – for their thumbs up or thumbs down. The European political and economic crisis presents the opportunity, or even makes it imperative, for voters to take part in an intelligent and serious conversation about the kind of EU integration project they want (Tsoukalis, 2003). Political contestation between different visions, ideas and ideological approaches is essential. The potential consequences of different decisions also need to be woven into this debate. An election campaign to the European Parliament, fought by the European political parties on common manifestos, with voters going to the polls on the same day in all member states, would present an ideal opportunity for this debate to take place. In Abraham Lincoln's memorable aphorism, 'democracy is the government of the people, by the people, for the people' (1863). The EU already carries out the 'for the people' element (Scharpf, 1999), but it is clear that the 'by the people' element needs bolstering. For this to happen, European voters must be given real choices.

4

Solidarity: Winners and Losers in European Integration

Europeans, and in particular European politicians, like solidarity. It has become a much-invoked, and at times much-abused, term that features widely in European political discourse as a distinctive element of European modernity and of its economic model (Outhwaite, 2008). Conceptually, it is pleasingly elastic in that it means different things to different people, and can therefore be easily employed as a rhetorical device for show or dramatic effect. Historically, it has also served as a political device to foster a common identity and support nation-building efforts (Fligstein, 2008). The frequency with which it is used suggests that, in general, it has positive connotations, which explains why the Commission, the Council or other EU bodies make such constant use of the term.

The increasing penchant for solidarity is a long-established trend that cuts across a number of policy areas. In foreign and security policy, the Maastricht Treaty of 1992 (Article 11, Title V) stipulated that 'the member states shall support the Union's external and security policy actively and unreservedly in a spirit of loyalty and mutual solidarity'. By 2000, solidarity had risen in status to become 'a universal value' in the Charter of Fundamental Rights with the declaration that: 'the Union is founded on the indivisible, universal values of human dignity, freedom, equality and solidarity.' The word 'solidarity' featured no fewer than 18 times in the ill-fated European Constitutional Treaty (ECT), and although French and Dutch voters killed off the ECT itself in 2005, 'solidarity' survived its metamorphosis into the Lisbon Treaty, maintaining pride of place in the preamble where the heads of state were 'intending to confirm the solidarity which binds Europe'. At Maastricht in 1992, they had merely desired 'to deepen the solidarity between their peoples'. This promotion to the preamble underlined that solidarity (exact meaning unspecified) should now be considered part of the European furniture, so to speak. Moreover, since the entry into force of the Lisbon Treaty, under the Solidarity Clause (Article 222), EU member states have been obliged to assist each other in the face of disasters, emergencies and crises on the European continent (Myrdal and Rhinard, 2010). Important as solidarity is in the aftermath of a terrorist attack, natural disaster or an emergency, understanding of what solidarity means in the EU goes far beyond this narrow field of collective action. So what does solidarity mean?

Solidarity is hard to nail down as a political concept, although most would agree in a normative sense that it is a good thing and consequently, there should be more of it. For socialists or trade unionists, solidarity is bound up with notions of working class unity or perhaps the principle of collective bargaining. Europe's Christians will also have their own interpretations of solidarity, linked to religious liberty and working collectively to ensure freedom from persecution. In Poland, as well as perhaps more widely in central Europe, solidarity evokes memories of the eponymous independent trade union – the first of its kind to be formed in the old Communist world – which led the heroic and victorious struggle against one-party, authoritarian rule in the 1980s. On the centre-right, solidarity also has its fans and adherents in Christian Democratic parties. Within the EU, solidarity can be cited as a justification for financial support to a member state (usually this is what the government of a net beneficiary from the EU budget means in calling for more 'solidarity'), perhaps to support economic convergence or to provide help for those who have got into trouble. For others, solidarity may be bound up with undertaking reforms to ensure that financial assistance is not needed in the first place. In other words, politicians and parties of the left and the right invoke the need for solidarity for a wide range of purposes.

There may appear to be universal, normative agreement that solidarity is to be encouraged, fostered and cherished, although matters are more complicated beneath the surface. It is based on people's acceptance that there exists a 'fundamental and consequential similarity' between them and that 'causes them to feel solidarity amongst themselves' (Brubaker and Cooper, 2000; Fligstein, 2008; Therborn, 1995). The choice to foster solidarity in a particular group however, in turn implies an exclusion of others who do not share this fundamental similarity. Surely not everyone can profit equally from solidarity at the same time. And why should some groups experience solidarity but not others? This chapter is concerned with the linkage between solidarity and European integration and addresses three questions that are equally trenchant in explaining the diverse linkages between solidarity and European integration. The overarching question of this analysis is the extent to which Europeans experience a shared bond of solidarity between themselves; in other words, the extent to which membership of a shared political community invokes feelings of connection between Europeans. The second question, which follows from this, is the degree to which Europeans support solidarity, understood as collective decision making within the EU and particularly its implications, such as the pooling of resources for redistribution within the political union. The absence of support for solidarity was underlined by Majone (2009) who argued that it would be impossible to transfer national welfare systems onto the EU level because of the wide differences in the kinds of social cleavages that exist in member states. The third question, which flows naturally from this, concerns who benefits from solidarity in the EU.

It is assumed that a majority of Europeans favour joint action in fields where their own member state is incapable of achieving a desired result by itself (e.g. on international trade or climate change). The extent to which Europeans favour the transfer of resources from wealthier to poorer areas is less clear, although this already happens within the member states to varying degrees. The supreme example of this kind of redistribution was the transfer of €1.3 trillion from west to east in Germany to fund reunification after 1990 (Graham, 2009). As always in a vibrant liberal democracy, there were some who protested that the cost was too high, but simply put, wealthy west Germans were willing to support their east German brethren who had found themselves stuck in an authoritarian Communist state for 40 years. The bonds of identity and solidarity between the 'two Germanies' were the strongest imaginable – one people living in two states. Until the Eurozone crisis, economic solidarity on this scale had not been discussed in the EU, although it is true that, since the first enlargement of 1973, European funds have been channelling resources to poorer member states. Back then of course, this meant not only transfers to the then largely agricultural Irish Republic, which of course benefited greatly from the Common Agricultural Policy, but also to a post-Imperial, but pre-Thatcher United Kingdom, which found itself living in less favourable circumstances relative to the rest of Western Europe. Cumulatively, the money transfers to Spain or Greece in the 1980s and 1990s or to Poland in the 2000s correspond to a transformational sum, but it must be borne in mind that the annual EU budget amounts to a little more than 1% of the combined GDP of the EU-28 (European Commission, 2013e). And the €67 billion that flowed to Poland during the period of the 2007–13 financial framework to build roads and update infrastructure is, in the grand European scheme of things, chickenfeed.

Solidarity between the member states will be severely tested in the aftermath of the Eurozone crisis. If the Eurozone survives, and much of the bad debt owed to other EU member states in the programme countries is written off, the necessary scale of transfers between member states will be closer to (but still substantially less than) the massive costs of German reunification than to the essentially minimal costs of structural funds. And this is without including the cost of any Keynesian pump-priming to boost the economies of the peripheral Eurozone countries. Solidarity on this scale will only be politically possible with far greater harmonization across the EU of social models, other areas of domestic politics *and* indeed perhaps of certain elements of political cultures. This is what makes the question of solidarity so pertinent for the EU at this juncture. However, harmonization of social models in particular constitutes a challenge – consider, for instance, Germans' annoyance at Greek retirement pension rules, in particular the legal retirement age (Charlemagne, 2010). Despite attempts to integrate this policy area – which was included in the Lisbon Strategy as part of broader economic and growth objectives – it is still the preserve of member states 'for good reasons' (Merkel, 2009). European publics have consistently opposed national welfare policies being taken over by Brussels (Fligstein, 2008). Consequently, it is hardly possible to move beyond basic issues and non-binding agreements, and social policy is characterized by the coexistence of different national models (Schmidt, 2002; Wincott, 2003).

The question of who benefits from solidarity is politically contentious because it is clear that solidarity within the EU is highly selective. The material as well as the intangible benefits of European integration have been felt far more by certain groups, including farmers, the owners of capital, particular industries, elites, certain member states, centre-right political parties and so on, than others, such as those countries excluded from membership (the outsiders, for example Ukraine, Russia, the southern neighbours, perhaps Turkey), trade unions, Europe's former colonies around the world, centre-left political parties and so on. Solidarity in its broad and pure sense implies three values that were present at the birth of the modern European nation at the end of the 18th century: liberty (as a unified front against persecution), equality and fraternity. In the 21st century, it is associated with political economy and transfers of resources. Yet as this chapter will argue, in practice, resources tend to flow to particular groups. To give the most obvious example, since the 1960s, there has been solidarity for European farmers through the Common Agricultural Policy (CAP). Since the outbreak of the sovereign debt crisis in the Eurozone, there has also been solidarity for affected member states, which amounts to solidarity for holders of certain countries' sovereign debt. In a European Union where there is to be more and more of this kind of selective solidarity at an ever greater cost to society as a whole, the questions of *who benefits from solidarity* and *why* – as well as who has lost from European integration – are absolutely crucial.

Before proceeding any further, it is essential to arrive at a workable definition of solidarity, and what it means in the context of the EU. The rest of the chapter first investigates who benefits from solidarity in the EU and then turns to the interlinked question of who supports the principle of solidarity understood as a kind of 'collective insurance' within the EU, thus observing who supports placing resources in a common pot for redistribution within the political Union.

What is Solidarity?

Solidarity is understood largely from a political or political economy perspective. It has three main functions. The first is the redistribution of resources within an economy to reduce or compensate for disparities in income between groups or individuals in society, or indeed between territorial units (i.e. provinces or regions) (Lowi, 1972). The second is the pooling of resources to provide support or redress when our circumstances change for the worse, or to protect the vulnerable whose circumstances may not have changed but have simply always been worse as a result of illness or disability (Marshall, 1950). These adverse circumstances can be universal and foreseeable, the most obvious being old age which is both predictable and (almost) inevitable. Or they could be risks that are unpredictable yet near-universal in that most of us have a high chance of experiencing one or more of these over our lifespans on a temporary or even permanent basis, such as poor health, unemployment or disability. Moving away from economic aspects, solidarity could also be interpreted as a kind of 'social glue' that binds us together as a community rather than as competing individuals (Fligstein, 2008). Thus our sense of solidarity, understood as common interest, prompts us to support and encourage activities that are mutually beneficial to society as a whole, but where the burden of carrying out such activities falls only or mostly on individuals or families, including education, the raising of families or possibly care of the aged. In other words, solidarity is a means of pursuing a common purpose.

Steinar Stjernø suggests that 'solidarity can most fruitfully be defined as the preparedness to share resources with others by personal contributions to those in struggle or in need and through taxation and redistribution organised by the state. It is not an attitude that is narrowly based upon self-interest' (2005, p. 2). Stjernø's concept of solidarity is derived from four supporting elements: (1) the basis or foundation of solidarity, in other words, where the urge to pursue solidarity springs from; (2) the object or function of solidarity, or the purpose that it serves; (3) the degree of inclusivity or exclusivity that a given concept of solidarity implies or requires; and (4) the strength or weakness of the collective driving it, which is concerned with the tension between the push towards the collective, on the one hand, and the pull towards the individualistic, on the other. These elements overlap with and complement the three main functions of solidarity sketched out above: redistribution of resources, pooling of resources, binding a community together.

The first of Stjernø's solidarity building-blocks requires the recognition of common interests or perhaps of sameness, interdependence or shared affiliations on the part of an individual and then a group of individuals. For an individual, this is about moving from thinking in terms of 'I' to thinking in terms of 'we'. For the states and citizens of the EU, this recognition of similarity or sameness is already in place. Clearly, it is already recognized that much is shared between Europeans in terms of their worldview, their values, customs, manners and habits. Pragmatically, there is a sense of common interests. Idealistically, for some Europeans there is a sense of a common purpose.

The second element that guides us towards a full understanding of this concept is the purpose solidarity serves. In its broadest sense, the intention of solidarity is to realize certain common interests that cannot be attained in isolation or individually. It may also be to increase our shared strength in conflict or confrontation with others. These two functions or objects of solidarity apply to European integration. Individual states in Europe acting in isolation are poorly equipped to manage whole swathes of policy, including trade, the regulation of the economy, migration, organized crime, defence and so on. Whilst the notion of collective

European solidarity providing strength through unity in the face of an external attack has become more abstract since the end of the Cold War, it still has a value for Europeans when they enter into confrontations with others. There may be no direct, military threat to the safety and security of Western Europe, but risks have certainly not disappeared. The threats that menace Europe today are more distant, less visible, less tangible and – frankly – less alarming than those of the 20th century. Contemporary dangers in the shape of climate change or economic obsolescence, for example, have an abstract quality to them; indeed there are bodies of opinion (Bradley, 2003; Lawson, 2009) which question whether they are truly threatening or dangerous at all. This hugely complicates the business of making the case for collective action in a way that pooling resources to resist the aggressiveness of totalitarian dictatorships, to provide security of food supply, or to secure peace, prosperity and cohabitation between European neighbours did not. Thus the argument about the necessity of action to resist the spread of a communist dictatorship militarily through NATO or economically, through the European Economic Community was easily won. It is far harder to win public support for collective action where the need for immediate and decisive action is far from self-evident. In other words, the case for solidarity for security's sake is not as clear-cut as it was between the 1940s and the 1990s.

Stjernø's third aspect of solidarity relates to inclusivity and exclusivity – the question of who benefits from solidarity and who does not, or who is protected by solidarity and who is not. In European politics, this is a moot point. It may in fact be the key challenge for the reconstruction of Europe in the aftermath of the Great Recession and the Eurozone crisis. Chapter 2 presented the idea that there are 'two Europes', effectively two separate European societies. One has benefited greatly from European integration, directly and indirectly. The other has not. Solidarity in terms of direct protection appears to be the preserve of far too few segments of society. The beneficiaries of the European budget who profit from solidarity are limited to: farmers and rural communities, lesser developed regions of the EU and some research institutes and education (particularly education about the EU). Emphatically, the budget is not well-placed to address many of the key policy challenges that are calling out for solidarity, including: intergenerational inequality; the vast growth of disparities in all kinds of income, wealth and resources between the two Europes as well as between the very rich and the rest since the 1970s; or the unfair differences between the treatment of labour market insiders and outsiders. Other areas in need of greater investment, or solidarity, could be: maintaining technological advantage through research; building and maintaining adequate infrastructure; or, more broadly, providing supply-side benefits that will boost Europe's competitive position *vis-à-vis* the rest of the world in terms of education, technology, innovation, know-how and infrastructure. The lively, and at times ferocious, debate on the question of the inclusiveness or exclusiveness of solidarity in the EU will be dealt with in some detail in this chapter since this is a matter on which there is no universal agreement.

Stjernø's final point concerns the degree to which individuals are prepared to relinquish autonomy in favour of the collective, i.e. the extent to which they are prepared to share resources. The answer to this question cannot simply be determined through an economic cost–benefit analysis since what is being shared goes beyond the material. For some member states, the balance to be struck at the EU level is between solidarity and sovereignty, and this is a calculation based as much on identity, legitimacy and political vision as it is on a pragmatic and purely economic calculation. The Conservative politician, Michael Heseltine, summed this up neatly for the UK in 1989 as a choice about:

> whether to cling to the sovereignty we know and value, exercising it, even as it shrinks, with all the resourcefulness we can find; or to strengthen that sovereignty by sharing it with others, acknowledging the hazard in order to grasp the greater opportunity. (1989, p. xi)

The existence of a potential risk in sharing sovereignty and thus extending solidarity is acknowledged, and subsequently cast aside by this pro-European politician. Many Europeans find it harder to overlook these risks, particularly those in the minority who do not feel a sense of affiliation or shared interests with others in their own country and/ or elsewhere in Europe. Thus, even where there exists an overwhelming rational case for European solidarity, based on a recognition of its function and the common interests which inspire it, for reasons of identity and perceived legitimacy it is not a foregone conclusion that solidarity will be supported.

In terms of who cares most about the principle of solidarity and its implications, Stjernø argues (2005) that solidarity is found in the discourse of academics, socialists or social democratic parties and in the Christian discourse of social ethics. This list of concerned parties could be broadened to include a much longer list of religions, especially the Abrahamic ones, since it is not just Christians who are concerned with such issues, but even this would be too restrictive. This book argues that the politics and policy of solidarity go beyond these narrow confines since, in a certain sense, we are all social democrats in Europe now. So many aspects of the social democratic project, in the shape of shared responsibility for healthcare and collective insurance against predictable or unpredictable life events, are embedded in European life that the discourse of solidarity has become a universal one of vital concern and interest to everyone living on the European continent.

The basis of solidarity is well established in Europe and its purpose is both understood and appreciated. What remains open to debate, however, are the interlinked questions of who should benefit from solidarity and the extent to which individuals are willing to relinquish autonomy in favour of collective action.

Who Benefits from Solidarity in the EU?

The beneficiaries of solidarity in the EU could be organized into two categories. The first – the direct beneficiaries – are relatively easy to identify if the qualification for membership of this group is receiving direct assistance from the budget. The second, much wider group of interest is composed of those who benefit from the kind of solidarity that stems indirectly from belonging to a polity. It has already been established that the purpose of solidarity is to realize certain common aims that cannot be attained in isolation or individually. A shared aim at the heart of the European integration process was the creation of greater prosperity through increased competition, facilitated by international trade, which would increase investment, productivity and income levels. By definition, the motor for this process, international trade, cannot be carried out by one country working in isolation. Increasing the living standards of Europeans was the very purpose of economic integration from the 1950s onwards, and an explicit aim of the Single Market which was intended to 'develop a dynamic society in which industry thrives and the activities which create wealth are encouraged' (Thatcher, 1984, p. 80). Several decades on from the optimistic launch of the Single Market, the focus is now upon those who have become beneficiaries of this process, in consideration of European society as a whole.

Direct Beneficiaries

An analysis of EU spending reveals that the principal beneficiaries of solidarity are predictably and predominantly farmers and those who live in poorer regions (although all regions of the EU receive some funding as a result of the general horse trading that produces a budgetary settlement every seven years), as well as the recipients of EU grants for training, research, and educational activities. The EU's seven-year budget, or multi-annual financial framework, is broken down into five categories: (1) 'competitiveness for growth and employment' (the Europe 2020 goals), receiving €89.363 billion or 9.1% of the total; and 'cohesion for growth and employment' which is assistance to poorer regions, with some €347.407 billion or 35.3% of the total; (2) 'market-related expenditures and direct payments' at €330.085 billion or 33.8%, in order words subsidies to farmers as price support; and 'preservation and management of natural resources' at €82.976 billion or 8.5%, which means direct income payments to farmers and fishermen; (3) 'freedom, security and justice' at €7.549 billion, which is for policies relating to policing, migration and so on; and 'citizenship' at €4.667 billion which is for consumer protection, public health, consumer protection, culture and dialogue; (4) the 'EU as a global player' or foreign and enlargement policies at €55.935 billion or 5.7% of the total; and, finally, (5) 'administration' at €55.925 billion or 5.7% of the total (European Commission, 2013e).

Thus it can be seen that 42.2% (€413.061 billion) of the budget is spent on the Common Agricultural and Fisheries policies (although this is down from 72% in 1984). Who receives this money? According to the Commission, the EU has 13.4 million farmers, which is almost seven times as many as the United States' 2 million. If the CAP funds were distributed evenly, over seven years each farmer would receive €30,825. Unfortunately, since 80% of Europe's farmland is owned by 20% of farmers, around 80% of the total budget is paid to only 20% of the total number of farmers. The largest landowners of course receive more; for example, in England, Queen Elizabeth received well over €500,000 in 2008 for subsidies, while the Dukes of Marlborough and Westminster, received around €1–1.5 million each in just two years. (The data for Scotland and Wales are secret; Baldwin and Wyplosz, 2012.) Eight out of ten farmers will receive less than €7,706 over the seven-year period or €91.72 per month, a very modest subsidy indeed. According to the European Commission, at the top end of the scale, 28,000 farmers received more than €130,000 in 2008, with the top 1300 each netting an average of €965,044 (in Baldwin and Wyplosz, 2012). In any case, out of the EU's 503.492 million people, 13.4 million profited from the CAP, but the overwhelmingly majority of these received very little. Therefore, meaningful direct benefits from the CAP in money terms appear to accrue to fewer than 500,000 people – a tiny fraction of the EU's

503.492 million people. It is hard to escape the conclusion that the CAP, which began in the 1960s with the legitimate and noble aim of modernizing a very out-dated and inefficient European agricultural sector, has become a mechanism for transferring large sums of European taxpayers' money to the very wealthy. This is not, however, to advocate abolition of the CAP. Agricultural subsidy is practised by all advanced countries except New Zealand and Australia (although Australian drought and rural assistance programmes look a lot like subsidies). Between 2008 and 2012 EU spending on the CAP fell from 31% of gross farm receipts to 19%. The 2012 figure is almost in line with the OECD average of 18.6% yet below the figures for Japan (55.9%), Korea (53.8%), Turkey (22.4%), Switzerland (57%) and Norway (63.1%). Outside the OECD, the EU figure is broadly in line with subsidies in China (16.8%) and Indonesia (21%). My suggestion, therefore, is merely that the effects of the CAP could be made less perverse.

What is most interesting about the CAP is its open-ended commitment to guarantee a decent standard of living for a certain section of the population – farmers and, to an extent, 'rural communities' – through a policy of stabilization. The policy has historically been seen as being motivated by economic and security concerns; yet its origins were also political in that it was observed that disgruntled farmers had provided a bedrock of support for non-democratic, authoritarian and totalitarian regimes in inter-war Europe, especially in Germany. Thus the matter that concerns us in rethinking the EU is the status of the CAP as a proto-social policy for the EU based on an economic *and* political rationale. The CAP established a precedent for using EU policies to compensate or win over particular interest groups that might be opposed to European integration or fear that they have something to lose from it.

Structural and cohesion funds paid to regions are the second largest item in the EU's budget line at €347.407 billion or 35.3% of the total. The ostensible purpose of these funds is to help poorer regions of the EU catch up, or converge, economically with richer ones. That said, some 40% of these funds (€138.96 billion) still goes to regions of the EU with a per-capita income above 90% of the EU-25 average (which continued as the base-line even after the 2007 enlargement to Romania and Bulgaria) on the grounds that everyone needs to benefit so that there is the greatest possible political support for this kind of solidarity policy across the EU. This argument is in line with the school of thought on the welfare state that argues that the wealthier must also benefit, even in a tokenistic fashion, in order to preserve the political consensus in favour of the principle of redistribution (Rosen and Gayer, 2010). The bulk of the remaining 60% (€208.44 billion) went to the 84 regions with per-capita GDP at less than 75% of the average of the EU-25 (Baldwin and Wyplosz, 2012).

All member states pay into the structural and cohesion policy and nearly all get something back in return. Whether they are net *contributors* or net *recipients* is dependent on how wealthy they are in comparison to the rest of the EU. In individual terms, at the top end of the scale, 1.34 million Estonians and 9.971 million Hungarians received on average €225–230 per annum for seven years. At the bottom end of the scale, the average Dane contributed a net sum of €125 annually in tax revenues to the funding of regions outside of Denmark. The average Briton or German contributed about €35–50 yearly between 2007 and 2013. On an individual basis, these amounts of money are small, both for the notional 334 million or so Europeans who are net contributors and the 170 million Europeans who are net recipients. Of course, structural funds are not simply an annual cheque for say €150 made payable to every Polish citizen for seven years. Rather, the direct beneficiaries of this form of solidarity are concentrated in construction companies (the owners and those who work for them) building roads and airports, upgrading railways, rebuilding sewerage systems or laying broadband cables. The beneficiaries of these projects are most obviously local to the project, but also European consumers and businesses who will profit directly and indirectly from, say, faster roads. This may be a small number of individuals, but it would be small-minded to pretend that the only beneficiaries of infrastructure or supply-side projects are those who build them.

The direct beneficiaries of EU integration as measured through the two largest areas of EU spending (the CAP and regional funds) are therefore, when expressed as a notional share of the EU population, about one-third or approximately 170–180 million people. Moreover, as we have seen, the amount of money notionally allocated to the overwhelming majority of them is tiny. And the numbers of those who benefit directly from EU spending on, say, agriculture or infrastructure is even smaller: fewer than 20 million. As Baldwin and Wyplosz put it: 'more than half the CAP payments go to big, rich farms, while for the vast majority of EU farmers, the CAP payments are just enough to keep them on the edge of bankruptcy' (2012, p. 251). The number of Europeans who benefit directly from the EU budget in any meaningful way is a miniscule percentage of the 500 million people who live in the Union.

It would be highly misleading to imply that only this very small number of directly-supported individuals and groups of individuals profited from EU solidarity. A far larger group of people benefits indirectly from the function of solidarity; in other words, working collectively to achieve certain aims that cannot be met individually. These common-purpose activities encompass a much broader scope of undertakings, including security against the risks of: external aggression expressed through trade boycotts, for example; inadequate food supplies; governments being unable to meet their commitment to pay interest to bond-holders (theoretically the EU does not do this – in practice, it does); exogenous economic shocks; changing global trade patterns; falling behind the technology frontier; natural disasters; international terrorism; fraud and organized crime; bank failures and so on.

Indirect Beneficiaries

This section focuses on just one aspect of EU solidarity because there is insufficient space to deal with every indirect benefit that Europeans derive from their Union: the question of who gains from the economic solidarity that principally derives from the Single Market. It is more or less taken for granted that all Europeans benefit in terms of the safety and the quality of what they buy, as well as the range of products and services available. The price of goods paid by Europeans is expected to be lower as competition increases. However, it is worth challenging this assumption of universal benefit. We would expect that a Single Market composed of many countries would benefit consumers more than a closed national economy. However, the world has moved on since the 1950s and, in an era of relatively free trade, it is worth re-examining whether the Single Market's benefits are as impressive as is commonly supposed – and, even more importantly, whether they are as widely distributed.

Basic economic theory about the nature of common markets with common external tariffs tells us that, in addition to trade creation, there is a great deal of trade diversion or distortion. It follows that, whilst participants within the Single Market benefit from it, nations operating outside are always at a disadvantage. In the early years of European integration therefore, it can be surmised that a certain amount of trade diversion took place in EU countries that had historically traded more with other parts of the world. An obvious switching was between the colonial markets of France, Belgium, the Netherlands, and, especially, the UK and the new European common market. In mitigation, however, it ought to be stressed that between the 1960s and the 1980s, when most of this switching took place, the European economy was growing far faster than former colonial markets. Companies operating within the common market benefited from this, as did consumers through lower prices for most goods, food being an important exception.

Much of the basic theory on preferential trade agreements is undermined by the fact that, in the context of a world economy governed in great part by WTO (World Trade Organization) and GATT (General Agreement on Tariffs and Trade) rules on non-discrimination in trade policy, the notion of trade diversion is much less important than it was in the mid- to late-20th century. Obstacles to trade between the EU and external countries or preferential trade areas (such as the North American Free Trade Agreement, or NAFTA) now tend to be more about health, safety, technical and environmental regulations than formal tariffs (with some important exceptions, including agricultural produce). In other words, in order to trade within the EU, EU rules (frictional barriers) must be complied with. Interestingly, the removal of these frictional barriers to trade caused by, for example, harmonization or mutual recognition of technical standards causes no trade diversion effect since it will always lower the price that a country pays for its imports (Baldwin and Wyplosz, 2012). The final piece of the Single Market jigsaw puzzle, the single currency, is also estimated to have had a very positive effect on both intra- and extra-Eurozone trade for the simple reason that companies operating within or outside Europe benefit equally from having to deal in one currency, as opposed to 17 separate currencies. According to Baldwin (2006), the Euro boosted trade between Eurozone countries by about 9%.

The consensus on the value of the Single Market is clear: in aggregate terms, Europeans benefit from the significant uplift to economic growth and prosperity that economic integration, increased trade and the Single Market have provided. Even where trade distribution took place, Europeans on average have become better off as a result of the creation of the Single Market, at least until the Great Recession of 2009 (see Figure 4.1 and Table 4.1). Yet it would be premature to conclude that the Single Market has been an unmitigated success that has benefited all Europeans equally. Despite the convergence process and the consolidation of the single market across *Europe as a whole*, inequalities in wealth and income have actually widened *within the individual Member States*.

Widening Income Disparities: who appears to have gained most from the Single Market?

It would be unrealistic to expect that the income gains that followed the introduction of the Single Market and the wider process of globalization

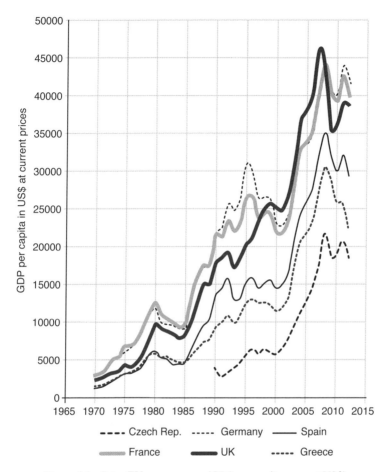

Figure 4.1   Intra-EU convergence (GDP per capita, current US$)

Source: Data from World Bank.

from the mid-1980s to the Great Recession of 2009 would be evenly shared by European society as a whole. Inevitably, those in possession of capital or those whose skills and experience were more in demand would be expected to profit to a greater extent than those whose skills were less in demand. This is a basic feature of a capitalist economy, and the economy of the EU is no exception. Moreover, there is general public acceptance that a certain variation in income levels and profits is both normal and necessary. Some people work harder than others, some people take more risks, some people have interesting or more workable ideas for new businesses and so on – and all these things are rewarded by the free market in a capitalist society.

Europeans are, at least by habit, capitalists and for the most part support the basic principles of a market economy – albeit with some variation between France and the rest of the EU (only 30–50% of the French agree that the free-market economy system 'is the best' as opposed to 60–70% of Germans and 58–65% of Britons, *The Economist*, 2011). In the central and eastern half of the European continent, many have experienced the altogether less agreeable alternative to capitalism of the planned economy. In consequence, Europeans like to think that the EU is a *social* market economy, or a system of 'capitalism with a human face' (Brittan, 1996).

In other words, at least since the Second World War, there has been a consensus that it is desirable for European societies to make sure that everyone gains from economic growth. Or in Adam Smith's eloquent and memorable phrase, 'the progress of opulence ... lifts all boats, large and small' (Smith, 1776). The underpinning value behind this belief in the social market economy is the imagined notion of 'fairness' which, despite its obvious subjectivity and relativity, is a powerful instinctive reflex and requires a sense of solidarity for it to be achieved. Europeans like to believe that they live in a system where hard work and playing by the rules are rewarded, and where everyone shares in the fruits of prosperity. But if this is what Europeans believe, is it actually true? Or is the notion of a social market economy more myth than reality?

In order to answer this question, I will analyze Organisation for Economic Cooperation and Development (OECD) data from Kaja Bonesmo Fredriksen's paper on the growth in total household disposal income from the launch of the Single Market drive in 1985 until 2010 (2012). Household disposable income constitutes an important indicator of well-being and living standards. It is the 'maximum amount that households can afford to spend on consumption goods or services without having to reduce their financial or non-financial assets or to increase their liabilities' (OECD, 2012a). It measures income dispersion between countries, thus giving a picture of the state and the evolution of inequality in the EU. These data, it should be noted, do not tell us much about causation, only about correlation. Another key point to emphasize is that this is part of a broader global trend (see Piketty, 2014), and not something unique to

Europe. However, as I will argue, this tendency, whatever its cause, runs contrary to what Europeans believe is fair and special about their economic system. It therefore undermines the principle of solidarity.

OECD data show us that total household disposable income grew more slowly on average in Europe than in the United States or the OECD as a whole between the 1980s and 2010, with a marked slowing by about one-third of the rate of growth after 1995. In some European countries, such as Spain, the UK, Finland or the new member states (after 1995), household income increased far more swiftly than others, particularly Germany and most of all Italy, where the rate of growth between 1985 and 2010 was less than one-third of the European average.

The data also show that the EU has concentrated on reducing income disparities between countries. In the quarter century between 1985 and 2009, the average annual growth rate in household disposable income in the sample of European countries was 2.5%. In Spain, which was poorer than other EU countries in the mid-1980s, disposable income grew by 3.97% on average, annually, between 1985 and 2010. In the UK over the same timeframe, the rate increased by 3.81%, again from a below-average level. This broad trend was evident when the data for each country was broken down into deciles. Whilst between-country income disparities have fallen since the mid-1980s, *within nearly all EU member states* income disparities have risen sharply. This is particularly true for the richest and most advanced European economics (such as Germany, the UK, the Netherlands or Sweden). In cumulative terms, the disparities have become hugely marked over time. The existence of a social democratic tradition here does not seem to make much difference: in Finland, the poorest 10% saw their incomes rise by 37% in real terms between 1985 and 2008. The richest saw theirs surge by 106%. In Sweden, the richest 10% saw their incomes increase by 116%, and the poorest by only 47%.

Breaking real disposable income growth down into within-country deciles, the picture becomes much less even than the inter-country situation. Across the EU countries included in the OECD average, the income for the wealthiest 10% of Europeans grew at almost three times the rate of increase for the poorest. Higher annual levels of income growth correlated with existing levels of income: the poorest experienced the least increase, the middle deciles a steadily rising level of annual growth, and the richest, the most of all. Incomes of the bottom 90% of Europeans grew at only half the rate of the top 10% over the 25-year period. It should also be remembered that these disposable income gains came on top of a higher pre-existing level of income, and therefore the compounded absolute sum was commensurately all the higher. Of the ten European countries, only in France, to some extent, and in Greece, to a great extent, did the incomes of the poorest decile rise faster than the richest. In the Netherlands, the disposable income levels of *the poorest households were 2.5% lower in real terms* over the 25-year period, at a time when the richest 10% had seen their incomes rise by 82%. The UK presented a similar picture, although the incomes of the very poorest continued to grow – albeit at only one-tenth of the rate of increase for the top 10% of the income distribution.

Table 4.1 compares developments in the evolution of real annual disposable income growth in the bottom three deciles with those in the top decile between 1995 and 2008. In all countries, the rate of growth in incomes for the richest 10% rose more than twice as fast as the incomes for the poorest. In the Netherlands, the incomes of the poorest 10% fell, but it is in Germany that the picture is most stark: the disposable incomes of the poorest 30% of Germans fell, whilst the incomes of the richest 10% continued to rise by almost one-quarter over the same timeframe. Only Greece and Italy bucked this trend.

Table 4.1   Average annual real disposable income growth, selected deciles, mid-1990s to 2008

Country	Decile 1	2	3	...	10
Denmark	0.30	0.77	0.84		2.69
Finland	1.38	1.38	1.72		4.79
France	1.21	1.39	1.37		2.36
Germany	−0.14	−0.20	−0.03		1.32
Greece	6.10	4.74	4.36		3.02
Italy	2.61	1.59	1.14		0.94
Luxemburg	1.26	1.66	1.91		3.71
Netherlands	−0.27	0.43	0.45		2.44
Sweden	0.75	1.33	1.97		4.28
UK	0.51	2.55	2.58		3.98
Weighted EU average	1.06	1.28	1.28		2.26
Hungary	3.79	4.25	4.09		2.91
Weighted EU average 2	1.15	1.37	1.36		2.28
US	−0.35	0.46	0.51		1.20

Source: Data from OECD Income Distribution and Poverty Database.
Note: Decile 1 = lowest income group; decile 10 = highest income group.

Taken together, these data show first that in many European countries, and especially Italy and Germany, economic growth slowed in comparison to the OECD average from the 1980s onwards, particularly steeply from the mid-1990s. Secondly, what economic growth there was did not benefit European society as a whole and inequalities in income widened considerably (Bonesmo Fredriksen, 2012), so that by 2008, income distribution in Europe had become more unequal than the OECD average. In other words, what little growth there had been in the slow-growing European states benefited only the rich.

Since the introduction of the Single Market, disposable income growth in many European countries has been concentrated in the hands of very few Europeans, a trend we would usually associate with emerging economies. The trend is even more pronounced when it comes to wealth, which is partly made up of income saved (Piketty, 2014). Globalization and the structure of an advanced capitalist economy in the 21st century may be just as responsible for these trends as European integration, but as Majone (2009) makes clear, increases in inequalities within member states are a side-effect of the lack of EU action to tackle them. The EU budget's provisions for regional aid are more a side payment to persuade poorer member states to accept economic integration than a tool of redistribution. By definition, the top decile of European society began with a higher level of income, but over the past 25 years they have been capturing a steadily increasing share of total income. This may be due to changes in taxation (and the reduction of the higher marginal rates of personal taxation), technological progress, changes in labour market institutions and, most importantly, globalization. Over time, this also leads to an ever-greater concentration of wealth at the top end of European society, which Thomas Piketty (2014) estimates for France is now greater than it was during the Belle Époque before the outbreak of the First World War. The social consequences of this can be catastrophic for the great mass of the population: in London, the richest city in Europe in both absolute and per capita terms, nearly 40% of children live below the poverty line (UCL, 2012).

A great many economists, when confronted with these data, would simply answer 'so what?' In response, I would argue that widening inequality – whether it is driven by Europeanization, globalization, both or indeed another cause – is politically, socially and morally hazardous. At least four important arguments may be brought to bear to support this assertion. First, excessive inequality is injurious to the social consensus. As Piketty argues, 'arbitrary and unsustainable inequalities undermine … the meritocratic values on which democratic societies are based' (2014, p. 1). When inherited wealth is perceived to matter for life chances far more than hard work, as it did in the 19th century and as it appears to in the 2010s, at least in the UK and France (Piketty, 2014), the notion of equality of opportunity is fatally weakened. Second, following on from this point, inequality is incompatible with the ideal of true equality between citizens living in a democratic system, and undermines the sense of solidarity that is born of shared experiences. When the lived experiences of those who own most of the wealth in a society differ so markedly from those of the rest, it is hard to speak of equality of citizenship. Third, inequality matters because it is the result of a public policy choice. Whatever free market economists may argue, rising levels of inequality are the product of decisions made by governments in regard to taxation and finance (Piketty, 2014). And finally, severe inequality serves to undermine a sense of fairness and the belief that there is a social contract that underpins European society. As was shown in Chapter 1, this sense of fairness includes a commitment to redistribution that is shared by a substantial majority of European voters.

Thus excessive concentrations of income, and consequently over the long term, wealth, in the hands of a smaller and smaller segment of the population is associated with negative consequences for the quality of democracy. It also has serious consequences for the imagined, popular notion of 'fairness' as a principle underpinning the social market economy, which most Europeans believe to be the optimal socio-economic model (see Chapter 5). In simple terms, if the benefits of the socio-economic market-based model that European integration promotes are seen as being too thinly spread, and only shared by a lucky few, then it follows logically that public support for solidarity will fall – although this would depend on the extent to which this reality were widely perceived (and resented). There is evidence to suggest that Europeans are becoming aware of these trends, with 77% of those polled in 2013 arguing that 'the economic system favours the wealthy' and 85% agreeing that the rich–poor gap had increased (Pew, 2013). There is less evidence to suggest that this is the cause of Euroscepticism, the roots of which lie more in perceptions of the EU's democratic deficit. Looking after possible discontents and losers in a democratic society and a free market economy is important, as the creators of the CAP understood in the 1960s. Excessive discontentment and the perception that society as it is currently ordered benefits only a minority have the potential to drive voters towards populist, extremist political parties. I examine this issue in more depth by looking at *who* supports the principle of solidarity in the EU.

Who Supports Solidarity in the EU?

We have already established that few Europeans benefit directly in material terms from the EU budget, and that the gains from economic growth in a system governed by the logic of globalization and the rules of the Single Market have been unevenly spread across European society. We now turn to the issue of public support for solidarity at the European level, which is understood as a collective insurance principle for member states that either need extra support to converge with the European standard of living or that get into trouble.

A fresh and interesting case study is provided by Michael Bechtel, Jens Hainmueller and Yotam Margalit's (2012) work on the attitudes of the public towards the bailout of Eurozone countries after the sovereign debt crisis. These have become a regular feature of European macroeconomic policy since the first Greek bailout of 2010. Public opinion was of exceptional importance for the politics of bailouts and it has been argued (Bechtel *et al.*, 2012) that this provided a constraint on EU member-state governments, by delaying or limiting the size of rescue packages. The controversy in the politics of the bailout centred on a number of, often incorrect, economic and political assumptions: (1) bailout funds transferred to a member state in trouble would entail cuts in public spending or higher government borrowing in the state providing the help; (2) bailouts were gifts, rather than interest-bearing loans; (3) some of the recipients were profligate and/or corrupt and incapable of getting their own house in order; or (4) funding was being used to pay for generous social protection, such as early retirement ages, that was not available in the states providing the funding. Public debate about the bailouts was often acrimonious and it should come as no surprise that only about one-third of the electorate in Germany and France, the two largest Eurozone economies, were in favour of bailing out the Eurozone member states which had got into trouble. But who were those in favour?

Bechtel *et al.*'s (2012) study found that a significant majority of the public who responded to their survey were opposed to transfers. Around one-quarter were somewhat in favour, and only 3% strongly in favour. When asked about Germany alone, fewer than one in twenty felt that Germany should pay more; and, once again, one-quarter felt that the contribution should be kept as it was. Two-thirds felt that Germany should be paying somewhat less (34%) or much less (33%).

So who comprised the proportion of respondents who were in favour? It might be assumed that the voters' preference on the bailout would be determined by their calculation of its likely effect on their own economic standing. In fact, this economic self-interest had little or no correlation with attitudes towards bailouts. Wealthier respondents, who might be expected to lose most, were generally more in favour than poorer respondents – although it could be argued that wealthier respondents could more easily be expected to take the hit to their wealth.

Fascinatingly, Bechtel *et al.* (2012) found that the identification with particular values, such as altruism and cosmopolitanism, were strong predictors of preferences over the bailouts. Where wealthier voters expressed a preference in favour, it was because they tended to have a higher propensity to hold these two values. Moreover, support for the bailout cross-cut the ideological spectrum. Centrist voters were more in favour of bailouts and supporters of extreme left or right parties were against. The key elements at play were not about domestic winners and losers, but rather about economic nationalism *vs.* sentiment towards other Europeans. Where voters expressed feelings of sympathy and solidarity towards other Europeans, they tended to support the bailouts. This is entirely in keeping with the argument put forward in Chapter 2 about the 'two Europes'. The prosperous, well-travelled, well-educated European who, as we have seen in this chapter, is far more likely to have benefited from the economic benefits of European integration supports the project, including economic solidarity that could be perceived as not being in his or her short-term interest. Poorer, less-educated and older Europeans are far less likely to support solidarity. This fits in neatly with the analysis of the supporters of the United Kingdom Independence Party (UKIP), a British Eurosceptic party, whose typical supporter is 'more likely to be male, old, working class, religious and to read the Daily Mail, the Express or the Sun than the electorate as a whole. They are less likely to have stayed in education beyond the age of 16, to have gone to university or to earn more than £40,000 [€48,000] a year' (Jones, 2013).

Conclusions

This chapter looked at the question of who actually benefits from the solidarity that is constantly evoked by Europe's political leaders. It argued that a relatively small group of individuals benefit *directly* from policies that are supposed to provide greater solidarity, although this has much to do with the fact that the EU has relatively few policies that directly target the objective of solidarity. It also argued that the benefits of economic growth became increasingly concentrated in the hands of the richest 10%

of people in Europe between the mid-1980s and the mid-2010s. This top decile is partly analogous to those who identify themselves as being 'European'. This was an interesting, yet not altogether surprising, finding since it is this group that appears to benefit in a disproportionate way both from globalization and from the Single Market. Yet this deep and increasing concentration of wealth in the hands of fewer and fewer Europeans (which more and more Europeans are becoming aware of (Pew, 2013)) has the potential to undermine the notion of fairness as a guiding and underpinning factor supporting the European model of capitalism that has been favoured in Western Europe since 1945. A more intriguing discovery is that the wealthiest 10% of Europeans are also more likely to support the practical expression of the principle of solidarity in the form of bailouts to struggling Eurozone countries. Identity, values and shared experiences certainly matter here, but so does material benefit from European integration. By illustration, in the case of a similar (but much older) union, some two-thirds of Scots have stated that they would back independence from the UK if it made them £500 (€600) a year better off. Only 21% would do so if they lost £500 as a result of independence (NatCen, 2011). Moreover, the relationship between European identity, the values it represents and material gain from European integration appears to be a two-way street. Those who benefit from European integration affect a European identity and vice versa.

A few conclusions are inescapable at this juncture.

First, for all the talk of solidarity in the EU, far too few Europeans actually benefit from it. This is not to argue that there are no universal benefits from European integration and there is obviously a distinction to be made between benefiting from European integration and benefiting from solidarity. Everyone benefits from greater consumer choice and protection through the single market, as well as peace, security and Erasmus student mobility, to give a few examples. As has been observed by McCormick (2013), the benefits of the EU are mostly taken for granted by voters. Moreover, all those living in the EU also benefit from, amongst other things, EU regulations against environmental degradation or dangerous working conditions. Whilst these benefits extend to those at the lower end of the income scale, it cannot be overlooked that Europe has become a much less equal place since the introduction of the Single Market in terms of both income and wealth – although this was largely a result of global trends and public policy decisions on wealth, finance and taxation at national level. There are far too few obvious winners from the European integration process as a total percentage of the population and the rewards of competition and enterprise are spread too thinly. In other words, there is a serious separation between the continued evocation of solidarity on the part of European political leaders and the lived experiences of the great mass of the European people. These trends are seemingly common knowledge (Pew, 2013) and globalization is often invoked as an explanation for why it is impossible to do anything about it, although as I argue in the Conclusion, this seems an inadequate excuse for the world's largest economy and trading power. As Piketty argues, 'it is possible to imagine public institutions and policies that would counter the effects of this implacable logic [of rising inequality] ... [but] establishing such institutions and policies would require a considerable degree of international coordination' (2014, p. 27). What international organization is better placed to lead on this public policy challenge than the EU?

Second, where Europe acts, it succeeds. In the 1950s and the 1960s, a serious economic and security challenge was the production of sufficient food for the population of Europe. Through the modernization and rationalization of agriculture, this challenge has since been met and no one could now argue seriously that agriculture is a top policy priority for Europe. This chapter has shown that Europe has also succeeded when it has applied itself to reducing income disparities between member states and Europe's regions, at least until the Great Recession and the Eurozone crisis. Between the 1970s and the Great Recession of 2009, the income disparities between the poorest member states, such as Ireland or Greece or Spain, and the wealthy core, such as Belgium, the Netherlands or Germany, fell considerably. The process has continued with great success since the enlargement of the EU to Central and Eastern Europe. This is to be celebrated.

Third, the challenge for Europe has shifted: in many ways the challenge for Europe in the 21st century is about finding ways of tackling the alarming income and wealth inequalities that have arisen between rich and poor in European society. If unchecked, these inequalities threaten to undermine the European social compact, and, in turn, to undermine support for European integration as a whole. Viewed from another angle, if Europe can turn its considerable powers and track record of success in delivering major policy objectives to this area, it will dramatically increase both the numbers of Europeans who benefit from what is currently a very selective policy of solidarity in the EU and of supporters of European integration.

What all of this entails is a shifting away of the focus of European policy from past problems, such as the modernization of agriculture, towards a policy agenda that is not only about creating prosperity, but crucially, is about sharing prosperity more widely. This is a serious challenge for Europe in the 21st century. Despite the convergence process aimed at reducing inequalities across the EU as a whole and the consolidation of the single market, inequalities in wealth and income have actually widened within many Western European member states. Instead of adopting a passive attitude to what many view as a consequence of globalization against which little can be done, the EU should adopt a more proactive stance. For instance, given its role as a sector that shares wealth and creates jobs, the further development of services through European integration must be aided. In other words, the objective should be about creating shared wealth and a lived experience of solidarity that benefits all Europeans as opposed to the lucky few. In turn, this could help to convert the opponents of change. The means by which this must be achieved is a re-examination of the social market economy, including the issue of the sustainability and reform of the European economy.

5

Sustaining European Capitalism

The final substantive theme of this book is sustainability. Like solidarity, sustainability has become something of a European buzzword, particularly since the beginning of the Great Recession. Promoting 'sustainable' growth is a core aim of the Europe 2020 ten-year growth strategy. Sustainability is also a watchword for environmentalists, trade unionists and many others besides, to whom it has different connotations. In essence, sustainability refers to the capacity to endure and the ability to maintain something at a certain level. Yet sustainability also has a secondary meaning, which refers to the ability to uphold or defend something – perhaps an idea, a set of practices, or a model. Sustainability is understood in both senses in this book: first as the ability of the European model to sustain itself; and second, as its capacity to be upheld and defended against critics. It also follows that it is a far easier undertaking to uphold and defend a European model that is successful than one which is clearly unsustainable.

The 'European model' is characterized in a domestic and an international sense. At home it refers to the sustainability of Europe's distinctive model of capitalism (also known as the social market economy; Albert, 1993). The chapter does not discuss the economic and social superiority of the European model but rather draws attention to the challenges that this model has been facing for some time as 'it has all the charms of an old provincial spinster, petrified in her traditions, rooted in her humanistic nostalgia, encumbered by scruples and foresight' (Albert, 1993, p. 296). What is also striking is the absence of harmonization between business cycles, tax rates and consumer prices which were supposed to be natural consequences of the introduction of a single currency (Outhwaite, 2008).

Abroad, the challenge to the European model is about Europe's ability to sustain, uphold and defend its interests and influence in a globalized world. Europe's influence in world affairs is looked at less in terms of war and peace and more as the capacity of the European Union to play a decisive role, or at least participate meaningfully, in those international debates that are important to its future, such as the regulation of trade. The central question here is whether, and how, Europe can continue to be a policy-maker, rather than a policy-taker. Each of these sustainability questions is of sufficient importance and distinction to warrant a separate chapter. Like charity, strength abroad begins with economic strength at home (Ikenberry, 2011). Following this logic, this chapter deals with the prospects for what I term 'European capitalism' and Chapter 6 builds on this premise to address Europe's capacity for influence in a dynamic international arena.

Before moving on to the question of whether 'European capitalism' is sustainable or otherwise, the term itself needs to be defined. This chapter begins with a brief explanation of the broad origins of European capitalism, followed by an overview of its main features, how it differs from other models and an assessment of its strengths and weaknesses. This is followed by an investigation into the sustainability of European capitalism, starting with an overview of the performance of the European capitalist model since the early days of the European integration process in the 1960s, and focusing on the quarter-century between the Single Market drive which began in the 1980s and the Great Recession. Here the spotlight is on the long-standing issues of low growth and high unemployment that pre-date the very particular economic problems stemming from the financial and sovereign debt crises, which were examined in Chapter 1. The final, normative segment of the chapter looks at what a possible response to some of these long-standing challenges.

European Capitalism

Origins

European capitalism is less distinct from other forms of capitalism than most Europeans imagine it to be in terms of the equality of outcomes that it produces, as we saw in Chapter 4. Nonetheless, there are solid reasons underpinning the assertion that the model for regulating the relationship between the economy and society that prevails in Europe is different from the practice of other highly advanced economies, such as the US (Martinelli *et al.*, 2007). An area of contention is the question of whether it is correct to speak of European capitalism as opposed to Swedish, German, Estonian or Italian capitalism, for example. This is a legitimate point, even if the analytical standpoint of this book is an examination of Europe's society, economics and politics as a whole. Gøsta Esping-Andersen (1990) put forward the notion of three stylized 'worlds' of welfare capitalism: Liberal, Corporatist and Social Democratic, which between them covered the differences between the approaches of the states of Western Europe that constituted the old EU-15. Other scholars have similarly pointed to a multiplicity of capitalist models within Europe (Amable, 2003; Crouch, 1999; Hall and Soskice, 2001; Sachs, 1990; Schmidt, 2002). To Esping-Andersen's three ideal types should also be added the Central and East European or Post-Communist models of welfare capitalism that underwent a considerable process of transformation away from the 'socialist alternative' over the 20 years after the fall of Communism in 1989 (Brada *et al.*, 2008; Deacon, 2000; Hay and Wincott, 2012; Wagener, 2002). It should also not be forgotten that the policy areas that constitute the commanding heights of European welfare capitalism, such as housing, pensions, in-work benefits, out-of-work benefits, child support, healthcare, and, of course, personal and corporate taxation, remain firmly the preserve of member states.

Important as these differences between European social models are, their similarities, especially viewed from an external perspective, are even more striking. There is something distinctive about European capitalism and the European social model viewed not only from, say, Mexico, India or Egypt, but also from the United States or Canada, which might be considered to resemble the European model more closely. Moreover, when it comes to the elements of the European capitalist model that are involved with the management of the economy, most government policy is enacted at the European level. This is achieved through the enforcement of the 'four freedoms' (goods, capital, services and people) through the Single Market, competition policy, and, increasingly, by setting parameters for macroeconomic policy-making at the member-state level which prevent too much deviation from the norm. If the so-called Fiscal Compact were to come into full effect, macroeconomic guidelines would become hard rules, enforced through fines upon the recalcitrant. Thus although the practice of capitalism may differ from one European country to another in terms of the details, the commonalities in the broad outlines of European capitalism are sufficient for a big-picture analysis to be carried out. It is also important to avoid the narcissism of small differences that informs too many of the more dramatic claims about irreconcilable differences between the various European social models. Viewed from an intra-European perspective, differences do exist – and they do matter, particularly in tailoring national-level responses to the various challenges facing European countries. However, from an extra-European standpoint the similarities are more obvious than the differences. As has been argued, there is strong evidence of gradual convergence, especially in certain sectors (Albert, 1993; Outhwaite, 2008; Schmidt, 2002). Schmidt argues that, under the combined influence of globalization and Europeanization, EU member states' practices have been moving towards a 'European economy much less distinguishable from the national economies that constitutes it' (2002, p. 305). This process has been driven by 'the internationalization of financial markets and trade, pushing the rationalization of governments and the diminution in their welfare state functions, and loosening the traditional ties of business with government and labour' (2002, p. 303) as well as the single currency, the single market, open methods of coordination for labour markets and the welfare states (2002). However, variations between Schmidt's three models of capitalism persist; first because differences between national discourses exist and do matter, second because the initial differences between capitalisms have paved the way to a lesser or greater extent towards convergence, and third because sectors are more or less open to convergence, depending on the representation and political-economic stakes attached. Schmidt concludes that different sectors are moving to different kinds of capitalism depending on what is at stake. For instance, the 'new economy' is moving towards market capitalism, characterized by a short-term focus, high-precision engineering prefers competitive managed capitalism and its preference for innovation and profits over the longer term, while defence looks at state-enhanced capitalism because it requires 'heavy investments with low rates of return over long periods of time' (2002, p. 307). In other words, the varieties of capitalism within Europe are not so much national in nature, as sectoral (although this is contested, see Hall and Gingerich, 2009).

'European capitalism' stems from the marriage of two competing political philosophies that originated in the European continent: liberalism and socialism. Europe's liberal inheritance is most evident in the consensus on the overarching centrality of the market – Adam Smith's 'invisible hand' (Smith, 1776) – as the best means of allocating scarce resources through the free price system. In the liberal tradition, freedom of contract and private property are guaranteed by the law, which also safeguards the principle of a level playing field on which economic players can compete fairly by preventing the formation of anti-competitive monopolies. Europe's socialist inheritance – understood broadly – originated as a critical response to liberal capitalism, and was founded on a rigid, Marxian view of class and the assumption that the poor, lower-class majority would always be exploited by the rich, higher-class minority. In this stylized account of the socialist perspective, escaping poverty is a near-impossibility in a completely free market economy, so wealth and income needed to be reallocated 'from each according to his ability, to each according to his need' (Marx, 1875). The brutal reality of Communism in the eastern half of the European continent and the patent economic failures of the Marxist-Leninist system gave birth to social democracy. The legacy of these socialist ideas is found in the Europe-wide consensus on the principle of economic fairness, which is to be achieved partly by direct redistribution of income and partly through the social democratic ideal of equality of opportunity, which is intended to overcome the problem of rigid class structures. Philosophically, European capitalism is a product of the compromise between these two competing worldviews of liberalism and socialism, politically expressed on the centre-left as social democracy, and on the centre-right as Christian Democracy and its secular bedfellow, compassionate conservatism. Thus a prominent European socialist such as Pierre Mendès France could support the basic principle of the market, albeit with more government control of key sectors, and a European conservative grandee such as Winston Churchill could speak in favour of both 'the ladder' up which everyone can climb, and the 'safety net' through which no one can fall.

Armed with this thumbnail sketch of the philosophical origins of European capitalism, albeit stylized and necessarily simplistic (Catholic social thought and non-socialist French statism also played a part) an analysis of the main features of European capitalism may be undertaken. This exercise is approached in two ways. First, a synthetic understanding of what European capitalism or what others call 'European welfare capitalism' (Hay and Wincott, 2012) is in theory will be set out. This is an important step since 'European capitalism' can mean very different things to different people. Second, we will look at the results or what European capitalism actually delivers through comparisons with the US and the OECD as a whole.

What is European Capitalism?

Government intervention in the management of the economy is the very essence of European capitalism. The actuality of state intervention is further buttressed by the normative assumption that active government is both necessary and desirable. Subjective attitudes towards government as a good or bad thing are important here: the archetypal European really does believe, *in contrast to* Ronald Reagan, that the man from the government is here to help. Furthermore, I would assert that this difference in *attitude* towards the government is the main marker of difference between capitalism as it is practised on either side of the Atlantic – as the examples of the US mortgage market or the farm sector show, in practice, government in America can be almost as interventionist as government in Europe. European politicians and civil servants do not, however, feel the need to apologize for doing their job. Europeans would also accept that the challenge for European capitalism is about 'whether and under what conditions the class divisions and social inequalities produced by capitalism can be undone by parliamentary democracy' (Esping-Andersen, 1990, p. 11). Americans may hesitate before accepting that this is a challenge that should concern the government at all. Statistically, around two-thirds of Americans believe that government should provide only 'basic' or 'the most basic' functions and just under one in five believing that it should 'take active steps in every area it can' (Gallup, 2010–13). In simple terms, it could be said that Europeans believe that their government should intervene in the management of the economy 'as much as is necessary', whilst their American counterparts believe that the government should intervene 'as little as possible'.

As Esping-Andersen (1990) noted, 'welfare capitalism' can be defined 'both narrowly and broadly'. The narrow school of thought sees welfare capitalism as income transfers, the provision of social services and perhaps a housing policy. Those who view welfare capitalism in broad terms also see the macroeconomic steering of the economy as integral. A sophisticated understanding of European capitalism includes the acceptance that many markets are 'politically created and form an integral part of the overall welfare state regime' (Esping-Andersen, 1990). Social structures, including family composition, the degree of social mobility, patterns of employment and the division of rights and responsibilities between individuals, families, employers and the government are all crucial determinants of the overall 'welfare regime', which in their details can be different from one European country to another. Yet it would be a mistake to focus too much on the 'welfare' element of European capitalism, important though it is.

European capitalism is much more than simply 'capitalism plus welfare'. Government intervention in the form of regulation is present at almost every level of the European economy. The purpose of this examination is not to make a judgement about whether regulation is a good thing or otherwise, not least because the policy goals and objectives of government regulation in Europe are themselves so diverse, and do not necessarily follow any particular ideological logic. Regulation abounds at the European and member-state level and appears to serve two diametrically opposite goals. First, regulation exists to boost competition, productivity, consumer choice and quality through free trade in certain sectors of the economy, most notably for 'visible' or tangible goods, from motor vehicles to dentists' drills to fruit-based liqueurs. Second, regulation exists to protect certain sectors of the economy through price controls, restrictions on market entry, and prescriptive rules governing opening hours and the ways in which businesses can operate, which serve to reduce competitive pressures. (On the specific case of Italy, see Emmott, 2012.) Sectors that are regulated with a view to protection are highly diverse, albeit with an emphasis on intangible services. Protection varies between member states, and all of the following can be found in this assortment: agriculture and fisheries, notaries, taxi drivers, pharmacists, on- and off-licence sales of alcoholic drinks and tobacco, groceries (by size and number of shops allowed), insurance, broadcasting, media, banking and other financial services. Regulation may well often be implemented for very good reasons, from the protection of public health to the preservation of the character of particular towns. It is to be hoped that regulation is in place because it is what the public wants, as befits a democratic society, although the most orthodox liberal ideologues such as Hayek would argue, like their 19th century counterpart, de Tocqueville, that excessive democracy is the enemy of liberty.

The sheer size and breadth of the government sector is the third prominent feature of European capitalism, since it extends beyond the provision of welfare into the direct government ownership of companies and other assets, including extensive real estate holdings. Variety across the EU's member states is strongly apparent in the range of companies and sectors where the state plays a leading role, including: water and gas supply; railways; electricity supply, especially nuclear power; defence companies; aerospace companies; bus and metro networks; mass market car manufacturers; radio and television broadcasters; airlines; and, particularly since the financial crisis, banks, which increasingly resemble a nationalized industry. When it comes to banking, it is salutary to observe that on both sides of the Atlantic it was these former paladins of the free market who squealed the loudest for government bailouts and handouts in the wake of the financial crisis of 2007–09.

European capitalism is a big tent. It is not particularly based on strong ideological convictions about what the government ought or ought not to do, so much as it comprises a series of pragmatic *ad hoc* decisions about the desirability of taking action to ensure a particular outcome in one sector or another. It is a variant of capitalism that contains so many inherent contradictions that it almost seems to be defined by paradox. Cognitive dissonance is at the heart of European capitalism. Thus the centre-right French President Nicolas Sarkozy could speak up for the principle of free markets, but as free markets that are 'regulated and controlled' (Archives of the French Government, 2008). To reiterate, European capitalism is a broad church but the one article of faith that is shared by the entire congregation is that government *should* play a significant role across the whole economy.

European capitalism in the guise of varied government intervention that both enables and restrains market forces has produced equally divergent outcomes. Fascinatingly, as a result, the EU economy is not singular and unified, but a multiplicity. It is not delineated by national boundaries but instead by sectors that have different levels of engagement with government, varying degrees of productivity and efficiency, and are situated closer or further apart from the technological frontier (Schmidt, 2002).

The sustainability of European capitalism is understood in a political and social sense as well as an economic sense, although it is this latter element that must be addressed first. European capitalism has already been defined as the marriage of liberalism and socialism. Whether the match is a success or failure will be determined by answering a number of basic questions:

1. Does European capitalism deliver prosperity that is shared more or less across all of society?
2. Does European capitalism provide adequate social protection for those in need of it?
3. Are there adequate funds in place to pay for the European model of social protection today?
4. Are there adequate funds in place to sustain the system into the future?

5. Does European capitalism enjoy the political support necessary to sustain itself?

These economic, social and political aspects are deeply entwined. They contain both positive and normative questions since the issue of fairness is central here, which is of course a thoroughly and admirably normative concept. The Anglo-Irish political theorist, Edmund Burke, would recognize European capitalism as not only a contract between the young and the old or those in work and those seeking or unable to work, but in the widest possible sense as an accord between 'those who are living, those who are dead, and those who are yet to be born' (1790). His memorable aphorism on society captures the heart of the debate about European capitalism and he correctly identifies true sustainability as a contract between those who pay into and benefit from the system, those who fought for the system to be established, and those who will suffer in the future if the system is not made sustainable.

The Sustainability of European Capitalism

Economic Sustainability

The overall performance of the European economy for quite some time has been less than spectacular. Even before the Great Recession began, it was clear that European capitalism was failing in three interlinked respects. First, economic growth was too slow and the process of convergence with the US had ground to a halt. If growth comes from three sources – total factor productivity, investment and labour market growth (which is linked to, but not quite the same as, population growth) – then clearly the former two will have to grow more briskly to compensate for a slowing or decline in the last. It is therefore important to establish what has been restricting productivity growth in the European economy. Second, partly as a result of this slow growth, unemployment has remained stubbornly high for a very long period. Third, as a direct result of both of these factors, the cost of providing high-quality social insurance and welfare was rising more quickly than the ability of the European economy to pay for them.

It is important at this stage to emphasize the danger of branding European capitalism inefficient and unproductive as a result of the social model on which it is based. From an economic perspective, there is nothing wrong with generous welfare provision – indeed it is of net economic benefit – provided that welfare is understood as investment in human capital and insurance against risks, that it does not discourage employment, that government spending on welfare is broadly balanced in the medium and long term and that the external current account balance is not in deficit. None of these elements need detract from economic freedom and liberty – rather they could be seen a complement to it and a way of compensating for market failures, such as the reluctance of firms to invest in training employees they worry may leave the company for higher remuneration elsewhere.

Before advancing any further, it is helpful to see some visual illustrations of the low-growth and high-unemployment trap over the very long term. Figure 5.1 shows the economic convergence of the largest European economies with the United States in terms of GDP per head between 1960 and 2013. Between 1945 and the oil shock of 1973, in aggregate Europe grew far more quickly than the United States (or the UK).

Data for the European economy as a whole do not exist, but in per-capita terms, the three largest West European economies increased their level of income relative to the US from 54% to 77% for France, from 40% to 70% for Italy and from 49% to 87% for Germany (Baily and Kirkegaard, 2004). This rapid catch-up relative to the US was exaggerated by the very low base from which the Europeans were starting in the

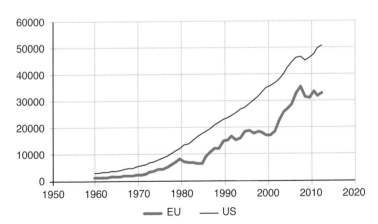

Figure 5.1   GDP-per-capita convergence between the EU and the US
(current US$)

Source: Data from World Bank, 2014a.

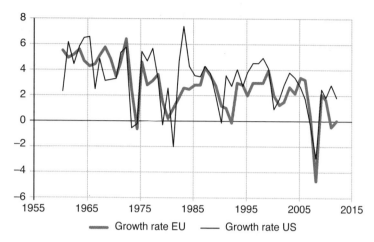

Figure 5.2   Comparative growth rate of GDP per capita US-EU (%)

Source: Data from World Bank, 2014b.

aftermath of the Second World War, the fact that the gap between average and best-practice productivity was so wide, the shift from agriculture to industry and the benefits gained from increasing economies of scale during the catch-up period (Denison, 1967; Temin, 2002). Olson (1982) argued that the war had helped to break up anti-competitive coalitions, cartels and monopolies in Europe, which allowed old industries to die and new industries to emerge. It could also be argued that Germany and other countries' model of cooperation and collaboration between managers and workers help maintain relatively peaceful labour relations, which provided a sustained and rapid level of growth. After 1973, the process of catching up with the US came to an end, and even reversed a little. Looking forward, by the early 2020s the EU is expected to have regressed in terms of its level of GDP per capita relative to the US to that of the early 1960s (World Bank, 2013d).

Figure 5.3 shows the high level of European unemployment since 1980. Figure 5.4 compares unemployment in the EU and US since the mid-1990s. In the 1960s in western Europe, unemployment rates around 2% were the norm, but these rose sharply from the 1970s to the 1990s, when rates averaged around 8–10% of the labour force (Baily and Kirkegaard, 2004). Economic growth rates never seemed to rise to the level necessary to bring unemployment down, which became known as 'Eurosclerosis' (Giersch, 1985). A number of factors have been put forward to

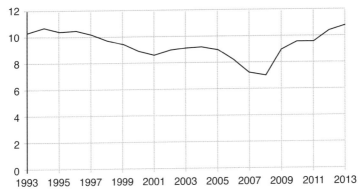

Figure 5.3   Unemployment rate in the EU, 1993–2013

Source: Data from Eurostat, 2013e.
Note: Rates approximated between 1982 and 1989.

explain the problem of unemployment in Europe (Baily and Kirkegaard, 2004), including: real wages were set institutionally, which made it hard for them to adjust or fall – and even that they continued to rise beyond what increases in productivity could pay for; transfer payments as unemployment insurance (especially when paid for a long time), disability benefits, welfare and early retirement discouraged job-seeking and reduced labour supply; restrictions in product markets after the 1970s

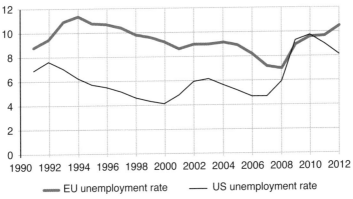

■■■ EU unemployment rate   —— US unemployment rate

Figure 5.4   EU and US unemployment rates

Source: Data from World Bank, 2013b.

discouraged new lines of production; and, finally, Europeans opted to work fewer hours in favour of greater leisure.

Numerous diagnostics have been undertaken to explain the low growth–high unemployment trap. At the turn of the century, the influential Sapir Report (Aghion *et al*., 2003) identified a European economy stuck in out-dated mass production, dominated by large firms, reliant on older technologies and blighted by long-term unemployment and a skills shortage. The Single Market for goods had long been completed, but progress in tradeable services integration lagged far behind. This, in turn was hindering an increase in competitiveness and employment levels. Two questions immediately come to mind: Where did these problems spring from?; why have they proven so intractable?

European capitalism's late-20th and early-21st century economic struggles need to be viewed in context. To begin with, Europe is a very rich and highly developed region of the world economy. Some areas of Europe have the highest per capita income in the world. The high-technology sectors of its economy, such as pharmaceuticals, aerospace, nuclear physics and the automotive industry, are situated on the very edge of the technology frontier and set the world standard for advances in quality and productivity. Europe has also been consistently prosperous since the beginnings of the industrial revolution in the 18th century. Where did this wealth come from? Older models of economic growth were based on the assumption that output flowed from the combination of three physical inputs: land, labour and capital. Under conditions of economic liberty – in other words, where economic actors can make their own decisions – increasing the volume of these inputs or the efficiency with which they were deployed would therefore lead to more growth. Matters are obviously more complicated than this, otherwise countries such as Brazil or Mexico with plenty of land and labour could simply have imported sufficient capital to become rich long ago. At the end of the 20th century, a more sophisticated 'endogenous growth theory' that drew in elements such as knowledge spill-overs and technology transfer was put forward to explain differences in growth rates. These again have proven to be insufficient in explaining diverse outcomes, which has prompted scholars to return to the questions, first raised in the 18th century by Richard Cantillon, Anne-Robert-Jacques Turgot and Adam Smith, of what constitutes economic liberty, and how it may best be guaranteed. This trio of liberal thinkers, to which might also be added the name of Edmund Burke, argued that economic and political liberty needed to be guaranteed by institutions, rules, norms and structures – the rule of law. The longevity of the ideas and theories put forward by these 18th century philosophers suggests rather strongly that they may have some analytical purchase in explaining the Europe's unemployment and growth puzzle in the 21st century. It might therefore be a worthwhile exercise to update these principles and apply them to the current situation, in order to see if any obvious shortcomings may be found. We will draw upon Steve Hanke and Stephen Walters' (1991) matrix of thirteen elements that in sum constitute a liberal economic order. They are presented in the first column of Table 5.1, followed by a brief description and a judgement about whether each applies to European capitalism.

As a tool for identifying potential restrictions on economic liberty, this exercise is a useful basis for further discussion and investigation. As can be seen in Table 5.1, European capitalism meets most of the criteria for a liberal economic order. Yet what is more interesting is that in many areas, the criteria are only partially fulfilled. First, as highlighted in Table 5.1, the opacity of government accounts and creative or false government accounting restricts economic liberty. This caused serious problems for Italy and Greece in their quest to join the Euro and for Greece in its quest to remain in the Eurozone. Second, Table 5.1 underscores the problems of running balanced budgets. This is partly a result of the low-growth and high-unemployment trap, and partly (as noted in Chapter 1) a result of the Great Recession. Third, restrictions are placed on economic liberty in international trade in agriculture and services. Fourth, more harmonization and simplification of tax regimes is needed in some member states. Fifth, subsidies and tax incentives for agriculture remain in place, distorting the market. Sixth, some European sectors, notably services, profit from privileges and immunities, again distorting the market. Seventh, price controls are in place in the agricultural sector. Eighth, bailouts have been introduced for banks, distorting the natural mechanism of the market. Finally, many companies in Europe are state-owned, although this may be far less of a problem than at first appears. Many of these industries, such as railways or utilities, are both natural monopolies and could also be considered as public services which might not be suitable for privatization.

The elements that stand out particularly strongly are the barriers to competition and economic liberty that exist in two sectors of the European economy: *services* and *agriculture*. Intriguingly, in service industries there is a correlation with high unemployment since they are by far the largest sector of almost any developed or developing economy in terms of jobs. Therefore, if there is inefficient or market-distorting behaviour

Table 5.1   Elements of the liberal economic order (Hanke and Walters, 1991)

Element	Stylized description	Part of European capitalism?
Private property and contract rights should be established	All resources should be owned or own-able and their owners should have the exclusive right to use these assets and to dispose of them	Yes
Fiscal order and transparency should be established	Governments should publish honest national accounts that include assets and liabilities to meet international standards	Yes – with some caveats for certain member states
Budget deficits and government spending should be kept under control	Governments should normally run balanced budgets	No – this element of a liberal economic order is contested
Inflationary pressures should be kept under control	Increases in prices should be low and predictable	Yes
The advantages of open international trade should be exploited	Trade helps boost competition and thus the allocation of economic resources and overall growth	Yes – with some caveats for certain sectors, including agriculture and services
Complex tax systems and excessive tax rates should be avoided	Simple tax systems are easy to understand and are less likely to distort economic behaviour	Generally, yes, with huge variety across the EU from member state to member state
Subsidies and tax incentives for private industry should be avoided	Subsidies distort the price mechanism, economic choice and the efficient allocation of resources	Yes – with some caveats for certain industries, including agriculture
Privileges and immunities should be avoided	Monopolies and closed-shop practices distort markets and hold back economic growth	Yes – with many caveats and exceptions, especially in services
Price controls should be avoided	These distort the price mechanism that is the heart of a capitalist system	Yes – with some exceptions, especially in agriculture
Restrictions on competition should be avoided	Anti-competitive practices politicize economic life and create inefficient enterprises	Yes – with some exceptions
State-owned enterprises should be privatized	Where the state operates industries that could also be run by the private sector, they will usually be inefficient	Yes – with exceptions
Blurred boundaries between public and private activities should be avoided	Governments should not bail out private firms	Yes – with exceptions for strategic or systemic sectors, such as banks
Manipulating or repressing private capital markets should be avoided	Manipulation distorts the savings process, discourages foreign direct investment and reduces economic growth	Yes

in place, it will have a clear effect on jobs. Agricultural employment in the EU has been falling continuously since the beginnings of European integration. Even in countries with large numbers of agricultural workers such as France (1 million), Spain (2.2 million), Poland (3.8 million), Romania (7.2 million) and Italy (3.3 million) (European Commission, 2013a), it is dwarfed by other sectors and is still declining. A preliminary conclusion is therefore, that, whilst agriculture should not be ignored entirely, the focus must firmly be placed on removing barriers to economic liberty in the employment-intensive service sector. A final consideration on the most effective means of improving economic liberty is that none of Hanke and Walters' (1991) elements of liberal economic order mean very much if there is no confidence in the government's ability to enforce them. Keynes' (1936) invocation of the importance of the 'state of confidence' is crucial here since the credibility of government policy, in terms of the design and implementation of social and economic policy, is firmly rooted in it. In other words, where there is no confidence in the capacity of a government to meet the kind of law enforcement and regulatory commitments identified in Table 5.1, the economic liberty that requires the protection of the rule of law is restricted, and therefore economic growth is reduced.

Is European Capitalism Politically Sustainable?

The Sustainability of the Present Situation: High Unemployment, Low Growth and an Ageing Society

As we have seen, the European model of capitalism produces a number of adverse outcomes. The first and most obvious has been an excessively high level of unemployment over the course of the past 30–40 years. The picture is not evenly spread across the whole of the European economy, and some member states perform much better than others, but overall, the level has been around 8–12% of the labour force for a very long time. Unemployment in Europe is made more bearable by the provision of social security, often for long periods of time, and by the trend towards shifting the unemployed out of unemployment benefits and into other kinds of assistance, including disability benefit or early retirement subsidies. By necessity, the level of taxes and insurance payments in Europe required to support the welfare state is higher than it would be otherwise. This last point does not *necessarily* imply that higher government spending has a dragging effect on the economy for a number of reasons that were highlighted by Colin Hay and Daniel Wincott (2012). These include the role that the government plays in training and re-training the workforce (which would otherwise be borne by employers – or simply not happen) and, of course, the automatic stabilizing effect that is provided by the payment of unemployment benefits during economic downturns. In essence this was what prevented the Great Recession of 2007–09 from becoming a 'Great Depression'. Generous government spending on welfare does not always produce higher unemployment provided that the incentives to seek work are not reduced through such payments. Yet there is no doubt that unemployment in Europe is far too high, and that it has been since the late 1970s. European capitalism has been far too tolerant of high unemployment, which in turn has led to much lower economic output, lower tax revenues from salaries, higher expenditure on welfare benefits and, most seriously, the rise in human suffering and misery that unemployment produces. These adverse effects are magnified by the fact that they have been tolerated for so long.

Another well-documented source of weakness for the European model of capitalism is the ageing society. Improved healthcare and safer lifestyle choices have lengthened life expectancy by well over a decade since 1970. The bulk of this improvement is due to a decline in the use of tobacco (around 29% of Europeans were smokers in 2010, less than half the level of the 1970s, when around two-thirds were regular smokers (Eurobarometer, No. 332, 2010)) with some additional gains related to improved diets and lower alcohol consumption (French alcohol consumption has halved since 1980; in Italy the fall is close to two-thirds, OECD, 2012b). Living longer in good health is to be celebrated. However, social policy across the EU has not yet caught up with this trend. Pensions policies were designed at a time when most retirees could only expect to live for a few years beyond 65. What is now needed is an increase in retirement ages to balance those who are paying into the social security system against those who are drawing upon it in old age.

The ageing trend is further exacerbated by the declining birth rate from around 2.5 children per woman in the 1960s to around 1.5 in the 2010s, which is below the estimate replacement level of 2.1 children (Eurostat, 2011c). Eurostat data show that the median age of the average European has increased over the first decade of the 21st century from 38 to 41. As a result, the old-age dependency ratio (the percentage of the population that needs to be supported by those of working age) has risen sharply from 20% to 27%. Between 2010 and 2050, it is predicted to rise still further from 27% to 50% (Eurostat, 2013f). Thus the full impact of the ageing society is yet to come. In some member states, the trend is more pronounced, notably Germany, where the average age has risen to 45, compared to 40 in the UK and France; and Italy where the old-age dependency ratio rose from 22% to 32% between 1990 and 2012.

The political support for the current model of European capitalism is based upon the myth of an imagined fair system and meritocratic society, which does not exist today, and has perhaps never existed in Europe. As was identified earlier, European capitalism ideally needs a welfare system in the Burkean mould that works and has fair objectives that meet the needs of the young, the old, those in work, those not in work and so on. This ideal system would enjoy wide, cross-party political support, could be paid for now, could be paid for tomorrow and would be adaptable enough to be reprogrammed to meet changing needs. In other words, it would be a sustainable economic system. Emphatically, this is not the socio-economic model that is in place today, which leads to inequality of opportunities, outcomes and high unemployment. The system's current deficits will only worsen as a result of the ageing of the population. The present system of European capitalism is 'sustainable' only in the absence of a clear and credible political alternative. Arguably, for 40 years after the end of the Second World War, an opaque but far from credible alternative did exist, in the form of one-party socialism and the planned economy in Eastern Europe and the Soviet Union. Coincidentally, this was also a period in which West European governments, perhaps mindful of the existence of an alternative on their doorsteps, undertook wide-ranging social and economic reforms aimed at reducing or mitigating the most damaging consequences of free market capitalism. Of course the challenges of the 1960s are not the same as those of today, but remaking the European welfare states in a sustainable mould is no less daunting.

The most disastrous effect or 40 years of high unemployment has been to make unemployment almost chronic or hereditary in some families and communities, particularly in the post-industrial areas that were at the heart of the 19th century industrial revolution, including the Ruhr, the North of England, Southern Belgium and North-Eastern France. Things worsen over the years because the children of the long-term unemployed are more likely to struggle to enter the labour market when their turn comes. As the pattern becomes entrenched, what is created could be termed 'a human zoo', whose inhabitants are fed, clothed and looked after but who are not really 'free' or supporting themselves in society at large. Indeed, over time, the very capacity of the inhabitants of the human zoo to support themselves declines as hard-to-reverse patterns of behaviour grow entrenched as a result of perverse incentive structures. Unemployment is not just an economic, or even a social, problem – it is also a moral one because both government and society have a responsibility *not* to keep people in involuntary idleness. It is for them to put in place policies that facilitate labour market inclusivity and empowerment – in other words, work. The question is how.

Setting an Agenda for Reform

Creating Jobs: Thorough Liberalization of Services and Labour Markets

The salient question that Europe's political parties and technocrats should be asking themselves is a simple one: How can the good life for the people of Europe best be delivered? The answer needs to consider the best balance of responsibilities between the individual, the family, the firm and the government. At the same time, it is reasonable to suggest that increasing the opportunity for participation in the labour market and lowering rates of economic inactivity needs to be at the heart of any programme for making European capitalism sustainable. In turn, this necessitates a dual effort both in terms of promoting policies that will lead firms to hire more staff and in equipping job-seekers with the skills that they require. The nature of this two-pronged approach illustrates perfectly that economic reform is not just about liberalization and free market forces; it is also about the government acting as an agent of personal empowerment.

The EU's Lisbon Agenda, launched in 2000, was designed to promote precisely this agenda of liberalization with intelligent social protection and welfare. Globally, the policy agenda sought to speed up economic convergence in the EU through a joint approach to supply-side policies which would boost the efficient allocation of resources and foster deeper and closer European integration at the same time. The aim of the Lisbon strategy was for the EU to become 'the most dynamic and competitive knowledge-based economy in the world, capable of sustainable economic growth with more and better jobs and greater social cohesion, and respect for the environment'. As noted at the time, the strategy was based on the premise that the primary goal for Europe was to 'overcome the differences in growth and productivity between the EU and its leading global competitors of the time, the USA and Japan'. Thus the emphasis was placed firmly on the knowledge-based economy and reducing or eradicating the perceived deficit with these other two advanced economies in terms of technological capacity and innovation, thus boosting 'European competitiveness' and a European 'knowledge society'.

An obvious problem with this basic knowledge-based approach is that it does not put sufficient emphasis on employment and the creation of jobs through liberalization of service industries, where most jobs can be found. Importantly, it is difficult for non-tradeables like restaurants, haircuts, nail bars, cleaning services and so on to be outsourced to emerging economies. The knowledge-based sectors of the economy are concentrated in manufacturing, which at its most productive creates a few very well-paid jobs for the highly qualified and a lot of work for robots (Bowman, 2013). This is not to discourage productivity, the high technology sector or manufacturing, but rather to question whether the principal policy goal for Europe should have been to boost the knowledge-based economy rather than to reduce long-standing unemployment.

A more jobs-oriented reform agenda would consist of something approximating elements from the Anglo-Saxon, Scandinavian or German experience of liberalization. None of these approaches were perfect in themselves, and all required further refinement, but an ideal model for intelligent liberalization would include the following elements:

1. creating flexible labour markets that encourage employers to take on staff by reducing the cost of having to let them go if times prove difficult (although see the point on pp. 147–8 about reforming the labour market sector in isolation);
2. reducing non-wage costs as a percentage of labour costs, thus reducing this so-called 'tax on jobs' (although this requires the burden of taxation to pay for future pension entitlements and so on to be moved elsewhere – but it can be done);
3. opening up certain industries to competition, notably the services sector (i.e. notaries, personal services, pharmacists, groceries, insurance, culture, broadcasting, media, financial services etc.);
4. boosting innovation (in line with the Lisbon strategy) to provide government support in research centres and universities for the kind of blue-skies research that will keep parts of Europe close to the global technological frontier;

5. providing support for the reform of national, regional and local administrations in order to boost their efficiency and most importantly, their capacity to make and enforce the rules that an advanced economy needs for the market to function most effectively and for economic freedom to be upheld.

It is this final element that is most often overlooked and will, like all the above reforms, need to be tailored to fit the national conditions prevailing in the 28 member states. It includes the capacity of states to enforce the decisions of courts (which is not always the case, even in the old EU-15, see Falkner, 2013); the transparency and fairness of the public procurement process; and on-going problems of corruption which, despite being more widely documented in newer member states (Vachudova, 2009), are also prevalent in old member states. It is on the issue of strong or weak institutions that the success of the other four dimensions of reform ultimately rests. The problem of the reforms that have been attempted in the southern member states at the behest of the Troika (composed of the International Monetary Fund, the European Commission and the European Central Bank) is that too much emphasis has been placed on implementing 'Northern European' policy solutions in environments where the 'Northern European' institutions that could support them do not exist. In other words, the Troika has put the cart before the horse in Europe's south. In doing so, it has inflicted unnecessary damage and undermined the future case for further reform. Whilst the Europe 2020 agenda that replaced the Lisbon strategy showed signs of having learned some lessons on how to reform – more emphasis was placed on strengthening national civil services and institutions – further progress must be made in policy-learning from the experiences of other member states, including Spain, Greece and, surprisingly, Germany.

The Perils of Partial Liberalization and the Sequencing of Reforms: Learning Lessons from Greece, Spain and Germany

The first lesson is that partial or incomplete liberalization has the potential to do far more harm than good. Contrary to popular belief, both Greece and Spain had undertaken some liberalization of their economies and welfare states in the 1990s and 2000s. Two interlinked problems were to undermine these attempts, however. In the first instance, both Spain and Greece exhibit symptoms of what Jonathan Hopkin and Mark Blyth (2012) call 'embedded illiberalism', where an instinct towards control or manipulation of markets for political reasons was deeply ingrained.

Good examples of this might be the endemic corruption surrounding the award of public tenders, or particularly at the local level, the need to pay bribes to obtain planning permission – which was allegedly highly lucrative during the Spanish building boom of the 1990s and 2000s. In other words, both Spain and Greece suffered from weak rule-enforcing institutions and strong lobbies in favour of the protection of special interests. Against this background, liberalization was carried out in a piecemeal fashion. In the case of the Spanish labour market, costly rules on employment protection were lifted for temporary workers, mostly new entrants to the labour market. When Spain experienced the significant downturn that signalled the beginning of the Great Recession in 2008, unemployment skyrocketed, climbing to almost 30% of the workforce (and more than 50% of the youngest workers) by 2013. The reason for this was that the unprotected workers could easily be sacked, and the protected could not. Under the terms of partial liberalization, those labour market outsiders on temporary contracts may be thrown out of work, whilst the labour market insiders, regardless of their efficiency and value, continue to keep their positions. Socially, politically and economically, this approach is intolerable.

The lesson from the experience of economic reform in Europe is that it is not just policies that are in need of reform, but also institutions. Liberalization measures 'interact with other social and economic institutions, sometimes with perverse effects' (Hopkin and Blyth, 2012, p. 14) and reform therefore needs to be a root-and-branch programme which is combined with support for structural institutional reform. Furthermore, to attempt structural reform in a fairly advanced economy equipped with weak institutions that have undergone only a partial transformation to state-of-the-art modernity, is to set out to fail. Reformed, strong, impartial, rule-enforcing institutions (courts, civil services, national regulatory authorities) that act as the referees of European capitalism are not just part of the reform process, rather they are the foundations, on which individual policies will stand or fall. (On the specific case of Italy, see Emmott, 2012). Liberalization cannot work in isolation.

What is so interesting about the liberalization agenda is that the European Commission is often cast as the unpopular schoolteacher urging and cajoling unwilling – and uninterested – pupils into concentrating on their studies. (The EU even refers to what the member states have to do as 'homework'.) This attitude is a natural extension of the Union's technocratic worldview, where for every problem there is, in a positivist sense, a 'right' answer. Yet, stepping back for a moment, we might wish to question whether this is a helpful approach. If such reforms are so useful, why should the EU have to force the recalcitrant member states to undertake them? The answer, perhaps, lies in the domestic structure of member states' institutions, their politics and their political culture. The impetus for reform really ought to come from the member states themselves; just as the 2004/07 accession countries were – to an extent – eager pupils, at times even actively seeking advice on transformation of their institutions to drive economic and political change. Therefore, a possible lesson might be that, instead of pushing unwilling countries towards reform, the EU should simply try letting them first fail and then come asking for help in exchange for concessions. This approach – which has been implemented in a clumsy way in the 'programme countries' – has some merit in the short term. However, what cannot be overlooked is that the member states themselves – their societies and institutions – must be looking to reform. In other words, there must be a demand for reform to match its supply. If this element is missing, the process of change will only ever be skin-deep.

The timing of reform is also absolutely crucial. As we examined in Chapter 1 on Europe and the crisis, where economic reform had been implemented *either shortly before or shortly after* the kind of narrowly-averted bank runs and government borrowing crises that we saw in Europe during the financial crisis, then the case for reform is undermined. The risk in making the case for reform before a crisis is that the sound arguments in favour of liberalization are ignored because it becomes tainted by its association with free-wheeling markets in financial services or 'casino capitalism'. Where reform is imposed as part of an austerity package, it is tainted by its association with a kind of 'collective punishment'. In this case, a degree of rebranding, both by altering the contents of the reform package (i.e. including some well-marketed sweeteners) and the style in which it is wrapped, could help lessen this effect. Another reason why structural reform is even harder during a crisis is that the alternative economic opportunities (new careers, new markets etc.) available to the losers from the reform process are far fewer than they would otherwise be – and thus resistance becomes more firmly entrenched. However, the overall conclusion is not that all is hopeless. Rather it is that, before experimenting with liberalization in southern Europe, it is necessary to *invest* in building the kinds of strong institutions at national, regional and local levels that can support a modern, liberal economy. Without strong institutions, it is difficult to see how liberalization can flourish. The sequencing of reform should be institutions first and policies second.

On the issue of institutional reform, it is sensible to add a word of caution about the benefits of reforming individual sectors (e.g. the labour market or financial services) in isolation along a one-size-fits-all model for the whole EU-28. The national economies have evolved individually over a long period of time and there are institutional complementarities between different sectors of each economy. For example, having a relatively inflexible labour market will encourage firms to pay particular attention to making sure that their workers have the right skills, and to maintaining those skills over time. In the case of Italy (Emmott, 2012), particularly strict labour market rules about dismissing staff come into effect when a company employs more than 15 people, which encourages an economy with a large number of small firms sub-contracting to one another. Thus, whilst the broad direction of travel towards liberalization of the labour market across Europe seems a good one, it needs to be done in a way that takes into account the wider economic 'ecosystem' that prevails in a given country and the possible, knock-on effects of reforming one sector in isolation. Piecemeal reform, in other words, is unlikely to be a viable and productive option. As Peter Hall and Daniel Gingerich note, '[t]he broader lesson is that those seeking to understand the effects of institutional change should pay careful attention to the potential for institutional complementarities across spheres of the political economy' (2009, p. 480).

Is Change Politically Sustainable? The SPD's Bitter Experiences in Germany

A reform that may be theoretically advisable from an economic standpoint does not always make sound political sense. Jean-Claude Juncker, Prime Minister of Luxembourg, summed up the attitude of Europe's leaders to economic and social reform with the words, 'We all know what to do, we just don't know how to get re-elected after we've done it', which was described in a moment of levity by officials in the European Commission as 'the Juncker curse' (Buti *et al.*, 2008). Social and economic reform is politically costly. It inevitably creates losers as well as winners. Economic reforms produce a classic political dilemma, well known to anyone seeking election to public office, in that the costs of reform are both concentrated and immediate, whereas the benefits are diffuse and delayed (Hopkin and Blyth, 2012). To draw a couple of concrete examples, whilst customers might benefit from the liberalization of pharmacies in France, Italy or Spain, in the form of lower prices and longer opening hours, the short-term losers are obviously the dis-possessed pharmacists who might be compelled to take strike action. In a similar fashion, the issuance of taxi permits cannot be liberalized without reducing both the income flowing to taxi drivers through higher prices and reducing the value of one of their most important assets, the licence itself which was expensive to buy. Here again, the general public benefits from lower prices and better service, but not immediately or even obviously. Therefore, the opponents of reform are far more likely to be politically mobilized than the potential beneficiaries (for the classic account, see Olson, 1965). This means that reforming governments have first to create as broad a coalition as possible, to sequence reforms around the political calendar, pick their battles carefully – and still risk ejection from office at the hands of frustrated, well-mobilized groups. Given the long-term nature of the positive effects from reforms, some politicians and political parties may find that it is their successors who reap some of the feel-good benefits of the reforms they carried out. This creates, quite understandably, a certain reticence towards reform on the part of Europe's political leaders.

In the short and even long term, creating too many losers can be dis-astrous for whole political parties, yet alone individual party leaders or ministers. Germany's SPD introduced the Agenda 2010 reforms, which included the Hartz programme of labour market reforms, during Ger-hard Schröder's second administration. The first few phases, introduced between 2002 and 2004, focused on training programmes, support for entrepreneurs, job centre reforms, the creation of 'mini- and midi-jobs' with scaled-back taxes and social insurance contributions. The contro-versial part, Hartz IV, was introduced in 2005, dramatically reducing unemployment benefits for the long-term unemployed, replacing them more quickly with so-called 'social help', payable at a very basic level. This caused outrage, especially amongst the SPD's core electorate of the German working class. Even though unemployment fell dramatically in the years that followed the reforms to one of the lowest levels in Europe from one of the highest, the SPD's popularity remained subdued for a very long time. Part of the party even defected to form a left-wing al-ternative. Ten years on from the Hartz reforms, with unemployment at a low (despite the Great Recession), it was the CDU under Angela Merkel rather than the SPD that benefited from Germany's economic revival. Other political leaders in Europe might look at the German experience and conclude that change would lead to a dramatic increase in their own chances of unemployment following the next election.

Why is Reform so Intractable?

A few words to summarize why reform in Europe is so intractable are important. In the first place, sectoral liberalization will create well-mobilised losers and diffuse winners. In the second place, perhaps most importantly in Western Europe, after more than sixty years of rising prosperity there remains an extraordinarily high level of invested capital in Europe, which creates a *douceur de vivre* unparalleled in human history. Quite simply, life is too comfortable for Europe's labour market insiders to contemplate reform. In the case of France, they would prefer to buy social peace by handing over almost half of what they produce to the state to support the labour market outsiders (Le Boucher, 2013). In the third place, anti-reformist sentiment is bolstered by the ageing population who are less likely to vote for policies that provide no short-term benefit to them. An ageing population is also associated with a more conservative and anti-change worldview. This is entirely logical. One cannot appeal to older voters by asking them to make short-term sacrifices for long-term gains since the old, by definition, do not have a long term to look forward to. In the fourth place, as we have seen, because reforms to labour markets are often partial in their nature, they only serve to increase the differences between labour market insiders and outsiders and have come to be associated in many member states with job cuts. In the fifth place, linked to this lack of success, there is a lack of political courage. Political parties may look at the experience of reforming governments elsewhere in Europe and conclude that such change is not for them. Sixth, the lack of thorough-going institutional reform in some member states has resulted in the persistence of patronage and clientelism which favours the short-term interests of political elites over those of society at large. Seventh, it is worth noting (Le Boucher, 2013) that there does not always exist a consensus on growth-oriented policies. Keynesians argue with supply-siders about the nature of what is needed to induce growth. The old Left worries that change would sweep away the welfare state. Ecologists and green parties opine that work and growth are false gods – such arguments have resonance in societies as wealthy as those of Western Europe. In many member states these seven factors combine to produce a coalition of denial and inertia that indirectly amounts to a preference for decline over change. This is most obviously seen in France, where it has been the case since the 1990s (Baverez, 2004). This is not to argue that other, perhaps more liberally-minded, member states do not have their own pathological problems. Within the UK, England increasingly appears to have an anti-development culture, stemming from its notorious short-termism as well as out-dated and excessively democratic planning laws, which are a feature of wealthy and ageing societies. It would take a Herculean effort even greater than the push to create the Single Market, the Euro or the Common Market to overcome these entrenched anti-reformists in Europe. As the experiences of Central Europe in 1989 or the programme countries during the crisis show, things will have to get rather worse before the public can be persuaded of the need for a change to the status quo.

Conclusions

At the outset of this chapter the question of whether European capitalism is economically, politically and socially sustainable was posed. As a corollary to this, the issue of whether it could be upheld or defended as a model or perhaps even an ideal was also raised. We have seen that European capitalism originated as a humane and pragmatic response to the profound social injustices that were wrought by industrial capitalism from the 19th century. One of the normative legacies of the marriage between liberalism and socialism was the belief that government – understood broadly – has a significant role to play in the management of the economy, and that this is a good thing. We have also seen that European capitalism, with strong state involvement in creating a level playing field for capitalism, steering the economy and managing a popular system of social protection, was remarkably successful as a means of organizing the economy and society in the post-Second World War period until the first oil crisis of 1973.

This evidence all points to a European model of capitalism that has only been partially successful in its aim of promoting inclusive prosperity as a result of two factors: the excessively high level of unemployment that has been tolerated since the late 1970s and the growth in inequalities that was charted in Chapter 4. Yet this chapter does not argue that it is European capitalism, with its emphasis on social protection and regulation, that it is to blame for Europe's lacklustre performance. It is also wrong to suggest that Europe is falling far behind the technological frontier in terms of what it produces: parts of the European economy are the most productive, prosperous and innovative in the world. Europe does not, therefore, need to emulate the US or the emerging economies in the way in which it treats social protection or the role of the government in steering economic development. Europe's welfare regimes are also affordable, if only a balance can be struck between those paying into the system and those receiving its assistance. This process will of course be complicated by the changing demographic outlook for Europe over the coming decades.

The real challenge for Europe is about labour market participation, in other words, it is about jobs. In terms of the balance between contributors to, and recipients from, the welfare system, it is about getting people into work earlier, keeping them there for longer through retraining and reskilling (which would allow them to move between different professions), and encouraging more people to work up to, and even a little beyond, the age of 70. This implies social and cultural change. The children of some Europeans who retired at the age of 55 may find themselves working 15–20 years beyond that age. In the past, too many economic strategies to boost the European economy have focused on the knowledge-based economy. This is a strategic segment of the European economy that should not be ignored, but if Europe is serious about the sustainability of its system, then it needs to widen its view. The employment potential of the knowledge-based sector is insufficient to redress the problem of unemployment, quite simply because it creates too few, albeit well-paid, jobs.

What Europe desperately needs in the 21st century is more mundane than the shiny allure of the high-technology industry with its modernist promises of a seemingly effortless future prosperity at the summit of the global supply chain. For Europe's people to be guaranteed a bright tomorrow of real and sustainable prosperity more of them need jobs. Many of these will not necessarily be at the cutting edge of technology, but which will be sustainable by simple virtue of the fact that they are not in the internationally tradeable sector, and therefore not vulnerable to competition from outside Europe. The best way to promote the creation of jobs is through an intelligent liberalization of the services sector to release its enormous potential for wealth creation. Services are the unfinished business of Europe's Single Market. They are certainly not 'low hanging fruit', however, and the obstacles to reform are formidable. Liberalization of service provision would be more likely to work if it were accompanied by significant deregulation of the European labour market and a concomitant reduction of non-wage costs as a percentage of labour costs. Such a reduction would give employers the allusive confidence they need to take on new staff, which is what federations of European employers are usually seeking (see Chastand, 2014). There is nothing particularly clever or exciting about liberalization of services and deregulation, but it is a policy that will lead to job creation. Deregulation also leads to a high degree of political resistance that is usually sufficient to see off any EU-wide measures aimed at such liberalization.

The EU has been here before (European Commission, 2000). For example, the Commission's 2004 proposal for a Services Directive triggered a highly politicized debate within the member states. Those opposed to the 'Bolkenstein Directive', raised the spectres of social dumping and 'forced privatization' of cherished public services. The figure of the 'undercutting Polish plumber' was used to crystalize opposition to the Commission proposal (Duval, 2006; *Le Monde*, 2005). Arguably, it was a strongly contributing factor to the negative result in the French referendum of 2005 on the proposed Constitutional Treaty (which had nothing to do with service liberalization). By the time the Directive was adopted in 2006, it had been shorn of its most controversial elements: financial services, transport, audio-visual services, radio broadcasting and others. Service liberalization is so touchy an area of reform because it is closely linked both to the provision of much-valued public services and to the system of contributions by which European welfare states are sustained. If a plan were to be set in place to liberalize (or rather to harmonize) the rules for service industries, the model of regulation would have to look more like a 'race to the top' in terms of the minimum standards to be guaranteed, than a 'race to the bottom'.

A similar story could be told about the various European Employment Strategies. The first was launched in 1997 as a response to the need for greater coordination of employment policies and labour markets in the run-up to the Economic Monetary Union (Rhodes, 2010). Based on non-binding, 'soft' law instruments such as peer review, benchmarking and persuasion, the aim was to reform labour markets by creating more flexibility and sustainability to boost investment in skills and to strengthen the European labour market in order to fully realize its potential. Yet the (deliberately) non-binding nature of the policy leads to a 'double standards game' (Rhodes, 2010) in which governments endorse European guidelines but fail to take responsibility for their implementation at home because they are fully aware of the adverse political consequences that would result.

The politics of economic reform are profoundly complicated, as the examples of the Services Directive and the European Employment Strategy show. Were they otherwise, the services part of the Single Market would have been fulfilled long ago. Yet in big picture terms, they are the best illustration of the way that overdue reforms can be overturned by the short-termism and conservatism of ageing, wealthy societies that are in denial about the need for structural reform. Overcoming short-term opposition to reform is not easy, and the risks of reforms being derailed by the protests of those who stand to lose out in the short term should not be underestimated. Here I return to the notion of sustainability, measured by whether the European model can be defended. Tough reforms are much easier to uphold where they can be shown to work effectively. Part of the problem of the German reform experience was that many of the poorest Germans and the working class did not share sufficiently in the fruits of growth. This is a salutary warning on the dangers of growing inequality.

In designing successful reforms, particularly for those parts of the European economy that are most in need of intelligent and sympathetic reform, two lessons are particularly valuable. Firstly, reform is not just about policy but also about institutions because policies that are designed and implemented by weak institutions tend to be undermined to the extent that they have perverse effects. This appears to have happened in the 'programme countries' in receipt of bailouts from the Troika where the kinds of policies that work well in a particular institutional setting were applied in states with very different, almost certainly weaker, institutions. As argued in Chapter 4, much of the process of institutional reform needs to happen at national level – and it should not always be the job of the European Commission to berate national governments for not doing what is in their own interest. (This particularly applies to the propensity of member states to complain about the Commission's tendency towards mission-creep and over-reach.) There must be a demand for reform at the national level to match its supply at the European level. Second, reform needs to be complete, involving root and branch in its scope. Reform should not create insiders and outsiders in labour markets. Nor should it protect some but ignore others completely. Here we return to the notion of sustainability in the form of Burke's 'intergenerational' contract. The experience of Spain is trenchant here. A partial reform of the labour market protected older and middle-aged workers and the retired at the expense of the young and new entrants into the labour market – with the disastrous consequence of seeing youth unemployment top 55.2% during the second quarter of 2012 – an increase of 13.6 percentage points compared to the 2010 rate (Eurostat, 2013e). This was not just a perverse effect of reform, it also served politically to undermine the case for structural reform of the labour market in the future.

Reform to make European capitalism sustainable again has been under discussion since at least the 1990s, and for much of that time, the opponents of change have made the political running, defeating serious budget reform, attempts to liberalize services and much else besides. Reformers have struggled to motivate the majority for whom life has been too comfortable to contemplate far-reaching changes or a new intergenerational contract. They have also struggled – and in many cases failed – to sell change as socially advantageous. The crisis of recent years has begun to challenge the consensus in favour of stagnation and the European appetite for radicalism is beginning to return, albeit manifested mostly in support for anti-politics parties. Before moving on to the opportunities that the crisis presents, and having taken a reading of Europe's strength at home, it is necessary to examine Europe's capacity to sustain its position in a globalized world.

6
Sustaining Europe's Global Role

European integration was conceived and nurtured against the backdrop of a bi-polar Cold War world (Lindley-French, 2007; Marsh and Rees, 2012; McCormick, 2008; Rees and Smith, 2008). The main fault line between communism and capitalism ran through the centre of Europe and the paramount interest of both sides was avoiding nuclear Armageddon and maintaining the *status quo* (Duchêne, 2008). This dangerous, yet ultimately stable, period of domination by two non-European powers, the Soviet Union and United States, helped Western Europe to undergo a relatively peaceful transition in its relationship with the rest of the world. It transformed from colonial hegemony to a more informal, albeit dominant relationship based not on military might and semi-authoritarian direct rule, but on a form of economic and 'civilian power' that emerged as an alternative to the power politics of the Superpowers in the early 1970s (Duchêne, 1972; Hill and Smith, 2011). A less optimistic view would be to suggest that, having exhausted the possibilities of holding on to imperial possessions using military means, in the latter part of the 20th century the Europeans opted for a relationship with the rest of the world that resembled an 'informal empire'. The Central and Eastern European countries were effectively subordinated to Moscow's foreign policy doctrine throughout the 45 years of the Cold War, constrained by the 'spheres of responsibilities' negotiated at Yalta in 1945 and obligatory membership of the Warsaw Pact (Staar, 1991). Their participation in international trade was coordinated by the Soviet-dominated Committee for Mutual Economic Assistance (COMECON). In common with the Soviet Union, the Central and Eastern Europeans could not be described as participating fully in the world economy until the 1990s.

What has changed fundamentally in international affairs since the early days of European integration is that the number of countries that make up the world economy has grown enormously. In the 1950s and 1960s, the term 'world economy' was used to refer only to the US, Western Europe and the western 'offshoots' of Canada, Australia, New Zealand and, perhaps, South Africa. Between the 1960s and the 1980s, this small club of rich trading states underwent a vast expansion to include Japan, Hong Kong, South Korea, Singapore and many countries in Latin America. In the 1980s, China led the planned economies in opening up to the world following the launch of the 'socialism with Chinese characteristics' programme in 1978 (Xiaoping, 1984). India moved decisively away from socialist planning after 1990 by dismantling the so-called 'Licence Raj', which removed many of the internal barriers to free market competition in the Indian economy (Aghion *et al.*, 2008). Between 1989 and 1991, Soviet and East European communism fell and the planned economy system that had been an intrinsic part of it was replaced with a post-communism variety of capitalism (Ellman, 2007). These changes added billions of new, admittedly poor, consumers to the world economy and, of course, billions of people to the global supply of labour, reducing the bargaining power of western workers. Today's challenge of static living standards and wage stagnation is neither a recent issue nor uniquely a problem for the economies of particular EU member states. It dates back to the 1980s and 1990s when new and large economies such as Russia, China and India 'plugged themselves into the world economy', constraining the evolution of workers' social conditions worldwide (Freeman, 2006; Ganesh, 2013). History is repeating itself: the adverse social consequences of globalization for workers remains a major concern in politics, but the responses so far have failed to tackle them satisfactorily. For instance, at the EU level, the 2005 Hampton Court summit led to the creation of the European Globalization Adjustment Fund to help workers who had lost their jobs as a result of changing global trade patterns in finding new jobs and developing new skills (Blair, 2005), but its €500 million budget did not suffice. The dramatic growth in the size and scope of the world economy, primarily driven since the late 1970s by the steady removal of barriers to the free movement of goods and capital, in turn drove forwards the much broader process of globalization, with its social and cultural, as well as economic, components. It is no exaggeration to say that globalization has changed the lived experiences of most of the world's population — in developed, as well as developing, countries — beyond recognition in little more than one generation.

The initial phase of globalization and the expansion in the number of participants in the world economy between the 1960s and the late 1990s did not, at first, appear to present any major challenge to Western, and with it European, pre-eminence in world politics. The economic preponderance of the US and the European Union persisted after the collapse of communism in the early 1990s. Despite temporary difficulties between 1993 and 1997, their combined share of world GDP remained steady at 55–60% until the Great Recession began in 2007. After this, their combined relative share of world GDP fell by 10 percentage points in just five years (Table 6.1).

In the first phase of globalization from the 1980s to the 2000s, expensive Western labour in relatively low-technology, yet labour-intensive sectors, such as textiles, chemicals or steel, was replaced with cheap labour from the world economy's newest participants in Asia, Latin America, and the former planned economies of Central and Eastern Europe (who were especially important for Western European firms outsourcing production). Cheap consumer goods flooded into Western economies and many of the polluting industries that had befouled the air of European cities for two hundred years relocated to other parts of the world. Superior employment prospects beckoned for the West's better-educated workers in the high technology or service industries, from pharmaceuticals to the aerospace industry to financial services. Globalization brought fabulous new opportunities for wealth creation in new markets, hungry for everything from the West's technology and expertise to its culture and finely crafted luxury goods. Globalization appeared in this early phase to be an unmitigated good for most of the peoples of the West, although there was a certain disquiet about what to do with the lengthening queues of seemingly unemployable workers who had been

Table 6.1   EU-US combined share of world GDP (current US$)

Year	GDP US	GDP EU	Combined GDP	World GDP	US-EU share of world GDP (%)
1990	5.75	7.32	13.0	22	60
1995	7.35	9.23	16.56	29.81	55
2007	13.96	17.04	31.00	55.91	55
2012	15.68	16.63	32.31	71.92	45

Source: Data from World Bank, 2014c.

unable to find work in the new, post-industrial economy. Even those whose skills did not equip them to participate in the best of the employment opportunities brought by globalization could still buy consumer goods, such as computers, fridges or DVD players, at prices that were a far smaller share of their wages than ever before. Even for the very poorest, who could not truly afford such goods, obliging banks were on hand to supply credit. In the first phase of globalization, Western economic dominance remained unchallenged and throughout the 1980s and the 1990s, more than 70% of growth in the world economy was generated in the US, Japan and the EU, despite fairly high levels of growth in the emerging economies (World Bank, database on GDP).

After 2000, this pattern of Western economic dominance began to change, albeit fairly slowly at first. In the first six years of the new millennium, the US alone accounted for 20% of output growth, but China accounted for almost half as much with 9% – a huge increase from less than 2% during the first phase of Chinese liberalization in the 1980s (World Bank, database on GDP). Yet the real shift occurred in the run-up to, and during, the Great Recession, that began with the credit crunch in August 2007. These changes were as sudden as they were dramatic: in 2007, for the first time since the first Industrial Revolution in Britain, China added more nominal output to the world economy than the largest Western country (World Bank, 2013c). This pattern continued as the US and EU slowly recovered from recession after 2010. If 2013 IMF forecasts are correct, over the decade to 2025, China alone will contribute perhaps one-quarter of new output in the world economy, and the US and EU combined will add between one-quarter and one-third (IMF, 2013a). This is an extraordinary turnaround over the course of a single decade between 2000 and 2010. Travelling back one decade more to 1990, the developed economies of the OECD had accounted for 70–80% of world output (Kharas and Gertz, 2010). The Great Recession served to hasten dramatically the shifts that were already taking place in the global economy. Quite simply, the US the EU and Japan are no longer the sole drivers of demand and growth in the world economy. By the 2010s they shared this role with China and increasingly with the other emerging economic powerhouses of India, Brazil and Indonesia. What these far-reaching changes in the world economy since the 1960s imply is the diminution of the *overwhelming* material advantages, as well as technological and financial ones, on which Western dominance of world politics has been based for more than 200 years (Ikenberry, 2011; Kupchan, 2012; Nye, 2011), although not as rapidly as the alarmists would suggest. Against this altered backdrop, the sustainability of any kind of leading role for Europe in a multi-polar world can certainly not be taken for granted, not least because, as Anand Menon (2014) points out, '[f]or the EU in particular, it hardly needs saying that an institution frequently referred to as an economic giant but a political pygmy would be gravely affected should ever its economic strength be called into question'. Perhaps as a sign of what was to come, the Copenhagen global climate change conference in 2009 was an excellent example of the way in which the Europeans suddenly found themselves shut out of conversations in which they had been used to playing a leading role (Kupchan, 2012).

Closer to home, Europe's foreign policy successes were most apparent between the mid-1990s and the mid-2000s through the EU's enlargement policy (an area of activity that begins as foreign policy and ends as domestic politics). Western Europe successfully exported its model of governance to ten new EU member states, eight of which were post-communist countries (Marsh and Rees, 2012). EU enlargement was a remarkably successful foreign policy tool that helped root the emerging former Communist states in peace, democracy, the rule of law and the free market economy. It is now apparent that this expansion of the EU was only politically possible against the completely benign international backdrop of that period. Since the Great Recession and the Eurozone crisis, enlargement has almost ground to a halt, with only Croatia joining the EU in 2013. In the rest of the Western Balkans – Macedonia, Serbia, Albania, Montenegro and now Kosovo – enlargement has slowed to a snail's pace as agreed in a 'silent pact between enlargement-fatigued EU member states and rent-seeking elites in the Western Balkans' (Bechev, 2012, p. 6). Game-changing enlargement talks with Turkey drew to a halt once it became clear that both France and Germany were planning to exercise an effective veto over Turkish accession – although negotiations on regional policy started in November 2013, after a three-year stalemate in the accession process (Pawlak, 2013). The issue at stake in the totemic question of Turkish accession to the EU was supposedly Turkey's capacity to fit in with 'European values', and for some French or German politicians, it was Turkey's cultural differences (i.e. its status as a Muslim country; Uras, 2013). The EU is a secular organization, so the religion of its population should not matter. In reality, they were concerned about the possibility of large-scale migration from the Turkish Anatolian hinterland to Western Europe. Both globalization and European integration have driven mass migration to and between the countries of Europe since the 1960s and 1970s. Some Europeans find these changes disconcerting, all the more so in times of economic strain, when jobs and other resources (such as welfare, housing or healthcare) seem to be stretched too thinly. In other words, migration, even in an age when the open expression of racial prejudice in Europe is a taboo, becomes a serious political issue during times of economic stress. The literature has produced wide-ranging estimates on Turkish migration to the EU ranging between 1 million and 4 million over a generation (Elitok, 2013; Erzan *et al.*, 2006; Flam, 2003; Krieger, 2004; Krieger and Maitre, 2006; Lejour *et al.*, 2004; Togan, 2002). EU enlargement is seen as leading to migration, which explains in great part the reluctance of the EU to accept more large, poor member states.

To focus too exclusively on the economic aspects of the present 'turn' in world politics (Ikenberry, 2011) risks falling into the classically EU trap of viewing globalization and transformation as having more or less exclusively economic consequences (Menon, 2014). This is just as foolish as the belief that power is exclusively military. As Joseph Nye (2011) makes clear, power is multi-faceted. The shift in the centre of world gravity, away from Europe towards Asia and the rest of the developing world, has deep political as well as profound economic consequences. The EU is not yet prepared to cope with these political consequences, even if it has become aware of the economic ones. It is even less prepared to deal with the military or defence implications of a new world order. At the centre of this crisis of adjustment is the way in which the EU persists in viewing governments of any hue apart from liberal democratic, or those transitioning towards liberal democracy, as illegitimate or less than fully legitimate. Europe may no longer be able to afford this narrow worldview in the coming decades. It will need allies in a multi-polar global system. It makes little sense to rule out swathes of countries as potential partners for Europe in a strategic or issue-by-issue sense on the basis of their form of government. Of course the EU would prefer to work with liberal democratic states when it can. And it should support (when invited) the social, economic and political process of transformation in third countries. In short, EU foreign policy will need to be about more than democratization.

One of the basic premises of my understanding of sustainability is that strength abroad begins with strength at home; although it certainly does not end there. The wider shifts in the world economy away from Europe and the US, that only began to make their presence felt after the 2000s, are linked, indirectly and directly, to Europe's capacity for foreign policy action. An inward-looking EU that appears stuck in a cycle of low growth and high unemployment and which is fearful of the future is unlikely to be a risk-taking, visionary player in world politics. Citizens fear the consequences of a widening EU for jobs, public services and their sense of identity. Economic factors and the perception of increased competition for jobs and resources also explain in part the increasing opposition to migration in many European countries. These underlying changes in the world economy, combined with the increasingly sclerotic performance of parts of the European economy (see Chapter 5), explain in great measure why the shine came off Europe's most successful foreign policy – enlargement – in the 2010s. As a result, Europe in the 2010s found itself incapable of deciding what relationship it wanted with the rest of the world and with the countries on its periphery, which it christened its 'neighbours'. Spanning all the states from Morocco to Belarus, the European Neighbourhood Policy (ENP), which was designed as an arms-length replacement for enlargement, has proven to be a poor replacement for a policy of bold and whole-hearted expansion of the Union. In many ways, the ENP is an example of the EU at its worst: a clumsy administrative solution to a problem which Europe has neither the vision, nor the will, to tackle effectively (Balfour and Missiroli, 2007; Lippert, 2008).

The ENP's lack of success was neither the fault nor the responsibility of the EU institutions, rather an illustration of the limited tools at their disposal. Under the right circumstances, the EU is capable of supporting long-term transformation in European countries, provided that there is no geopolitical rival in place and that there is a demand for the EU's reform agenda to match its supply. But long-term transformation is almost the only tool at the EU's disposal. It struggles to address short-term crises because it cannot make snap decisions, often finds it hard to arrive at a united position and has no armed force to make credible threats. In part, this explains why the ENP appeared to be in tatters by 2014, when Russia annexed Crimea (part of Ukraine) with scarcely a whimper from the EU (which was too busy worrying about its gas supply). In the southern neighbourhood, the EU failed to provide even basic guarantees of security in the aftermath of the Arab Spring of 2011, and was forced to sit on the sidelines as the situation across the wider Middle East worsened dramatically from Iraq, to Syria, to Libya, to Israel and Palestine.

Any investigation into EU foreign and defence policy is instructive in highlighting the serious limits to European integration. It is in this policy sphere that the EU and its member states wrestle most with the balance between national sovereignty and integration (Allen, 2012; Giegerich and Wallace, 2010; Gnesotto, 2004; Solana, 2004; Wallace,

2005). Declarations 13 and 14 annexed to the Maastricht Treaty on European Union (TEU) are only one illustration of the continued salience of national sovereignty in this policy area (see Hill, 2006). The loyalty obligation and mutual solidarity clause set out in article 24.3 of the TEU cannot mislead the reader: EU foreign policy does not replace national foreign policy and a common policy is not the same as a single policy (Koutrakos, 2013). It is also a realm where the former world powers of 20th century Europe – France and the UK – are struggling to come to terms with their loss of independent influence. The issue of the EU's representation at the UN and the protection of national representation at the Security Council is a case in point (Hill, 2006; Lehne, 2012; Wallace, 2005). An analysis of this part of the European integration project also provides a degree of clarity about what the *finalité politique* of the European project might be, as will be shown throughout the chapter.

In investigating Europe's place in the 21st century, this chapter proceeds in three steps. It begins with an overview of the many and varied European sources of strength, which are the basis for European influence in world politics, most of which are economic. It then turns to the shortcomings of the more political aspects of European foreign policy, with a focus on the degree to which the Lisbon treaty helps to address these. It argues that the EU is increasingly in need of a grand strategy (Howorth, 2012; Renard and Biscop, 2012a) for foreign policy and serious review of the means by which such a strategy's objectives could be delivered. As Thomas Renard and Sven Biscop argue, 'the international order of the twenty-first century – multi-polar, multilateral, volatile, interconnected and unequal – reveals the inadequacy of zero-sum thinking to deal with contemporary challenges and calls for renewed reflection on the international order' (Renard and Biscop, 2012a). Of course, a grand strategy would not resolve all the EU's problems, not least the challenge of implementation. The core problem is that the member states are not able and willing to cooperate. As Catherine Ashton underlined in 2013:

> [W]e should not delude ourselves – Lisbon left [the Common Foreign and Security Policy] CFSP as intergovernmental and subject to unanimity decision making: in situations where there is an absence of political will or an agreement amongst the member states there are limits to what the Service can deliver. (European External Action Service, 2013c, p. 3)

Nonetheless, a grand strategy would be a start, not least because, if all 28 member states were publically to agree to it, it would be harder for them to undermine it at a later stage. This chapter proceeds with an analytical summary of what could be termed 'the common European interest' and how this has changed since the 1950s. It then brings these two elements together by asking whether Europe's changing strengths will allow it to protect its interests and thus sustain a position of influence in world affairs.

The central argument of the chapter is that, imperfect as European integration may currently be, it offers the peoples of Europe their best, indeed only, chance of being able to cope successfully with the big-picture economic and global challenges that they are facing in the 21st century issues which are one of the root causes of so much collective, European angst about the future, at least at the elite level. Europeans over the age of 30 grew up in a world dominated by Europe and a few of the countries – such as the US and Canada – that they had colonized. Put simply, the world was run either by Europeans or by Americans who shared a largely similar worldview. The world has changed, but Europe does not have the institutions, the means, the ideas, the policy, nor the resources to deal with the challenges of multi-polarity and the emergence of a non-European world order.

The origins of Europe's failure to keep pace with changing times are historical. The Europeans' attitude to the developing world from which they retreated as colonial rulers after the Second World War spawned the expectation that the world would become a kind of informal empire of the West, at least for the foreseeable future. The arrogance of this period was encapsulated by General de Gaulle's scathing and possibly apocryphal pronouncement that, 'Brazil is the country of the future; and will always remain so' (quoted in Burnett, 2010). The future is arriving in many countries that West Europeans and Americans once dubbed 'second' or 'third' world to distinguish them from their own 'first world'. The rapid economic, and occasionally, political development that globalization has brought should be a cause of celebration everywhere in the world, as the peoples of the world become richer and better governed. Yet to Europeans who grew up with the certainty of always being on top, the 'rise of the rest' is unsettling because it is seen to imply a fall in their own relative influence, and perhaps, their prosperity. This seems too pessimistic an outlook.

Without European integration, the influence of all the individual European states on global affairs would be scant indeed (European Convention, 2002a, 2002b; Fabry, 2013;). On the one hand, the EU offers its *peoples* the distinct possibility that the polity in which they live will remain relevant, influential and a powerful force in world politics. On the other hand, European disintegration offers the certainty of irrelevance in world politics for both the peoples and all the *member states* of the EU. It is this question of relevance versus irrelevance that is by far the strongest argument in favour of the European integration project in the 2010s. Globalization has already changed the world economy beyond recognition. In the future globalization could change world politics in an equally significant fashion if there were global regulations on both existential, cross-border threats, such as climate change and environmental degradation, and on global social and economic challenges, such as migration or regulating market failure internationally. A sustainable role for Europe in world politics is not only about Europeans being present during discussions about the future of the planet, but also about their capacity to produce outcomes that are aligned with their interests and values. As this chapter will argue, the EU currently has no such capacity.

Europe's Sources of Strength

Analyzing influence is a complicated and fraught process, not least because of the age-old problem of establishing causality between a particular action and an outcome. Even establishing a framework to investigate the capacity to exercise influence is almost as tortuous, particularly for something as broad in scope as world politics. (See, for example, Moravcsik, 1991, 1993, 1998; Tallberg, 2008; Wallace *et al.*, 2005; on the power and influence of a member state within the EU; and Allen and Smith, 1990; Bretherton and Vogler, 2006; Jupille and Caporaso, 1998 on the influence, 'actorness' or presence of the EU.) This chapter draws on the approaches to 'soft', hard and smart power developed by Nye (2004, 2008, 2011), combined with the work of Steven Lukes on power and influence (2005) and my work with Karolina Pomorska (Copsey and Pomorska, 2010, 2013). Nye sees power as 'hard' and 'soft'. Those who seek to use power effectively to achieve their objectives need to know how to deploy both kinds. Influence, following the logic of Lukes, is understood in three dimensions. The first is the simple power of persuasion, either by deploying threats or by winning the argument. The second is concerned with agenda setting, in other words, determining what will be discussed and what will not. The third, which is almost certainly the most potent form of influence, is the ability to influence the behaviour of others in such a way that they act in the way we want them to, without further prompting. In other words, this third dimension of power is concerned with setting norms or determining what is deemed to be expected, customary behaviour. This framework can equally be applied to the international arena and this chapter will focus on Europe's capacity to exercise these three different kinds of influence, by looking at the various sources of European strength in external affairs.

This chapter first reviews the foundation of Europe's international strength over the long term, working on the premise that the capacity to exercise influence abroad begins with economic power at home. The analysis draws on data relating to the size of the European economy relative to other major economies in the world, and the population of Europe relative to that of the rest of the world between 1950 and 2008. It also looks ahead to 2030, asking what Europe's position in the world economy is likely to be. The purpose of this exercise is contextualization. The rest of this book has reviewed European integration in a 'domestic' or European perspective, and this picture is completed through comparison with other parts of the world. In looking ahead, the section takes into account Europe's underlying strengths, which are not only its economic weight and location alongside the US at the edge of the technological frontier, but most crucially, the quality of its human capital in comparison to other parts of the world economy. It also looks at Europe's role as an investor (and source of foreign direct investment (FDI)) and as the leader of the world's banking and financial services industries. It concludes that reports of the impending demise of Europe in the world economy may be somewhat exaggerated in comparison with those states that Europe is most frequently accused of falling behind. Yet international power or influence is about more than just economic power at home and includes diplomatic range and sophistication, strategic purpose, vision and grand strategy. Such a grand strategy should take account of the need to combine both 'hard' and 'soft' instruments of power projection.

Second, this chapter looks at Europe's supposed institutional capacity to exercise influence in the world, by analyzing European participation in significant multilateral institutions, such as the UN, the International Monetary Fund (IMF), the World Bank and the World Trade Organization (WTO). It argues that without a plan and a common European strategy, the resources available to Europe's politicians and diplomats do not amount to much, although Dermot Hodson's (2011) study suggests that in multilateral forums, the EU and its member states have the capacity to achieve what they desire, almost despite themselves. This could be seen as an example of the EU paraphrasing Garrett Fitzgerald's memorable aphorism, 'It sounds great in practice, but how will it work in theory?'.

Third, it looks at Europe's 'hard power'. Military strength has long been Europe's Achilles heel. An increasingly pacifist mindset, the absence of any credible external threat, the habit of relying on US protection and the reluctance to form serious single European expeditionary forces have combined to ensure that Europe punches well below its weight in diplomatic exchanges where military muscle plays as big a role as civilian power. The best example of this is the Israel–Palestine conflict, which is on Europe's doorstep, yet the major external player in the peace process remains the US. Europe can deliver few credible threats, even economically as the 2014 Ukrainian crisis showed. This chapter argues that the situation is likely to continue until the emerging challenges to Europe's security – which stretch all the way from the Sahel to Crimea – begin to influence the political debate in a serious way, and trigger a wider discussion both about the idea of a grand strategy for the EU and the pooling of sovereignty that would be needed to deliver it. From the end of the Cold War until the 2010s, Europeans lived in a part of the world that was remarkably free of potential conflict. In the wake of the Arab Spring, the Syrian civil war, the collapse of order in Libya and Iraq and Russia's annexation of Crimea, this no longer appeared to be the case. The chapter concludes that the absence of 'hard power', mostly as the result of intra-European domestic political squabbling and the arrival of what has been termed the 'post-heroic' era, remains the most significant drag on Europe's capacity to exercise influence in the world.

A central argument of this chapter is that the EU-28's numerous strengths and potential sources of influence when deployed collectively, actually amount to less than the sum of their parts. This is largely the result of the Union's inability to act in unison, to forge a grand strategy, agree common positions (and stick to them) and put in place an institutional framework that reconciles competing national interests in favour of the collective European good. For years, scholars have been debating why it should be harder to achieve consensus on foreign policy than, say, monetary or trade policy with a focus on the continued relevance of varying national interests that are hard to reconcile (Gordon, 1997/98; Hoffmann, 1995; Menon, 2014). This remains a debate with no conclusion, although it has been observed (Copsey and Haughton, 2009; Copsey and Pomorska, 2010) that in some of the new member states continual reference is made to the defence of national interests, without necessarily knowing what those interests truly are.

In assessing the strengths and weaknesses of European foreign policy, the chapter concentrates more on economic and institutional or even 'hard power', than what might be termed Europe's 'favourite' kind of influence: normative power (Manners, 2002; Nicolaïdis and Whitman, 2013). This is arguably the most potent force of all: the ability to make others act as we wish them to, without further prompting, by changing their view of what is customary behaviour. Moreover, there is evidence to suggest that it does work in some cases (Noutcheva *et al.*, 2013). Much has been said about Europe's insistence on a new kind of world order, based on norms and values rather than *Realpolitik*. The argument for marginalizing normative power is that, although Europe's holy trinity of democracy, respect for human rights and the rule of law have spread around the world, it would be wrong for Europeans to attribute too much of this coverage to their own actions. In the first place, European norms and values could be seen either as Western (the United States' revolution of 1776 preceded France's by some 13 years), or indeed universal, considering that the protestors who brought about the Arab Spring of 2011 were calling for justice, freedom and democracy. The origins of these values may be uniquely European or at least Western, but their ownership has become more widespread. It is true that normative power facilitated the imposition of European modes of governance on the Central Europeans in the 1990s, but this was as much about a desire to close the gap in living standards as anything else. (Doubters would do well to read the demands of Polish workers at the birth of Solidarity in 1980, two-thirds of which relate to material conditions; Weschler, 1984.) The weakness of Europe's normative power is further illustrated by its lack of success in supporting democracy in its neighbours, notably Ukraine, Belarus and Russia, but also in the south. It was not European pressure that threatened the Arab strongmen in 2011; on the contrary, Europe was initially at pains to prop up the various 'presidents-for-life' (Whitman and Juncos, 2012). As will be argued in greater depth in Chapter 7, Europe's economic and political travails since the mid-2000s have to a certain extent weakened the power of attraction of the European way of life. This point is expressed succinctly by Edward Luce: 'Europe is no longer the universal standard by which other societies measure their progress' (2011, p. 309).

A critical examination of normative power could go even further by arguing that the concept itself, or rather the way in which it was enthusiastically seized upon by senior EU politicians, represents a net negative for the construction of an effective EU foreign policy. Normative power provided the EU with a false sense of security about its own place in the fast-changing world of the 2000s. The convenient notion that the EU was a normative power distracted attention from the need to think critically about the other forms of power, which would need to include, as Nye (2011) argues, both 'hard' and 'soft' instruments. Moreover, the idea that the EU's main foreign policy objective should be to spread its norms and values undermined its ability to build alliances with states whose form of government could not be recognized as liberal democracy. For the EU to exercise power *with* others rather than *over* others (Nye, 2011) it will need to extend its list of potential partners beyond liberal democratic states to include those countries whose leaders aspire at least to better the lot of the people they govern (Kupchan, 2012), which is an important minimal condition. This does not mean that the EU should work with any kind of regime, merely that it would profit from being less prescriptive about who it views as legitimate. To give an illustration of how this differs from current policy, the EU insists on human rights clauses in all trade agreements with third countries (except the US). Powerful democracies with strong liberal traditions, such as India, find this insulting and indeed would be justified in perceiving such a policy as 'regulatory imperialism'. The EU needs to understand that it is possible to be liberal without being western.

The European Economy in Global Context

Since the EU's capacity for influence rests on its economic weight (see Damro, 2012), it is essential to present a sketch of how the EU's relative economic position in the world economy has evolved since the 1950s. Table 6.2 and 6.3 present the basic data that relate to Europe's place in the world economy since the dawn of European integration after the end of the Second World War. Table 6.2 presents the total size of the European economy relative to other large economies in constant 1990 US dollars at purchasing power parity. Since the EU did not exist in 1950, the figures are an aggregation of the statistics for 25 of the 28 EU member states in 2013. (Cyprus, Luxembourg and Malta are missing, although they are too small to affect the picture presented.) The European economy was the largest in the world from 1950 to 2008, although it was projected to fall to third place by 2030 when it is overtaken by the US and China. However, it should be remembered that, because these GDP statistics are at purchasing power parity, Europe's leading position in the world economy will be retained for much longer at prevailing market exchange rates. Purchasing power parity (PPP) tells us something about the life of the average citizen and what he or she might buy in the way of vegetables or haircuts, but it needs to be borne in mind that many items from aeroplanes to oil cost more or less the same across the world, and therefore nominal GDP data are also helpful. The European Commission's *Global Europe* report (2011) estimates that Europe's share of world GDP in 2050 will be between 15% and 17%, against 16–18% for the USA, 23–28% for China and 8–11% for India. A note of caution should be sounded in that the statistics for China and other parts of the emerging world economy assume that these states succumb neither to serious political unrest nor to the middle income trap (Eichengreen, 2012; Eichengreen *et al.*, 2013), whereby the process of economic catch-up stalls. This occurs largely through failure to move up the technology ladder (Eichengreen *et al.*, 2013) which, I would argue, is also due to fundamental institutional weaknesses, such as corruption and weak law enforcement. China and the other emerging economies may avoid the fate of many other developing countries, but the odds are not necessarily stacked in their favour. Table 6.2 also illustrates the speed of the changes that took place in the first decade of the 21st century. The economy of China more than doubled in size over an eight-year period from 2000, and there was also very rapid growth in India, Indonesia and the countries of the former Soviet Union.

Demographics lie behind most of the significant changes in Europe's share of the world economy, particularly in the 21st century (Table 6.3). At the onset of European integration, Europe was the second most heavily populated region of the world, after China, with a total population more than twice that of the US and even more so compared with India. The rate of increase in Europe's population slowed very sharply after the mid-1970s and ground more or less to halt in the 21st century. Between 1975 and 2008, Europe's population (and that of the former Soviet Union) increased by less than 10%, whilst that of the US rose by 42%, China by 44%, Brazil 79% and India by 89%. Given these huge increases in their total population, the emerging world economies were fortunate to be able to sustain a level of growth higher than that of the rate of population increase and high enough to lift some of their people out of extreme poverty.

Table 6.4 presents the data for per-capita GDP in PPP terms since 1950. This statistic is most relevant to the average European, because it correlates most closely with his or her lived material experience. Here we can see that Europeans constituted the richest society in the world, after the Americans, and were predicted to remain so at least until 2030.

These data show that Europe and the US have moved, and will move further, away from a position of economic hegemony. If this trends continues, they will simply be two players amongst many in a multi-polar

Table 6.2 The European economy in global context, total GDP (trillions 1990 US$ at PPP)

	EU[a]	USA	China	India	Brazil	Indonesia	Russia and former USSR
1950	1.489	1.456	0.245	0.222	0.090	0.066	0.510
1975	4.494	2.516	0.798	0.544	0.456	0.196	1.561
2000	8.210	8.032	4.319	1.899	0.975	0.672	1.288
2008	9.766	9.485	8.988	3.415	1.262	1.007	2.242
2030 projected	13.825	16.662	22.983	10.074	n/a	n/a	3.239

Notes: [a] Aggregate figure for 25 EU countries, includes all members as of 1 July 2013 except Cyprus, Malta and Luxembourg.
Source: Data from World Economics, 2013.

Table 6.3 Population of Europe in comparative perspective (millions)

	EU[a]	USA	China	India	Brazil	Indonesia	Russia and former USSR
1950	377	152	546	359	53	83	180
1975	453	216	916	607	109	131	255
2000	487	282	1,272	1,022	176	205	289
2008	494	307	1,324	1,147	196	228	284
2030 (projected)	490	374	1,462	1,532	240	289	272

Notes: [a] Aggregate figure for 25 EU countries, includes all members as of 1 July 2013 except Cyprus, Malta and Luxembourg.
Source: Data from World Economics, 2013.

world economy by the middle of this century. Moreover, the lived experiences of most Europeans will remain comfortable, and are even forecast to improve somewhat. In essence, what is happening is that a rising share of global economic output is being generated by those parts of the world where the great majority of its people live. This may imply additional competition for European firms in much the same way as the rise of the United States in the late 19th century brought competition for Western Europe, and Japan's post-war economic miracle forced the Europeans and Americans to raise their game. In fundamental terms, however, Europe is at no obvious risk of economic marginalization, as becomes all the more obvious from the data presented in Tables 6.5 and 6.6, which show Europe's overwhelming domination of both the global banking industry and foreign direct investment.

Tables 6.5 and 6.6 are testament to the depth of European capital markets and the role of Europe as a driver of investment in the world economy in the 2010s. Table 6.5 shows that, out of the total of more than \$25 trillion worth of foreign claims on the world's banks in 2012, some \$16.4 trillion, or two-thirds were owed to European banks. Just over half of the world's total claims for derivatives, guarantees extended and credit commitments were owed to European banks. The European banking sector accounted for 61% of the claims outstanding from the US and just under half of those outstanding from China. A similar picture of European dominance can be observed in the statistics for foreign direct investment (FDI) (Table 6.6) with the total European stock in 2012 amounting to more than \$8.6 trillion against \$3.9 trillion for the US and \$832 billion for China, just under 10% of the total figure for Europe. By way of comparison, France and the UK each accounted for more than \$1 trillion of total FDI stock in 2012. These data on Europe's role in the global financial services sector are an important legacy of Europe's long-held position (jointly with the US since the early 20th century) as the most developed region of the world economy. Such legacies are also to be found in Europe's theoretically disproportionate influence within multilateral institutions.

Europe's Capacity for Influence in Multilateral Institutions

Together with the Americans, the Europeans played a leading role in the creation of the world's multilateral institutions for global governance, including the UN, the IMF, the General Agreement on Tariffs and Trade (GATT, which would later evolve into the World Trade Organization)

Table 6.4   The European economy in global context, per-capita GDP (US$ at PPP)

	EU[a]	USA	China	India	Brazil	Indonesia	Russia and former USSR
1950	3949	9561	448	619	1672	803	2841
1975	9920	16284	871	897	4187	1497	6135
2000	16858	28467	3421	1892	5532	3276	4460
2008	19769	31178	6725	2975	6429	4428	7904
2030 (projected)	28124	45550	15280	6575	n/a	n/a	11908

Source: Data from World Economics, 2013.
Notes: [a] Aggregate figure for 25 EU countries, includes all members as of 1 July 2013 except Cyprus, Malta and Luxembourg.

Table 6.5 European dominance of global banking: consolidated foreign claims and other potential exposures (millions of US dollars)[1]

	Total foreign claims[2]	Vis-à-vis European banks	Vis-à-vis non-European banks	Total other potential exposures[3]	Vis-à-vis European banks	Vis-à-vis non-European banks
All Countries	25,026,678	16,408,940	8,617,738	15,551,684	8,017,278	7,534,406
	100%	66%	34%	100%	51%	49%
United States	5,486,089	3,362,541	2,123,548	2,586,878	2,126,614	460,264
	100%	61%	39%	100%	82%	18%
China	610,054	303,168	306,886	158,078	61,652	96,426
	100%	49%	51%	100%	39%	61%

Source: Data from Bank of International Settlements, 2013.

Notes:

[1] Ultimate risk basis. End June 2013, millions of US dollars.

[2] Foreign claims (public sector, banks, non-bank private sector, unallocated by sector);

[3] Other potential exposures (derivatives, guarantees extended, credit commitments).

Table 6.6   European dominance of the total stock of FDI (inward and outward stocks combined; millions of US dollars)

Country/Region of world economy	Total stock of FDI (inwards + outwards) in 2012
Developed economies Europe	8,676,610
United Kingdom	1,321,352
France	1,094,961
Germany	716,344
Developed economies America	4,570,442
United States	3,931,976
China	832,882

Source: Data from UNCTAD, 2013.

and the World Bank (Jørgensen and Laatikainen, 2013). Of course, it was not the EU or its predecessors that created these institutions, and with the exception of the WTO at which the EU represents the interest of all 28 member states, the EU shares representation of Europe abroad with its member states. As Knud Jørgensen and Katie Laatikainen argue, the EU's presence in multilateral institutions is both 'in-determinant and shape-shifting' (2013, p. 2). Sometimes the EU will be working along-side its member states, as is the case in the UN General Assembly, where the EU has had enhanced observer status since 2011 and can represent all 28 member states where there is a common position. Sometimes a few member states will represent the entirety of the EU, as is the case in the negotiations between the EU-3 and Iran on its nuclear energy programme. One trend is clearly observable however. Since the birth of the European Political Cooperation in 1970, the EU has become an increasingly omnipresent, if far from omnipotent, player in international institutions (Emerson *et al.*, 2011). When cooperation between the member states and the Union works effectively, it might be theoretically possible for Europe to engage in 'double-dipping' in international institutions, as a source of strength rather than weakness.

Path dependence, in combination with the sheer weight of numbers that the 28 member states of the EU bring to international organizations that are still based around supposedly sovereign states has given the EU a disproportionate share of influence. In the UN, the EU, through the permanent membership status of France and the UK, has not one, but two vetoes on the Security Council. Within the IMF, the EU has some

32% of the voting rights, against 17.7% for the United States and 11.5% for China, India, Brazil, Russia and South Africa to share between them (*The Economist*, 2011; see also Pisani-Ferry, 2009). Europeans are not the only over-represented group in these multilateral forums; North Africa, Middle East and smaller Asian states are also over-represented (*ibidem*). The difference is that these other smaller states (Morocco, Qatar or Singapore) are allocated an over-weighted share of the votes because they have no larger, integrated regional body to speak for them like the EU. To these in-built advantages in the EU's institutional representation should be added fact that officials from the member states and the Union are accustomed to sharing or pooling sovereignty, making trade-offs to achieve what they want, and effectively navigating the relationship between different layers of governance. These habits come almost instinctively to all those officials who have worked within or with the European institutions which, after 60 years of Europeanization, includes more or less any senior bureaucrat from any of the member states (Checkel, 2005; Jørgensen and Wessel, 2011). In human resources terms therefore, the EU again has a decisive advantage in theory.

Measuring the effectiveness or performance of Europe within the international institutions is much harder. In the words of one European Commission official, citing the UN as a case study, 'impact is extremely difficult to assess, because political objectives in UN are rarely spelt out clearly and demonstrating causal links can be impossible' (Jørgensen, 2013, p. 86). Where objectives are not explicit, it is difficult to analyze whether goals have been achieved. Moreover, even where objectives are clear, reciprocity – you vote for my proposals and I will vote for your proposal – is a familiar characteristic of international organizations and confuses any attempts to measure outcomes and performance (although Hodson, 2011 is an interesting case study of multilateral influence). There is limited literature on the EU's effectiveness in international institutions and the mainstream international relations materials remain state-centric. Part of the problem is that, for a long time, the objective of the EU in international organizations was simply *being* rather than *doing*. In other words, the goal was simply to be present around the negotiating table and thus implicitly or explicitly recognized as a legitimate player in state-dominated international organizations. (See, for instance, the debate preceding the adoption of the UN General Assembly resolution 65/276 on the EU's participation in the work of the UN in May 2011; Serrano de Haro, 2012.) Actually *achieving something* was a second-order goal that in any case was dependent on securing a presence in the first place.

Academic attention followed suit and concentrated on analyzing the EU's 'presence' (Allen and Smith, 1990) rather than its activities, with some emphasis on the issue of whether the EU member states were coordinating their positions in, for example, the UN (Youngs, 2010). More recently, attention has turned to the question of whether the European External Action Service (EEAS) will improve Europe's capacity to pool its resources (Allen and Smith, 2010; Barber, 2010).

Looking forwards, the task for the EU is changing. Europe's capacity for influence in multilateral institutions is very high, chiefly as an institutional legacy of the mid- to late-20th century order, where Europe and the United States predominated (and the USSR and COMECON self-excluded themselves, Cutler, 1992). Newcomers to the WTO and similar international organizations have to accept rules that were put in place principally by Europeans and Americans. Some have argued that one of the challenges of managing the global 'turn' (Kupchan, 2012; Renard and Biscop, 2012) is coopting other countries successfully in such a manner that they too support these multilateral institutions (Ikenberry, 2011). The risk of Europeans continuing to have disproportionate influence in international forums is that organizations such as the IMF will lose their legitimacy (Saxer, 2012), and in the worst case, will be replaced by other forums in which Europeans do not predominate. This is likely to be a slow process, but it is already happening. A good example is the shift away from the 1970s-era G-7 group of major economies, later the G-8 when Russia joined in the 1990s (until it was expelled in 2014), towards the G-20, which was created in 1999 but only became a significant international forum during the Great Recession in 2008. Another risk is that emerging powers reject institutions that were not designed for them and, some would argue, were actually intended to perpetuate deeply resented Western hegemony. The task for Europe in the 21st century is three-fold. In the first place, sufficient voting rights in international institutions such as the IMF need to be ceded to other countries around the world if those institutions are to retain credibility. It is the willingness of the EU to cede these voting rights to other players that is the acid test of the European commitment to multilateralism for many countries (Youngs, 2010). Secondly, the EU itself needs to move beyond the goal of simply being present in international forums towards setting itself objectives that can be achieved through collaboration between the member states and the EU. Ambitiously, the EU has set itself the target of reforming international institutions to take into account the changed circumstances of 21st-century world politics. This is a brave move that risks allegations of hypocrisy. Europeans were not only late converts to reform, at a time when their economic weight was gently declining, but when it came to reforming voting rights in the IMF or exchanging permanent seats on the Security Council, they have not backed up their reform-minded sentiments with concrete actions. That said, the present is an ideal time for the EU to attempt this, whilst it still has the cards stacked in its favour in terms of voting weights and influence – in other words, whilst it still has a lot of bargaining chips.

Europe's Hard Power

The EU is not in possession of any 'hard power' because it is not a military organization (Biscop and Whitman, 2013; Koutrakos, 2013; Marangoni, 2008; de Vasconselos, 2010). It has no military forces in the shape of an army, a navy or an air force independent of the member states, although it does have so-called 'battlegroups' comprising 19 battalions or 28,500 soldiers out of a total of about 1.6 million across the EU. Only two of these battalions are ready for deployment at any given time, so in practice, the member states tend to act alone as France did in Mali in 2013, or not at all, as was the case after the Russian annexation of Ukraine in 2014. Collective agreement is needed to deploy the battlegroups, which are supposed to undertake the so-called 'Petersberg tasks' of a humanitarian or peacekeeping nature. The idea of a single European army has not been discussed seriously since the rejection of the European Defence Community by the French National Assembly in 1954. Over the twenty years since Maastricht, it did, however, develop a Common Security and Defence Policy (CSDP) as a branch of the Common Foreign and Security Policy (CFSP) (Merlingen and Ostrauskaité, 2008). By 2014, the EU had undertaken 34 CSDP missions of a policing nature – border missions, training of local staff, security support for reconstruction and so on – mainly in Africa, but also in Europe and Asia. The CSDP was therefore not entirely irrelevant to European defence, but it was the most striking example of the way in which the collective might of the EU amounted to far less than the sum of its 28 member states.

Consensus over the future of European defence has been even more conspicuously absent than consensus over the future of Europe's civilian foreign policy, not least because some of its member states – Austria, Finland, Ireland and Sweden – are neutral. Many member states, including France, Germany, Poland, Italy and Belgium, advocate deeper European defence cooperation, whilst others, such as the UK, favour NATO and the

Transatlantic Alliance to remain the major provider of European security (Grevi *et al.*, 2009; Howorth, 2007; Longhurst and Zaborowski, 2007).

In the US in particular, the EU is often accused of spending too little on defence (Bandow, 2013). The US Secretary of Defense's words in the wake of the shortcomings of NATO military operation in Libya illustrated well this criticism (Gates, 2011). Another way of looking at the issue would be to suggest that the US spends too much on defence, at around 39% of total world defence spending for a country with less than 5% of the world population (SIPRI, 2013). The EU, taken to be the combination of its 28 member states, spends about half this amount, which puts it in the second spot behind the US. In 2010, the EU had 1,620,188 active military personnel, not counting reserves, of which some 66,313 were deployed on missions (European Defence Agency, 2011). It spent around €194 billion on defence in the same year, broken down into about 20% on equipment, 51% on salaries and other payments to personnel with the balance on operations, maintenance and other expenditure. Only 1.1% of the combined defence budget was spent on research and development, and a small percentage (between 9.6% and 16.6%) of public procurement spending on defence was devoted to collaborative projects between 2006 and 2010.

According to Sven Biscop (2013), 'hard power' for the EU in military terms would consist of four main capabilities:

1. A permanent strategic reserve of troops, over and above all on-going operations, that could be readily deployed as a rapid reaction force (which implies a total of at least 120,000 soldiers, sailors and airmen ready for combat operations in the European neighbourhood);
2. A naval force of sufficient strength to allow Europe to achieve command of the seas, whilst retaining a sufficient reserve to be able to engage permanently with other partners;
3. Regional strategic autonomy that would allow for transportation and air-to-air refuelling without having to rely on American assets;
4. A strategic planning staff able to engage in permanent contingency planning on the use of all available civilian and military instruments in collaboration with the EEAS.

Capabilities 1, 2 and 4 are barely met in the mid-2010s, and 3 seems far away.

If Europe wishes to boost its military or 'hard' power the challenge is less about increased spending – particularly since most military spending goes on pensions and salaries for personnel that cannot be deployed in any kind of useful military intervention – and more about making better use of its very considerable assets through much closer collaboration. The obvious areas for improvement are procurement (which is exempt from Single Market rules, allowing member states to apply protectionism to national defence industries) and research and development (to avoid duplication and, crucially to benefit from economies of scale and scope). This would also provide a boost to Europe's high-technology industries and produce spinoffs that could be exploited for civilian purposes. Procurement is sensitive both theoretically, because it involves sharing secrets relating to national defence capabilities, and in practice, because the rationalization of the European defence industry could cost a lot of jobs (and save a lot of money). To support these processes, in 2004 the EU launched the European Defence Agency (EDA) to support the development of defence capabilities in crisis management, to promote and enhance cooperation on armaments, to strengthen the European defence industry's technological base and to create a competitive European defence equipment market. This move was a step in the right direction, although it was imperilled by the threat of a UK decision to leave the agency in 2012. In this area, Europe is much further behind than it is in terms of collaboration between the member states in multilateral forums.

What is most striking across all three dimensions of power – economic, institutional and military, but especially in the case of the latter two – is that, for all its strength on paper, Europe actually *achieves* rather little as a foreign policy actor. It is as if the whole of the EU amounted to less than the sum of its parts. The EU clocks up solid successes in negotiating trade deals, but achieves less elsewhere. Once again, the EU can cope with economics, but does less well with politics. Enlargement of the Union (with the exception of the Western Balkans) has ground to a halt. The much-vaunted ENP has not led to much peaceful democratic transition in the Mediterranean or Eastern Europe. If anything, the security and governance situation is deteriorating across the neighbourhood. The initial promise of the Arab Spring led to a bitter rollback of democratic elections in Egypt. Syria descended into civil war. Algeria failed to liberalize. Part of Ukraine's territory was annexed to Russia in 2014, mirroring the way in which Georgia's Abkhazia and South Ossetia fell under Russian 'protection' after the war of 2008. Armenia lined up with Russia's plans to create a Eurasian Union in 2013. Belarus failed to democratize. These failures so close to home, to say nothing of the Palestine–Israel conflict, undermine Europe's claims to power and influence – normative, 'soft', 'hard' or otherwise.

Furthermore, as Lorenzo Fioramonti (2012) demonstrates, there is an equally large gap between European rhetoric and reality when it comes to the perceptions of the emerging powers of the world. Few have even heard of the EU, let alone credit it with much power and influence. Whilst elites in emerging powers may express support for the EU's pursuit of multilateralism, they differ from Europe in seeing multilateralism primarily as the best means of preserving carefully-guarded national sovereignty. It is also important to offset against support for the EU's defence of multilateralism the emerging powers' resentment at what they perceive as a selfish and restrictive European trade policy, as well as their irritation at being lectured by rich countries on the dangers of climate change when many of their own people have no access to electricity.

The Common European Interest in World Politics

Europe's essential interests in world affairs have remained remarkably constant since the beginning of the push for European integration at the 1948 Hague Congress: the promotion of peace, democracy and liberal values to be achieved through greater multilateral cooperation (Edwards, 2011). External relations have become an inevitable dimension of this project (Vimont, quoted in Bindi and Angelescu, 2012) and today the promotion of peace, democracy and liberal values are still grand objectives of the EU's external action (article 21.2 TEU). In the early years of integration, peace was to be achieved in Western Europe step by step through the economic and political integration first of states, and then of people (the 'Monnet method' or functionalism; Sandholtz and Stone Sweet, 2012). The first of these has been achieved, although as discussed in Chapters 2 and 4, in the mid-2010s the second has some way to go. Peace through unity was the dominant discourse of the late 1940s and early 1950s when memories of two world wars were still fresh in the minds of most Europeans. This was also the logic behind the creation of the European Coal and Steel Community (1951); through joint control of the raw materials needed to produce weapons, the build-up of military capacity in any member state for another European conflict would become impossible (Schuman Declaration 1950). The European idealists of the 1940s and 1950s sought redemption from the horrors of the 20th century's two global conflicts that had left tens of millions dead, flattened many towns and cities in Europe as well as bringing economic, political and social devastation and profound human misery (Smith and Stirk, 1990; Churchill, 1950–1954).

Having exhausted the possibilities for violent, nationalistic conflict between states and peoples over the 31 years since 1914, the European movement pushed for internationalism, cooperation and peace. They also sought to provide an acceptable alternative to Communism. The legacy of the Second World War would continue to exert a palpable influence on European integration beyond the Cold War, right up to the late-1990s, by which time the last generation of European leaders for whom the war was relevant (Andreotti, Kohl, Mitterrand, Delors and Thatcher) had moved on. The transition from Kohl to Schröder in 1998 appeared to mark the end of this phase (except in Poland) as the new Chancellor made it clear that he would not be prepared to put the interests of other countries above Germany (*The Economist*, 2014).

As European integration evolved, Europe's interest extended not only to the promotion of peace within Europe, but also to the extension of its norms and values, wherever possible, to other parts of the world. At times there were tensions, as noted above in the case of India, about the extent to which it was possible or desirable for the EU to foist its own norms on other countries without seeming imperialist. This perhaps was the best example of the disconnect between the way the EU saw itself and the way that other countries saw the EU – which was frequently negative, as a neo-colonial liberal imperialist. By the 21st century, according to the EEAS, Europe's interests in the world extended to peace-building, development assistance, the promotion of good neighbourliness, human rights, multilateralism, cooperation in response to international crises, security, action on climate change and the enlargement of the EU to those European countries that had not yet joined (European External Action Service, 2013b; article 21.2 TEU).

A second trend in strategic thinking about Europe's global role since the 1950s is the notion that Europe could become some sort of qualitatively different 'new force' in world politics. For some, this implied that a united continent could escape the dominance of the US in the West, and perhaps, rather more tentatively, by creating a nuclear-free, non-aligned Europe, free the East from the evils of authoritarian, one-party state communist rule (Lindley-French, 2007; Smith and Stirk, 1990). Others saw the future of Europe as a 'third force' in Cold War-era world affairs, in addition to the Soviet Union and US (Dietl, 2006). In part this was reflected in the idea of the European Defence Community in the 1950s. For two of the early West European member states, France and the UK, European unity offered a path back to Great Power status and a meaningful place at the top table for European statesmen (Lindley-French, 2007;

McCormick, 2008). This was certainly a part of the European vision of Harold Macmillan, Edward Heath or Charles de Gaulle, although it was not necessarily a Danish, Belgian or Irish vision of Europe's place in the world.

Over time, the 'third force' or 'new force' narrative morphed into the idea of Europe as a 'civilian power' (Duchêne) in the 1970s and then a 'normative power' (Manners) from the time of Fukuyama's 'end of history' in the late 1980s to the early 21st century. The period between the drive for the Single Market in 1985 and the launch of the first Euro notes and coins in 2001 appears almost to be a 'golden age' of European integration. It was a time for the most idealistic visions of a completely united Europe, certain not only of its own liberal values, but of its economic strengths and its place in the world, progressively expanding the benefits of European integration wider and wider, first to Europe – and then perhaps to the rest of the world. This brief 15-year period appeared to be the dawn of the age of a European Liberal Superpower and the identifiable tendency was to think of the EU as being part of a new world order in international politics, where rules, norms, values and ideas took the place of crude *Realpolitik*.

In the first decade of the 21st century, the Liberal Superpower notion became increasingly discredited as Europe came under steadily growing pressures, both internally and externally. Outside the EU, the attacks of 11 September 2001 on the US brought an end to the peaceful period in international politics that followed the West's triumph over Communism at the end of the 1980s. Once again, Western Liberalism had an enemy that it could not, unlike Saddam Hussein's Iraq in 1991 or 2003, defeat through a military campaign (Rees and Aldrich, 2008). Unlike the Soviet Union, fundamentalist terrorists were not interested in conservative, peaceful coexistence, but in radically shaping the world through a campaign of violent intimidation, designed to undermine Western liberal institutions (Rees and Aldrich, 2008). On the European frontier, as the price of oil and gas rose steadily in the first decade of the 21st century, Russia's interest in the ENP countries of Ukraine, Moldova, Belarus and the southern Caucasus was revived (Giusti and Penkova, 2012; Smith, 2011; Vogler, 2011). The splits between Europeans about the nature of their relationship with the US became obvious at the time of the 2003 invasion of Iraq. The campaign pitted France, Germany, Austria, Belgium, Greece, Slovenia, Finland, and Sweden against the UK, which actively participated in the invasion, and Denmark, Poland, Italy, Spain, the Czech Republic, Hungary and the Baltic countries, which joined the 'coalition of the willing' (Gaffney, 2005; Lequesne, 2012; Sedivy and Zaborowski, 2005). Within the Union, the economy continued to perform badly after 2000, with Germany in particular stuck in recession and very slow growth for much of the decade. Cracks in European unity were equally apparent in the squabbles over the creation of the European Constitution, which had been designed to launch a bold new phase in European integration with the EU, through a foreign minister and President, speaking 'with one voice' on the world stage. Four years were spent in creating the watered-down European Constitutional Treaty (ECT) only for it to be rejected by French and Dutch voters in 2005. The French 'no' resulted from social concerns over job losses and the perception that the ECT represented a step of 'integration furthering globalization' with the ghost of the Bolkenstein directive (Mazzucelli, 2007). In the Netherlands, the 'no' campaigners instilled a sense of threat to the social model, to liberalism and to national identity (Taggart, 2013). It then took another four years for the replacement Lisbon Treaty, which created a President of the European Council and a High Representative for Foreign Affairs and Security Policy (who is also Vice-President of the European Commission) to come into force.

Several structural problems relating to Europe's capacity to act in world affairs became apparent over the course of the first decade of the 21st century. First, it was clear that the member states could not agree between themselves on how much sovereignty in international politics and diplomacy would be pooled at the European level. The poor compromise that was finally agreed created the possibility for a single European voice (or several competing EU voices as it turned out) in world politics, but preserved the principle of unanimity in foreign policy, which made reaching agreement on what Europe's spokespersons should say nigh-on impossible. Symbolically, the change from the Minister of Foreign Affairs in the ECT to a High Representative in the Lisbon Treaty illustrated a retreat from the daring move to create a centre of gravity for foreign policy in Brussels. Second, the gap that was opened up between the European elite and the European people at the time of the Maastricht referendums of 1992 was not closed by the ECT and Lisbon Treaties but widened further, as the French and Dutch voters were denied a say on the Lisbon Treaty that they had rejected as the near-identical ECT. The Irish electorate voted against the Treaty in a first referendum and were only persuaded to endorse it in a second, after being promised unspecified legal guarantees on national tax-raising powers and the preservation of an 'Irish' European Commissioner (Commissioners are supposed to be independent of their member states – and usually are) (BBC, 2011b). The legitimacy gap, that has only worsened since the Eurozone crisis, weakened further the case for a single European voice on the world stage.

If the European project started as a means of reconciling European nations, external relations became an increasingly important dimension of it (Vimont, quoted in Bindi and Angelescu, 2012). Progressively expanding both its geographical reach (to the former colonial empires of its member states, the stabilization of the Balkans, the association and accession of eastern and central European countries, defining relationships with emerging players as well as the conclusion of strategic partnerships) and its policy scope (from the trade policy and development cooperation to a foreign policy including a security and defence dimension), the EU aimed to establish its position in international affairs. To strengthen the Union's effectiveness, its visibility and its credibility as an actor, the Lisbon Treaty reformed its institutional architecture, setting up the enhanced position of chief of the EU's diplomacy – the High Representative/Vice President of the Commission (HRVP) (article 18 TEU) – and a diplomatic service – the EEAS (article 27.3 TEU). Almost immediately after the implementation of the new treaty, these institutional innovations were required to respond to the Arab Spring's anti-authoritarian uprisings with far-reaching political, economic and social consequences.

The HRVP faced many challenges and indeed its own mid-term review of 2013 was only lukewarm in its assessment of the success or otherwise of the EEAS (European External Action Service, 2013a). The reasons for this were legion. First, the TEU provided for too extensive a mandate (*EPC*, 2011). Catherine Ashton, the first incumbent, was not only in charge of the CFSP, she was also one of the Vice-Presidents of the Commission in charge of external relations and of the coordination of external action within this institution. In addition, she was the permanent chair of the Foreign Affairs Council, a new Council formation to deal with external affairs specifically. The HRVP's triple hat, including both internal and external responsibilities, was probably too demanding. Second, if the mandate were overstretched in theory, it was scarcely possible to implement it and Ashton often had to choose between her different responsibilities. If the HRVP were to play a major role in the stabilization of the neighbourhood, to lead the Iran nuclear talks and host the conference on 'a new deal for Somalia' all at the same time, there was clearly a risk that she would be perceived at best as a part-timer in her other attributions and at worst as an outsider in either forum or institution (Grevi *et al.*, 2005). In practice, the position is not an easy one because it requires member states to give the incumbent the political space necessary to make his or her voice heard (Marangoni, 2012). Lastly, the position was weakened by repeated attacks against the first incumbent's involvement or commitment to the job (Mahony, 2009). Catherine Ashton's hearing before the European Parliament, her brief Brussels experience and the tensions with member states in the setting-up of the EEAS were all subject to criticism, in turn weakening the position – although her international counterparts were more positive than the European media (Barber, 2010; Mahony, 2010; Merritt, 2009; Waterfield, 2009b; for an opposite view, see Rettman, 2010a). Moreover, the balance of evidence seemed to suggest by 2014 that, when left alone to carry out the job without interference, the HRVP was quite effective, as the Iran nuclear talks seemed to show.

The second major institutional innovation introduced by the Lisbon Treaty was the EEAS, a supporting diplomatic service for the HRVP (article 27.3 TEU and Council decision 2010/427/EU). The EEAS pools the experience related to external relations of the Commission, the Council and member states. It was structured along geographical and thematic lines, including EU crisis management structures and a large network of delegations abroad, in an attempt to enhance the consistency of EU external action. Initial difficulties of staffing and appointments (Rettman, 2010b) and budgeting (European Commission, 2010), as well as the challenge to establish its position in the institutional triangle and to generate new working relationships between the EEAS and the other institutions, have drawn much attention (European Commission, Secretariat General, 2011, 2012; Marangoni, 2013). At the same time, the diplomatic service had significant potential to materialize as the hub of EU external action. The EEAS was intended to play a decisive role in the definition of strategic guidelines and orientations of EU external action, building on the full range of external policies and instruments of the EU (for instance article 9 Council decision 2010/427/EU on the programming of financial instruments; European External Action Service, 2013a). Yet in reality, performance was less than spectacular.

After several years of major setbacks in European integration, as was discussed in Chapter 1, the mood of doubt about Europe's place in the world intensified as the European economy dived precipitately during the worst economic downturne since the 1930s. What had previously been concerns about Europe's economic and political prospects gave way to *Kulturpessimismus* or a Spenglerian sense of palpable European crisis after 2009, particularly since European and Western relative (and absolute) economic decline came at a time of rapid expansion in the other rising economic powers of the world. On the eve of the Great Recession in May 2008, Gideon Rachmann put forward the notion of Europe in the 21st century as a globalized version of Switzerland's place in Europe: small and politically marginal, yet secure and rich at the same time (Rachman, 2008). The previously rosy picture of the European future stemmed from an idealistic vision of world politics which, during the crisis, was exchanged for realist notions of eternal, cut-throat competition between states, causing greater worry – particularly because Europe suddenly seemed to be on the losing side in this Manichean world. The drift backwards towards a realist understanding of world politics in turn did not restore confidence 'but merely engendered further doubts over the EU's capacity to shape a liberal world order' (Youngs, 2010).

Contrasts in the prevailing mood between the late 1980s and early 1990s, on the one hand, and the perspective of the 2010s on the other, seem stark. Between 1985 and 1992, the European economy expanded by 2.5–3% annually and created 15 million new jobs (Delors, 2013). Communism fell. Delors reported that he had 'rarely known, inside the Community, such a euphoric atmosphere' (p. 173). Fast forward to the 2010s when, in addition to the Eurozone crisis, the EU economy was stagnant and 26 million were out of work. Yet these two periods could simply be seen as two ends of the same spectrum, which make little sense when viewed in isolation. In the late 1980s, it was argued, wrongly, that liberal democracy had won the ideological battle and marked the endpoint of mankind's political development. In the 2010s, there were worries that European capitalism was broken and that future generations would live in far worse conditions than those of the late 20th century. This pessimistic view of the European future seemed likely to be equally misplaced. Positive or negative sentiments about Europe's place in the world change over time and often have more to do with what is going on outside the EU than what is taking place within it.

Continuity in European interests boils down to four elements. First, Europe's fundamental interest in world politics is the promotion of its values, especially peace. It is harder to say precisely what its interests, as distinct from its values, are and there is a need for a fuller analysis of the bigger picture of the collective EU interest, especially beyond the economic sphere. Second, it seeks a world where trade in most goods and services is as free as possible. This is normal for a trading hegemon (and often comes at the expense of poorer countries or regions) and it could be subject to change as Europe's position in the world economy evolves. Third, the European interest is in a multilateral world, where decisions are made collectively and not by coercion. In other words, in the 2010s Europe sought the successful transformation of an international order that was designed by the West for the West towards a multi-polar order whilst preserving as many of the underlying principles as possible. This was a particularly big ask given that many of the emerging powers were deeply resentful of the world order that had been created by America and Europe after the Second World War. Fourth, and this is perhaps where there has been most change since the late 1940s, it sought in the 2010s a world that looks as far as possible like Europe: minded towards cooperation, liberal, democratic, pluralistic, secular and governed by the rule of law. If this was not possible, and Europe's attachment to secularism and a particular interpretation of liberty seemed likely to make this ultimately impossible, then it sought a world that would be either friendly towards, or tolerant of, Europe's way of working.

Identifying Europe's common interests would be a necessary first condition for a grand strategy setting out what the EU should deliver in foreign policy terms. For this reason, Chapter 7 suggests this question as a research avenue. The issue is fiendishly complicated, since it touches on the extent to which 28 member states with supposedly varying interests would be prepared to accept a joint strategy towards, for example, Russia, which looked unlikely in the 2010s. And of course the major problem here, as Jolyon Howorth (2012) noted, was that the whole notion of grand strategy is at odds with the EU's iterative mode of decision making. Moreover, a second condition for the drafting of a grand strategy would involve the evolution of a hierarchy of importance between the EU's competing values and interests. The case of the Ukraine in 2014 was instructive. For the first time since the Second World War, one European country, Russia, annexed the territory of another European country, Ukraine, on the basis of a hurried referendum and a military occupation dressed up as a local rebellion against Ukrainian rule. Clearly, this violated both European values (the promotion of peace, the rule of law, respect for human rights) and some European interests (safe and secure neighbours). Yet the protection of other interests (notably European commercial and financial ties with Russia, and most importantly, security of energy supplies) meant that the EU's response was extraordinarily feeble. The key question for any grand strategy must therefore be: Precisely what values or interests are to be promoted and at what cost? Confronting

this issue would put the EU face-to-face with many of its own hypocri-
sies and contradictions, but it would contribute towards the creation of a
credible foreign policy.

Conclusions: How Sustainable is Europe's Global Role?

Over the sixty plus years of European integration, the world has changed
enormously. There can also be no doubt that, as a *result* of profound
changes in the world economy, Europe's position *vis-à-vis* the other players in world politics shifted over the 30 years between the 1980s and
the 2010s, especially after the 2000s, away from 'co-hegemony' with
the United States towards being one, particularly important, actor among
many. Economic decline matters most to powers whose claims to importance are exclusively rooted on their economic or trading weight. Viewed
from the vantage point of the 2010s, sustaining Europe's position of influence in a changing world looked set to grow a little harder still over
the coming generation, although the strong economic fundamentals that
form the basis for continued European influence seemed highly unlikely
to evaporate.

In addition to the above points about GDP, finance and investment
in particular, the EU in the 2010s remained in a prime position in international trade. Trade policy was one of the founding external policies
of the EU (Niemann, 2012) and the competence of the EU had been
extended and strengthened over time. The size of its internal market and
the openness of its trade policy (except in agriculture, defence and services) established the Union as the biggest player worldwide. Merchan-
dise exports amounted to €1,686.8 billion and imports to €1,791.7 billion
in 2012 (European Commission, DG Trade, 2013b). Both in terms of
exports and imports, the EU represented the largest share of world trade,
before other the US, China and Japan, as illustrated in Figures 6.1 and
6.2. The picture was more clear-cut on the share of exports than on the
share of imports. Since the 1970s, the EU has remained the world's largest exporter. If the total volume of exports has significantly increased
(despite a drop in 2009), its share of world exports has consistently declined over the same period. The trend is the same for the US and Japan,
while Chinese exports are are likely to represent the largest world share
by 2020 if Chinese dynamism is maintained. The EU's import position
was not left uncontested. Both in volumes and in terms of share of world
imports, the EU and the US were very close in the 2010s (Figure 6.2).

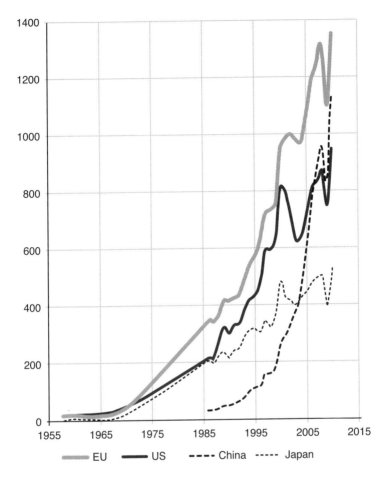

Figure 6.1   EU exports in the global context (billion €)

Source: Data from Eurostat yearbook 2011.

Overall, the EU's position in world trade remained a leading one in the 2010s. The size of its market justified this claim, as well as explaining the leverage that the Union may have on its partners (Meunier and Nicolaïdis, 2006). However, signs of economic slowdown were perceptible. Internally, trade was a policy area of increasing tension between member states, both with regard to intra-EU and extra-EU trade. As was noted in Chapter 1, some member states run what amount to mercantilist

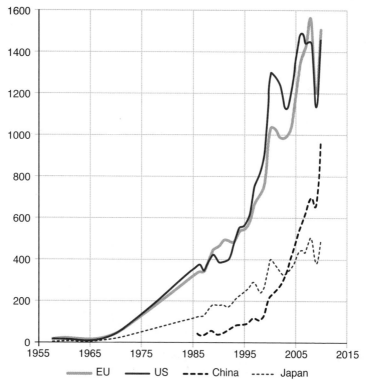

Figure 6.2   EU imports in the global context (billion €)

Source: Data from Eurostat yearbook 2011.

trading policies, and through the pressure and policy change exerted on the 'programme countries' seemed to be encouraging other Eurozone countries to do the same. Whilst individual member states' contributions to the EU's international trade position tended to vary a great deal prior to the Eurozone crisis, thereby adding to imbalances between national situations within the EU (Hall, 2010), one of the consequences of austerity was to reduce current account deficits quite sharply across the Eurozone periphery. Although this may not have been good policy, it did mean that the EU was structurally moving towards a (misguided) policy of export-oriented growth across the whole Eurozone, rather like a developing country.

In concrete terms, being influential in world politics is about whether Europe will continue to be a policy-maker, rather than a policy-taker, when it comes to tackling the social, economic and political problems that result from globalization. These problems can only be dealt with at the world level in multilateral institutions which are themselves under threat from the emerging powers who resent their role in promoting what is seen as Western hegemony. Herein lies the weakness of thinking about the EU's position in world affairs exclusively in terms of economics. Some of these issues are very familiar, and for that matter are already handled internationally, such as trade. Others are emerging areas for world policy-making, including environmental protection, climate change, international terrorism, organized crime and migration. What is interesting about this list, and which will be familiar to students of European integration, is that some of these areas were precisely those in which European states decided to cooperate between the 1950s and the 2010s, as the weakness and inability of their own nation-state to act effectively in isolation became apparent. The challenge of the 20th century was to Europeanize the response to these issues; the challenge of the 21st is to globalize policy-making in these areas.

As this chapter has argued, in foreign policy terms Europe's collective strengths actually amount to less than the sum of their parts when assessed by effective outcomes. The EU mishandled not only the Arab Spring, but also the Ukrainian crisis of 2014. To misquote Oscar Wilde, to mishandle one may be regarded as a misfortune; to mishandle two looks like carelessness. For this reason, a change in the structure of Europe's capacity for international action was needed in the 2010s. However, it was less apparent whether the political will for greater collaboration between Europeans existed at either elite or popular level, and that must be the cornerstone (Schweller, 2006) on which any possibility of serious European influence rests. This attitude was what needed to change. The Eurozone crisis and the rise of new powers meant that Europe could no longer afford the luxury of so much squabbling between countries that hold generally similar views about the kind of world governance structures that European foreign policy is designed to promote and build.

The rationale for 'more Europe' internationally is beautifully simple. As was observed at the outset of this chapter, closer collaboration in foreign policy offers Europe's *peoples* the distinct possibility that the polity in which they live will remain relevant, influential and a powerful force in world politics. A failure to cooperate means the certainty of irrelevance in world politics for both the peoples and all the *member states* of the EU when measured against the emerging titans of the 21st century. It is this question of relevance versus irrelevance that was by far the strongest argument in favour of the European integration project in the 2000s.

Moreover, there may even be grounds for optimism, since protecting Europe's interests in the world, or foreign policy more generally, is an area in which the public can best appreciate the case for collective action. No one European country will be able to tackle greenhouse gas emissions in isolation. Moreover, combined with the relatively low salience of foreign policy issues to the general public, advancing Europe's collective cause in the world may indeed be an area where the permissive consensus on European integration is not yet exhausted.

Having completed a substantive survey of the practice and outcome of European integration, it is appropriate to review the state of the academic debate on European integration and the extent to which the crisis implies a change of course in the study of the EU before considering what Europe's choices in the 21st century might be.

7
Rethinking European Integration

In the Introduction, it was observed that the mid-2010s is a good time to rethink European integration, in both a practical and academic sense. The process of systematic reflection and rethinking in Chapters 2 to 6 was empirical in nature, taking a broad look at the results of over half a century of polity-making, driven by deepening economic, political and social integration between European peoples and countries through the lenses of identity, legitimacy, solidarity and sustainability. The effects of the Great Recession on European integration were considered in Chapter 1, highlighting as a source of concern the incomplete nature of the transition of European institutions – at the national and European level. It was noted that a critical debate has begun about what the choices for Europe are, or should be, with interventions from politicians, former senior officials and academics (Aglietta and Brand, 2013; Beck, 2013; Goulard, 2013; Goulard and Monti, 2012; Habermas, 2012; Heisbourg, 2013; Herzog, 2013; Piris, 2011; Streeck, 2013).

Answers to questions of what should, or ought to, happen are by definition, subjective and fall within the remit of normative studies in political science or political philosophy. For that reason, such normative debates are usually located beyond the frontier that separates the study of political science from practical politics. That said, the business of making choices on the basis of competing normative viewpoints is at the very heart of a liberal democratic system of government. Reconciling the two becomes plausible when we ask ourselves whether political science matters to policy-makers and citizens. If we accept that it should, as most political scientists do (Gerring and Yesnovitz, 2006), it follows that we have a responsibility to promote the practical application of political science by ensuring that it plays a role in informing the democratic exchange of opinions. When political science becomes apparently irrelevant to the rest of society it becomes vulnerable to external assaults, such as that mounted successfully by Senator Tom Coburn in the US, which led to a brief ban on using federal money to fund political science research from 2013–14. Following this logic, the study of European integration has a role to play by informing political and policy debates about the future direction of the EU.

Before engaging in a normative debate, however, it is essential to establish what the contribution of the academic study of European integration, particularly theory, over the past 50 years has been to our understanding of the politics, polity and policy of the European Union. No single chapter can hope to provide a *précis* of the sum of human knowledge about European integration. Rather, the central aim of this theoretical overview and discussion is to provide a deeper context in which to assess what the substantive content of the book implies for the future study of the EU. Given the sheer volume of material that has been produced by political and other social scientists working on European integration since the 1960s, the approach is synoptic in nature and is structured according to two basic questions.

The first and most substantial is: What does the existing body of theory tell us about European integration? Theory informs the way academics conceive of and interpret European integration, at the same time shaping and determining the research questions they ask about the nature of European construction. As Ben Rosamond points out, theory cannot be 'cordoned off' in EU studies (2000) and, in the words of Andrew Moravcsik, 'only by deriving competing hypotheses from general theories ... can we transcend ... indeterminacy and bias' (1998, p. 11). In essence, theory is what helps researchers to formulate better questions. In this first segment of the chapter, I do not purport to reinvent and to supersede the canon of European integration theory. What I do attempt is to *summarize* some of what has already been investigated.

The second part of this chapter asks what the new research questions in European integration theory should be. Given the arguments that have been presented in the chapters on identity, legitimacy, solidarity and sustainability, it asks whether, and how, the model of market-based integration needs to be rethought.

A central argument of this book is that the EU has outgrown the notion of a market-based integration project. Technocratic regulation and market-making provide an insufficient basis on which to build a European identity, not least because the economic benefits of integration are unevenly spread. It is also manifestly impossible to fall in love with a single market. In other words, extending the EU's activities into areas closer to citizens' hearts, as well as their minds or their wallets, will build the affective ties that are essential for the creation of an EU political system that enjoys the same quasi-automatic, instinctive legitimacy as the European nation-states that until now have been seen as the sole guarantors of democratic process. Once this step, along with increased political contestation (Hix, 2008), has been accomplished, it should be easier – or at least possible – to address the many dilemmas and challenges of economic, political and social reform that are bound up with the degree of solidarity that exists between Europeans.

As we have seen, the many and varied challenges to European society, to the European capitalist model and to the sustainability of the European way of life pre-date the Great Recession and the Eurozone crisis. These two severe economic shocks have exacerbated and magnified Europe's long-standing problems. Europe's experiences in the Eurozone crisis underlined boldly what had been becoming more and more evident since the Maastricht referendums of the early 1990s: the technocratic model of governance within the EU has become inadequate, both in terms of its efficacy and its legitimacy. Synthetically, the chapter investigates the advantages and shortcomings of the present model of politics and policy-making and asks what changes might improve the system.

What does Theory Tell us about European Integration?

The Concept of Integration

European integration has been understood throughout this volume as an open-ended process by which, in the words of Haas, 'political actors in several, distinct national settings are persuaded to shift their loyalties, expectations and political activities towards a new centre, whose institutions possess or demand jurisdiction over the pre-existing national states' (1958, p. 16). This is a thorough, demanding and idealistic definition of integration to which I subscribe. What is interesting in a long-term perspective is the extent to which, despite the jurisdiction of European institutions over national states, loyalties have been transferred both reticently and unevenly (see Chapter 1). Haas's definition of European integration differs from the perspective of intergovernmentalists who see integration as the process of creating institutions to which member states subscribe, that is, without a transfer of loyalties away from the national level. Michael Hodges described integration as 'the formation of new political systems out of hitherto separate political systems' (1972, p. 13). Antje Wiener and Thomas Diez (2009) see integration as a process that has both political and social aspects. Since the 1980s, there has been a rise in scholars concerned with the *outcome* of European integration rather than the process itself (Marks, Hooghe and Blank, 1996; Marks, Scharpf *et al.*, 1996). Since European integration is such a vast area, the notion of a theory that purports to explain it is necessarily 'an elusive concept' (Rosamond, 2000). This book has been concerned with the *process* and the *outcome* of European integration, albeit with more of an emphasis on the latter as well as the linkages between the two.

The Role and Value of Theory in Social Science

Theory serves several purposes in this chapter, yet its capacity for explanation is treated cautiously and perhaps more modestly than is fashionable in the 2010s. Wiener and Diez introduce the varying interpretations of theory in social science by drawing on the work of King *et al.* (1994) and Przeworski and Teune (1982) to define it as:

> a causal argument of universal, transhistorical validity and nomothetic quality, which can be tested through the falsification of a series of hypotheses. (Wiener and Diez, 2009, p. 3)

Causality is vital and yet fiendishly difficult to establish in the social sciences. The insistence on universal applicability, timelessness and the notion that a theory should form a kind of 'law' (the nomothetic quality) sets the bar very high indeed. Such an understanding of theory is idealistic and representative of a 'gold standard' or benchmark for scientific enquiry by which, for reasons of academic vigour, all social science should be measured. Yet at the same time, it has an element that is a little bombastic, even dangerous, since all theory in social science ultimately ends in failure, broken on the wheel of Karl Popper's dictum of falsifiability. That the endgame for theory is always falsification is the case for the simple and obvious reason that there are no natural laws about human behaviour waiting to be uncovered by even the boldest and brightest of social scientists (Popper, 1957).

A more modest and, I would argue, accurate definition of social science theory is as a means of explaining patterns of political or social behaviour. As Gerry Stoker puts it, 'good theories select out certain factors as the most important or relevant ... without such a sifting process, no effective observation can take place' (Stoker, 1995, pp. 16–17). Relating particular events to broader trends or patterns through this process is essential for good social science, encapsulated by asking James Rosenau's (1995) simple, yet highly effective guiding question: 'Of what is this an instance'?

Ideally, social science theory should also have some, obviously limited, capacity for prediction. Going beyond this can lead the social scientist to exaggerate the value of the findings of his or her enquiries. This has happened to some extent in economics, where the great strides forward in computing power since the 1960s have provided researchers with enormous data sets and emboldened the discipline by encouraging the impression that incontrovertible proof about the nature of economic relationships, set out in neat mathematical notation, can be established. In fact, nothing can be proven incontrovertibly in social sciences. This is also a trend that is just beginning to be questioned (Carlin, 2013; Piketty, 2014) – what social scientists do is to point towards what is more or less likely to be the case in quite specific circumstances. To re-iterate, this is a point of basic difference between the natural sciences and social sciences. At sea level water always boils at 100 degrees Celsius. No such hard and fast rules exist in social sciences.

In synthesizing these various perspectives, our understanding of theory amounts to a process of abstract, yet systematic, reflection. Its purpose in social science is to explain policy choices and outcomes, decision-making behaviour and to problematize generally observable trends and to match particular developments to them. Theory provides grounding or context to the business of academic enquiry and is a means of explaining the assumptions that lie behind all empirical observations. Abstract thinking in this mould is what allows social scientists to ask better questions in the first place. As Rosamond puts it, theory is a 'fundamental prerequisite for the proper study of the social world' (2000, p. 3). Thus, equipped with a joint understanding of the concept of integration and the role of theory in social sciences, the two may now be usefully combined and their role in the development of European integration studies explained.

The Development of European Integration Theory

European integration theory has been in existence for as long as people have reflected deeply on the possibility or the desirability of a political union between European countries. Normative 'proto-theories' of

European integration that would not be seen as 'functionally-equivalent' (Rosamond, 2000) to contemporary political science emerged over the thirty-year period between the end of the First World War and the launch of the European Coal and Steel Community in the 1951 Treaty of Paris. Better-known exemplars of this include Coudenhove-Kalergi's *Pan-Europa* (1923), Ortega's *The Revolt of the Masses* (1929) or Mitrany's *A Working Peace System* (1944). There is a perhaps overlooked value in both the aims and the nature of the work of this early generation of thinkers on European integration by painting their ideas onto an entirely blank canvas – and it is fitting that one such exponent of a European federation, H.G. Wells in *The Way to World Peace* (1930), is primarily known for his works of science fiction.

The development of what a political scientist would recognize as European integration theory did not really begin until after the signing of the Treaty of Rome that created the European Economic Community (EEC) in 1957. Since then, the discipline has advanced considerably in four main directions of enquiry, which Wiener and Diez (2009) classified as: different explanations of integration (i.e. why the EU is the way it is); conceptualizations of European governance (i.e. theoretical analysis of European government, what it is, what it does and why); critiques of the status quo (usually stemming from a particular worldview); and, normative debates about the future of the European integration project that centre on what Europe needs or ought to become.

That the last of these four directions of enquiry is the most neglected is a reflection of fashions in political science. The concern of political scientists, proto-political scientists and other theorists with drawing up blueprints for an ideal future polity was a long-established trend, albeit one that fell out of favour as political science has became gradually positivist and 'scientific' in nature. Yet it need not always follow that the advocates of dispassionate objectivity should have the monopoly on professionalism (and indeed value-free political science cannot be said to exist). For example, Alexis de Tocqueville, as a proto-political scientist, historian and politician, was not only concerned with the analysis of the system of government of France under the *ancien régime* (de Tocqueville, 1856); he was also setting out a case for how the institutions and practices of French government in the mid-19th century *should* be organized. That his work is studied in the 21st century would indicate that it continues to have some intellectual value.

The declining importance given to idealized 'system design' of the EU was not only the result of changing trends in academic fashion, but also a natural process responding to the fact that the European integration process had taken deeper root and its institutions, politics and policies established firmer patterns of behaviour. Prior to this, embedding the European Communities as a new way of doing business, the European integration project was not only something genuinely novel, radical and qualitatively different to what had existed previously in terms of international cooperation, it was also a project in its infancy. European integration provided a fertile test-bed for the development of theory. Practical opportunities for political scientists (and other social scientists) to test their ideas about optimal institutional design, politics and policy are rare, yet not entirely unheard of. One large-scale example was the immediate post-communist era in Eastern Europe, when academics were asked (with varying degrees of success) to design policies for what was then known as political and economic transition. (See Sachs, 1994, for the best account of this kind of practically-applied academic theory, providing a racy narrative of Poland's jump to the free market.)

With the embedding process complete, from the 1960s onwards, theoretical enquiry into European integration developed following the logic of three schools within political science: international relations, comparative politics and policy studies. The first generation of scholars was anxious to explain European integration and why it was taking place from an international relations perspective (Deutsch, 1957; Haas, 1961, 1967, 1970; Haas and Schmitter, 1964; Hoffmann, 1966) with liberalism, realism and neoliberalism informing the theoretical approach to their questions. Prompted by the launch of the Single Market drive and the paradigm-shifting Treaty of Maastricht, during the 1980s and 1990s, grand theories sought to explain why European integration had undergone a dramatic revival and to identify the longer-term drivers of European integration, understood broadly (Milward, 1992; Moravcsik, 1991, 1998; Pierson, 1996; Sandholtz and Zysman, 1989; Stone Sweet *et al.*, 2001; Weiler, 1999). Overlapping the latter phase of grand theory-building in the tradition of international relations came a comparative politics approach to the study of the EU. By the 1980s, the European integration project had demonstrated its durability as an international organization, but at the same time, it had not morphed into a quasi-super-state. The focus of scholarship moved towards understanding what kind of a political system the European Communities and the EU represented, or in other words, 'understanding the nature of the beast' (Risse-Kappen, 2008). Moving away from international relations towards the disciplines of comparative politics and policy studies was an entirely logical shift. By the 1990s, the EU was clearly something much more than a classical international organization and the 'European policy' that originated

in Brussels was more a matter of domestic politics than foreign policy for the Union's member states. Scholars interested in this theoretical
approach to European integration have tried to discover what kind of
political system the EU represents and how its processes and regulatory
approach can best be described, categorized and theorized.

After the French and Danish Maastricht Treaty referendums in 1992
and 1993, and even more so after the abandonment of the Constitutional
Treaty following the 2005 plebiscites in France and the Netherlands —
notwithstanding the fact that voters use referendums to punish unpopular
governments and reward popular ones — it had become clear that European integration had, in the eyes of many, negative social and political
consequences. Or perhaps it was more that voters associated the EU with
the adverse consequences of globalization. In any case, apparent changes
in the attitude of voters towards Europe (or the salience of the issue to
them) led international relations scholars to study the social aspects and
consequences of European integration. This wave of scholars drew on social constructivism, post-structuralism, international political economy,
normative political theory and gender studies to inspire their approaches.
They were interested in what European integration truly was, the resistance that it generated and how it was constructed. From a comparative
politics perspective, the empirical observation of public attitudes towards
European integration and voter behaviour in the post-Maastricht era led
a new generation of political scientists to turn their attention to the intriguing phenomenon of rising Euroscepticism (Taggart and Szczerbiak,
2008).

It would be too simplistic to suggest that the development of study
of European integration was driven exclusively by the progress and advancement of the European Communities and the EU. Rosamond (2000)
provides a salutary and insightful critique of the argument that real-world
developments, such as the Maastricht referendums, the introduction of
the Schengen area or the launch of the Euro, drive European integration studies independently. He reminds readers that in addition to the
inductive approach (i.e. asking research questions based on our empirical observations) there exists also the deductive approach by which our
observations are 'seen as useful sites for the examination of theoretical
propositions or the competitive testing of theories against one another' (Rosamond, 2000, p. 2). He also indirectly makes the point that our
understanding of the EU through theory is driven as much, and maybe
more, by intra-disciplinary debates and gatekeeping about how knowledge may be generated. Some academics have both very strong views

and powers of enforcement over what is deemed *admissible* as research, how it should be *conducted* and what the *borders* of the discipline are.

For example, the theory of neo-functionalism (the idea that integration produces positive 'spillover' effects that require further integration in other sectors) emerged from the efforts of a community of American scholars who applied pre-existing and functionalist thinking to a clearly delimited international region (Rosamond, 2000).

It is both natural and appropriate for the furtherance of science that academic norms and rules should be established. However, these rules and patterns of acceptable behaviour and practice also serve to constrain and delimit what may be considered admissible as science, or even what may be considered worthy of investigation in the first place. At the micro-level, academic careers, reputations and rivalries are based on the application of these norms and rules. It is a marker of great prestige among an academic's peers to be the author of a grand theory. Yet as Rosamond's fascinating historical account of trends in theoretical approaches to the study of European integration shows, such theories rise and fall over time as the result both of changing evidence and of changing modes of thought. Many careers have been built on 'engaging in "dissenting" forms of work'; yet other scholars might argue that knowledge is 'accumulated in the context of ... paradigms, not by challenging their assumptions' (Rosamond, 2007). A third group of Young Turks champions the arrival of 'professionalism' in the discipline, welcomes the import of 'research standards' and laments past work that was 'wholly descriptive'. Present high standards of practice are contrasted with the lack of rigour in what unhappily passed for science in times past. These patterns repeat themselves endlessly.

Yet all theory may one day be falsified and washed away with the tide as future generations raise their eyebrows at the inexact standards and woolly thinking of their forebears. For every Adam Smith, Max Weber or Karl Marx, there are tens of thousands of scholars, eminent in their day, who are either forgotten entirely or, at best, remembered as standard-bearers of social science orthodoxies that succumbed to new evidence and/or to changing disciplinary fashions. It follows that those who seek to understand the development of European integration theory and of the avenues of investigation that have been pursued in the first half century of European studies must have a grasp of this background and all the motivations of the scholars at work. There is certainly nothing discreditable in recognizing the at-times decisive role played by changing fashions within political science; after all, every profession has its norms, standards and patterns of acceptable or unacceptable behaviour. A frank and honest examination and analysis of the internal workings of academia is thus the final piece of the jigsaw puzzle in understanding the role of theory.

In summary, ideas, concepts and theories cannot be separated from the historical or intellectual contexts in which they were generated (Skinner, 1978). The morals, manners, habits and behaviours of societies change dramatically over time and future generations will doubtless find certain aspects of liberal western society as distasteful or abhorrent as we consider slavery in Ancient Rome or the 18th-century West Indies, for example. In consequence of the inseparability of historical and intellectual context from academic practice, no social science theory is timeless in nature, and we would do well to be mindful of this in our approach to theoretical insights generated from European integration studies.

What Does Theory tell us about European Integration?

European integration theory, in common with all theory in political science, serves three basic functions, which provide: (1) a means of understanding or explanation; (2) description and analysis through classifications, typologies and labels; and (3) a critique and normative intervention providing principles for the future. The domain of political science theory extends to questions related to polity (the political community and its institutions), policy (the analysis and comparison of content; reflection on the normative underpinnings of policy; why technocracy prevails over participatory approaches and so on), and politics (the struggles and strategies of political actors dealing with one another). This section will examine the extent to which these three functions have been served.

As one might expect, the polity, policy and politics of European integration have been studied in great depth and detail since the 1960s, passing over the course of that time from being a 'boutique to a boom field' (Keeler, 2005). In addition to the approaches and areas of work cited in the preceding section, there has been extensive enquiry into explaining, for example, why EU integration proceeds at different speeds, in which ways the EU is more like a state and in which ways it is more like an international organization and why European integration is uneven. In truth, one can no sooner hope to provide a comprehensive review of the literature on European integration since 1960 than one could for American politics over a similar period, just as one can no sooner arrive at a 'general theory' of EU politics than one could a general theory of American politics (Hix, 1996). What *can* be done is to overview what has been studied in thumbnail form with a view to understanding what has been very well covered and what has been neglected.

In terms of describing, analyzing and explaining the polity, policy and politics of the EU, Rosamond (2000) argues that the canon of European integration theory characterizes the EU in four ways. Firstly, the EU is an international organization similar to the UN or the WTO. From a legal perspective, this is indeed the case. From an international relations perspective, international organizations are created and developed by their members in order to further common interests so the dominating backdrop is one of converging state interests.

Secondly, European integration has been seen as an example of regionalism in the global economy (Rosamond, 2000). This school of thought is more interested in comparing the EU with other regional cooperation initiatives, particularly the NAFTA or Mercosur, but also more broadly the Arab League and more recently, the Eurasian Union. This field of study is dominated by scholars from the disciplines of international relations and international political economy. They address such questions as whether regionalism arises under very similar circumstances in all instances, the relationship between regional integration and wider international cooperation, or the extent to which regional economic groupings accelerate or hinder the spread of free trade (on comparative regionalism, see Börzel *et al.*, forthcoming).

A third group of scholars have studied the EU as a highly complicated instance of the dynamics of multi-level policy-making. Here questions are asked about the interactions between different actors – national civil servants and politicians; courts; political parties; European bureaucrats; interest groups and social partners such as business federations and trade unions; regional and local actors; and, external players coming from outside the EU system, including third countries, would-be members and strategic partners – in the policy-making process of agenda setting, policy formulation, implementation and so on. Academics with an interest in this aspect of the EU game are asking Dahl's famous question, 'Who governs?', and considering where power and influence are located, the role of institutions and the overlap between national and supranational locations of power.

Fourthly, the EU has been understood as *sui generis*, i.e. of its own kind and therefore unique in its characteristics and not comparable to anything else. This is the officially endorsed EU view of itself and is rooted in the irrefutable fact that the EU has uniquely independent institutions and supranational powers. Not only is the EU quite unlike any other international organization, its institutions are unlike the national political setup of any of its member states. In this *sui generis* understanding, there is no sense in attempting to use the EU as a test-bed for theories and insights generated in other fields of international relations and political science because the Union has neither 'historical precedent' nor 'contemporary parallel' (Rosamond, 2000). Some would argue that this uniqueness line of argumentation has the tendency to lead towards excessively detailed empiricism, or, even worse, the most damning judgement of academic study as mere 'journalism'. Rosamond (1995) argued that this view of the EU automatically excludes the possibility of offering deeper theoretical insights. Hix (1996) also argued that it distracts scholars from a focus on the 'real' problems that Europe and its citizens face. One conclusion might be that the EU is not a state; it is 'just' a polity, albeit one quite unlike any other. Perhaps it is best to accept that it is unique – and that there is nothing wrong with that, since this kind of analysis fits best with what can be observed.

What could be concluded from this briefest of sketches is that European integration theory has served very well in its first two functions: providing a means of understanding or explanation as well as description and analysis through classifications, typologies and labels. Less work has been carried out in the domain of *critical and normative interventions* with principles for the future. The next logical step is to consider the nature of those new research questions.

What Should the New Research Questions in European Integration be?

Normative and critical insights into European integration are not worth very much unless the issues discussed are built on a more dispassionate, positivist foundation. What would be hugely useful and most welcome in the study of the EU at present is more work that combines the profoundly valuable, rigorous and important theoretical and empirical insights into European integration, including more adventurous work on normative matters. This is not to advocate a form of social enquiry where all pretensions to scientific objectivity are discarded in pursuing the Will-o'-the-Wisp of originality. Rather, it is a call for a more inclusive approach that draws a little of its spirit and inspiration, if not its substance, from the earliest forms of proto-theory about European integration which were loaded with idealistic subjectivity. In part it is also a suggestion that there should be more academic work that is even more closely related to the needs of the European polity, its policies and its politics – and which does not limit itself to describing and analyzing what can be observed, but also dips its toe cautiously into the hot waters of what could happen and considers the options for change. Such a normative approach would greatly serve to illuminate public debate on the future of the European continent, and has been acknowledged as 'being back on the table' by Wiener and Diez (2009). Before spelling out what the questions could be, it is sensible to say summarize this book's approach to the study of the EU.

Towards a More Normative Approach and the New Avenues for Research

This book assumes that all academics are seekers of truth, even if they may disagree about what constitutes truth, and how it can best be discovered through investigation or contextualized within the boundaries of pre-existing human knowledge. With good reason, its approach to the study of European integration would have to be that of the *sui generis* perspective for the elementary reason that there really is no historical or contemporary parallel. Imprecise or haphazard parallels could be drawn by stretching the most elastic concepts one could find in order to compare, say, the effect of 70 years of integration within the Soviet Union on understandings of identity, solidarity and legitimacy in Russia, Ukraine and Belarus. Or one might look at the impact that the creation of India and Pakistan had on these self-same three issues in those two states. Yet this would be an inadequate, even pointless, exercise since all of these examples refer to states and we would be looking at the process of state- or nation-building. The EU is not a state; it is 'just' a unique polity-in-the-making.

What is perhaps not currently needed is any further work on the nature of the EU that is confined to the state or international organization dichotomy. Lots of attention has been given to this question, arriving at the valid but insufficient conclusion that the EU is 'less than a federation – more than a regime' (Wallace, 1983), which in turn is already an advance on Jacques Delors' description of the Union as '*un objet politique non-identifié*' (Schmitter, 1996). For the moment it might be best to stop there, whilst acknowledging that there will be a need to return to this question as the EU evolves (see for example Schmidt, 2004, 2009).

Following this line of reasoning, using Rosenau's (1995) simple yet highly effective guiding question – Of what is this an instance? – may not be appropriate for the study of European integration. In the worthy pursuit of scientific rigour and excellence, we may end up asking the wrong kind of questions by limiting ourselves only to explaining the world as we perceive it. As social scientists, this approach also involves giving up any attempt to change the world, even in a modest way. This seems a pity since it acts to exclude much lively, enlightening and valuable discussion of normative questions that are pertinent to our society today. Provided that the conclusions that are drawn from normative discussion are presented in that light – i.e. as informed opinions, but opinions nonetheless, rather than the conclusions of positivist scientific enquiry – there can be no harm in them. Moreover, as argued above, normative academic debate in turn stimulates a better quality of public discussion, which by degrees improves the quality of democracy and government. Since social science is supposed to be for the good of society, and not just for the benefit of social scientists, this can only be a good thing.

What is needed is more research on the EU that combines analytical and methodological rigour of the academy with a more practical, hands-on approach to informing Europe's political and policy debate about the current existential crisis that draws its inspiration from the think-tank world. Academic research sometimes offset at far too high a level of abstraction to be comprehensible, let alone relevant. Think-tank analyses have been known to suffer both from a bias in their approach to a problem and from an insufficiently rigorous approach – which could be categorized as 'assertions with footnotes'. Some academics have begun to bridge this gap (Tsoukalis, 2014) and it would be beneficial for others to begin do so too. At this time of existential crisis, governments and societies across Europe are in dire need of academic studies that not only diagnose the true nature of the European integration project's current malaise, but also propose – even in general terms – some fresh ideas about what might be done to remedy the situation. I now turn to what some of these emerging research themes could be.

New Avenues for Research

In terms of the subject matter of a critical and normative intervention, the list is long, but it would seem obvious to limit proposals to those areas that have been suggested by the substantive content of this book. Areas for possible further investigation might include the cross-cutting issues outlined in the Introduction and Chapter 1 on the Eurozone crisis, and those that were described in Chapters 2 to 6 on identity, legitimacy, solidarity and sustainability.

This book's central argument is that the EU has advanced as far as it is possible a model of political integration based primarily on the removal of economic barriers to trade and competition within a single market. It has further contended that a widespread European identity is unlikely to emerge as a side-product from a process of technocratic, largely economic integration. I have argued that not all Europeans benefit equally from the Single Market and European integration. Thus whilst the current model may capture some citizens' minds through an appeal to their wallets, it has created few affective ties to their hearts. Such emotional bonds are the first building block for a robust and fully legitimate EU political system underpinned by the same quasi-automatic, indeed instinctive legitimacy of the nation-states that have claimed a monopoly on the democratic process until now. If this emotional underpinning can be achieved and greater political contestation injected into EU politics, it should become possible to begin to tackle the many challenges and conundrums of social, political and economic reform that are interwoven with the broader debate on the presence or absence of solidarity between Europeans. The research question that suggests itself here relates to the basis on which European integration might fruitfully proceed, apart from removing the barriers to the free movement of goods, services and people.

The myriad challenges to the European capitalist model, European society and indeed the European way of life existed before the Great Recession and the Eurozone crisis. The main consequence of these two severe shocks was, as has been argued, primarily to worsen Europe's long-standing problems. In turn, Europe's post-2007 blight highlighted clearly what had been becoming more and more evident since the referendums on the Maastricht treaty of the 1990s: that the technocratic model of government and integration has become exhausted and inadequate. This exhaustion has knock-on effects, not only on the efficacy of technocratic integration, but also on its legitimacy. This chapter investigates both the advantages and shortcomings of the present model of European politics and policy-making and asks what existing academic insights and further research can usefully bring to this debate. Here the obvious question that springs to mind relates to the possible alternatives to technocratic government.

Chapter-by-chapter, the research questions that were raised are as follows. Chapter 1 dealt with the effects of the Eurozone crisis, which was caused by the financial crisis in the banking sector and the build-up of excessive debt. The questions that spring directly from this observation relate to the urgent need for more research into the full effects (economic, social and political) of the increasing size and scope of the financial services industry on the European economy, and an investigation of the increased risks as well as the gains from this process. Chapter 2 on identity noted that those segments of European society who benefit most from European integration tend to identify more closely with it. It also observed that identification with Europe has not penetrated the attitudes of the non-elite segments of European society. This is mostly because European identity has apparently not managed to transcend the rational and reach out to the sensibilities and emotions of most Europeans – and when it does so, the emotions it taps into tend to be more Eurosceptic than pro-European.

Two very interesting avenues of research suggest themselves here. The first is about the question of the links between material benefits from European integration and support for the project at a time of profound economic, political and social crisis. The second is linked to, but separate from, this first question. It would be useful to investigate how attitudes towards the EU as a polity-in-the-making develop at an individual level, both cognitively and emotionally. This question is suggested for two reasons. Those Europeans who engage in cognitive reflection about the EU and its value to them tend to be more favourable towards it whereas emotional responses towards Euroscepticism rather than pro-Europeanism. Yet not everyone has the ability or the desire to engage in abstract reflection. It would be useful to have a pan-European, 360-degree view of attitudes that charts their psychological, emotional and irrational roots and development at the popular level. (Some excellent work on emotion in politics has already been carried out, see Guibernau, 2013.) It would be equally fascinating to understand why national elites in some member states are so obstinate in their desire to remain ignorant about the EU project. It would also be interesting to have some insight into the possible 'Damascene' moment when an individual realized that he or she was a Eurosceptic. Hypothesizing these moments as 'Damascene' conversions is not mere sophistry; it has value because Eurosceptics seem to harbour their views with such ferocious intensity. Why? One of the most interesting, and perhaps dispiriting, features of modern Europe for the Europhile, is that the zealots are mostly to be found in the anti- rather than the pro-EU camp. Again, why? This would be a worthwhile addition to previous work on the pragmatic, rational and ideological reasons that may lead politicians and political parties down this path.

Charting Euroscepticism, or indeed any strongly-held political viewpoint, from an affective perspective would necessitate going beyond the disciplinary frontiers of political science. Once we start to ask slightly different questions, we may need to draw upon the alternative toolkits of other disciplines to answer them. Emotion in politics is a really fascinating field for future research; instinctively, we know that it plays some role in determining who we are, where our loyalties lie and the way we relate to others. Yet we draw away from it instinctively because it is so hard to measure, whilst all the time knowing that what is measureable is not necessarily meaningful. Emotion is something more than the study of political rhetoric, and whilst we, as social scientists, may not have the tools to hand to investigate it, others do. This implies experimenting with the importation of new methods and approaches from other disciplines such as psychology. There is nothing wrong with this, not least because embracing a range of disciplies means following a path worn by earlier generations who seized on the exciting possibilities of quantification and mathematical notation. These have become standard features in political science as well as economics and the natural sciences, but we should not limit ourselves to quantitative methodologies since they may not be appropriate for the investigation of every hypothesis.

Chapter 3 argued that, objectively judged, the EU is democratic, legitimate and accountable in the vast majority of its work. However, as was underlined in Chapter 1, the creation of the Euro marked a decisive step in the transformation of the EU's domain from low to high politics. The Eurozone crisis exposed a flaw in EU democracy because saving the Euro required both bailouts and a tough programme of austerity measures which had not been democratically approved. Thus there is a need to look into the means by which decision making in the EU can be legitimated. This must include a significant injection of visible political contestation into the EU's consensus-based system of decision making, as has been argued by other scholars (Follesdal and Hix, 2006), and an increased role for the European Parliament. Yet, given the complexity of decision making and the reality of power sharing and overlapping competences that result from the multi-level nature of EU politics, there is also a need for multiple and alternative means of providing legitimacy. Thus the question relates to what constitutes appropriate democratic legitimacy under conditions of supranational – even intergovernmental – integration (as highlighted already by Wiener and Diez, 2009). In other words, by what means can a supranational organization best legitimize itself, its decisions and its actions (or inaction)? Some initial work has been carried out by Gerda Falkner (2013) but there is a pressing need for much more to be done in this area, linked as it is to questions of growing public scepticism about the political process and why it is that societies seem to be becoming progressively anti-political. If we accept the unique nature and novelty of the EU as a polity, we must also accept that the means by which it legitimizes itself must also be original.

Following on from the argument in Chapter 3 about the need for a legitimacy-building pact to be forged between the EU and both the member states and the European electorate as a whole about *how* the EU is to operate, Chapters 4, 5 and 6 flagged up the need for a new deal on the substance of *what* the European polity should concern itself with. The challenges for Europe's society and economy that relate to solidarity and sustainability have evolved almost beyond recognition since the 1960s. Therefore, the policy fields with which the EU concerns itself need to change to reflect this – not least because the EU is operating a currency union with European-level responsibility for financial and monetary stability, without comparable powers and responsibilities for other aspects of macroeconomic policy-making. The broadest question for academic enquiry, then, is about the policy options for the future management of the European economy, and what the likely consequences of their implementation could be. Bringing back the 'political' aspect to this political economy question is important because policy-making in the EU has always been dominated by a technocratic mode of thinking that assumes that there is an optimal policy out there waiting to be discovered, without too much reflection on the assumptions that lie behind this supposition.

Linked closely to this question are the issues related to Europe's 'reform trap'. The challenge for Europe has already been identified as the incomplete nature of the institutional transformation, especially at the national level in the southern European Eurozone member states of Italy, Spain, Greece and Portugal. Where further research is needed, it is again linked to critical and normative interventions about possible policy strategies that could deliver institutional transformation at the national and at the European level. We know a great deal about how institutional transformation can be supported in pre-accession countries (Schimmelfennig and Sedelmeier, 2005) but we now need policy studies on how this could be put in place to promote on-going reform and transformation within current member states. It has been also noted that in some cases, when faced with a choice between reform or decline, the majority of the public in certain member states (of which France seems to be the most obvious exemplar; Le Boucher, 2013) chose decline. Three pertinent research questions that suggest themselves here are as follows. First, how might the government of Europe's polity-in-the-making be rethought in such a way as to provide carrots and sticks that will chivvy reluctant national governments towards a thorough-going process of institutional reform to help prepare their countries for the challenge of globalization? The second question is political in nature and highly relevant for the years to come because it concerns the effects of an ageing society on political and policy debate at the national level. To what extent do older voters – for whom the promise of future gains is unattractive because of biological imperative – constitute a veto block on reform of the member states' social models? Is this casual empirical observation misleading or simplistic? It is indisputable, in any case, that more research into the politics of structural reform is needed (see also Pierson, 2001).

Another question which springs from the data presented at the end of Chapter 4 is whether, and under what conditions, the dramatic increases in inequalities within member states of the EU can be reversed. It could be argued that this was nothing to worry about, but I would retort that a large equality gap has highly adverse consequences for meritocracy and the ideal of democratic equality between citizens. One assumption, that underlines the attitude of many to this problem, is that it is a global phenomenon, unstoppable and uncontrollable. This seems inadequate, even lazy, given just how many of the rules for the management of the global economy are set by, or at least with the agreement of, the Europeans. Indeed, as Piketty (2014) notes, the decisions on the regulation of finance, capital and taxation that created the conditions for the growth in equality were just that: decisions. And decisions can be reversed or different paths chosen. Such policy studies need not confine themselves to the optimal means of conventional redistribution of income by taxation and spending. They should also consider wider questions, such as whether the real attention must now be paid to finding ways to better enable Europeans to recover from some of the destruction that globalization has caused in particular sectors (i.e. the tradable sectors of the economy) through a re-investigation of the notion of a workable globalization adjustment fund. A secondary issue is the means by which sustainable economic prosperity can best be generated. It would be worth investigating whether, instead of transferring resources through structural or cohesion funds, it would be better to invest the money – counter-intuitively – in the richest parts of the EU with the most developed 'knowledge-based economies' where such funds can best be absorbed.

Chapter 6 discussed Europe's capacity for effective action in international affairs and concluded that it often amounts to less than the sum of its considerable parts. It also underlined the way in which the EU tends to see the 'turn' in global affairs of the 2010s and the shift of power eastwards (Ikenberry, 2011; Kupchan, 2012) in exclusively economic terms. It is therefore time to bring politics and grand strategy back into the policy of EU external affairs. Europe's weakness in international politics is partly to do with the unwillingness of its member states to pool sovereignty on foreign policy and defence matters between them, partly as the result of the current institutional structure of foreign policy decision making at the EU level and partly connected to the absence of a grand strategy. There is a need therefore for further academic studies, both into the extent to which the EU-28's interests are compatible with one another and, into what the elements of a workable grand strategy should be (Howorth, 2012), incorporating defence, trade, educational exchange and traditional foreign policy. Moreover, an additional new research avenue could be found in looking at why defence or foreign policy should be more sensitive in sovereignty terms than, for example, monetary or trade policy.

When it comes to achievements in foreign policy, the EU can claim effectiveness only in supporting long-term change in the enlargement -and-conditionality mode. As we have seen in the case of the ENP, socialization strategy does not always work without the back-up that comes from different elements of a grand strategy. If deeper cooperation on 'hard power' matters, such as defence integration, is too complicated for 28 member states, a starting point might be a thorough study into the extent to which such integration could begin with the EU's two largest military powers, UK and France, and the conditions under which they could be joined by other member states over time. Thus there is also need for research into the kind of grand bargain that would need to be struck in foreign policy to provide elite and popular support for a thoroughgoing grand strategy.

In addition to these intra-EU studies, there is also a need for much more work on the interests of the emerging powers of the 21st century. It is commonly observed that their interests do not necessarily align with those of the EU, and that it should not be assumed that they would support the continuance of a liberal multilateral order that was designed by the West for the West. If we espouse Kupchan's (2012) idea that multiple versions of modernity exist, it would be very helpful to know much more about what these amount to. What, for example, is a well-run autocracy? Does it exist? How does it legitimate itself? What does this mean for Western-style liberal democracy? This is all the more important since it is not immediately clear what the emerging powers would like to see in place of the existing multilateral, rules-based international system. For this reason, there is a need for a new body of work on the extent to which the emerging powers' *values* and *interests* align or differ from those of the EU. Given the difficulties of accessing data and sources in many emerging powers (the two most obvious examples are Russia and China), there will be need for a degree of old-fashioned Area Studies empirically-detailed work, complemented by mainstream International Relations insights to overcome the problems that Area Studies research has in 'going native'.

Although this book has argued that the limits of a market-based European integration process have been reached, it is not clear what comes next. And given increasing public dissatisfaction with European integration, a new area of enquiry might be the need for further integration that is driven by these functional concerns and how it can be balanced against the absence of popular support, if at all (Leuffen *et al.*, 2013). It is to be hoped that the answers to some of these research questions will allow academics to provide at least a rudimentary idea of some of the options for a European integration project that goes beyond removing the barriers to free markets. Thus armed with an overview of the new research questions in the study of the EU, we may proceed to examine, in both a positive and normative sense, what some of the new choices for Europe are in the wake of the Great Recession, the Eurozone's travails and the existential crisis of European integration.

Conclusion: Rethinking the Choices for Europe

This book was written during the depths of the European Union's first existential crisis; a period of recent European historical development marked by a sense of intractability, failure, loss of purpose and general drift that challenged and undermined much of what has been understood and written about the EU and the European integration project. Its objective was two-fold. First, it sought to investigate what the true effects of the Great Recession and the Eurozone crisis have been. Second, in no small part prompted by the sense of deadlock, inertia and general *Kulturpessimismus* that went hand-in-hand with the crisis, it aimed to explain why the political, social and economic situation across the EU and its member states remained both so grave and yet so irresolvable at the same time – the apparent contradiction of a situation that was, as the Viennese used to say, 'desperate but not serious' prompted further enquiry.

In reflecting on why Europe's leaders should seemingly reject reform and change in favour of inertia and stagnation, the initial search for explanatory factors explored the problems caused by path dependence that have been analyzed at length by scholars of historical institutionalism. A supplementary observation made at the outset of the analysis was that the conditions for breeding the inefficiencies, and even pathologies, to which path dependence leads are more readily found in the EU than elsewhere. This is in a great measure due to its uniqueness as a political system, where sovereignty is shared in some areas and jealously guarded in others, and where there is a great profusion of political players from 28 member states who have influence, powers of delay, powers of veto, varying interests and differing ideological viewpoints. Moreover, many individual political deals in Brussels are small parts of larger 'package deals' agreed as a result of numerous trade-offs between diplomats and MEPs, or even the result of 'grand bargains' struck after long months, even years, of intense talks between Europe's heads of state and government. Whilst none of this means that the political system of the EU is impossible to reform and adapt to changing circumstances, it constitutes a political order in which it is much harder to unpick what has already been agreed in institutional, political and policy terms. And what is already an inelastic political system has become progressively more so over time as the sheer volume of path-dependent decisions (and non-decisions) rises and number of political players continues to grow. It was perhaps an exhaustion borne of fruitless attempts to reform the Union that made Europe's leaders in the 2010s so cautious of any serious attempt to rethink the EU's purpose.

In the Introduction, two overarching explanations were offered to explain the true nature of Europe's great existential crisis and why it seemed so intractable. The first involved incomplete institutional transformations at the European and national level that have locked in political systems and policies that are incapable of dealing with the economic, social and political challenges that the EU-28 faces. The consequences of this were the twin problems of market failure and government failure across Europe, that became so exposed and apparent after the beginning of the Great Recession, and were most clearly visible in the mid-2010s in what the European Commission referred to as the 'programme countries'. Thus, unfinished or incomplete institution-building at the European level lay behind the Eurozone crisis, whilst at the member-state level the crisis was more closely linked to building national institutions on half-dug or even rotten foundations. The second path dependence-based explanation about the intractability of the on-going crisis concerned the intellectual underpinnings or ideology on which the decisions taken by Europe's political leaders are based. Since the Treaty of Rome in 1957, that ideological underpinning has been rooted in progressively lifting barriers to free trade and competition between member states, whilst protecting the rights of consumers in the process. This book argued that the EU in the 2010s was experiencing the crisis of a market-based system of European integration that had simply reached its limits. Market-based integration no longer provided an adequate ideological foundation behind decisions and policies to drive the EU forwards. This ideological vacuum was a significant contributor to the sense of crisis during the Eurozone's severe economic downturn. These two overarching, path dependence-based explanations were developed in Chapter 1, which looked at the current crisis in depth, and throughout Chapters 2 to 6. These arguments may be summarized in ten, interconnected points as follows.

The starting point was the proposition that the EU's crisis extended well beyond the travails of the Eurozone. Its deeper, path-dependent roots lay in decisions that were taken long before the financial crisis that began in 2007, the Great Recession and the sovereign debt crises. This point was not widely understood during the worst phase of the Eurozone crisis in 2010–12, when the narrow focus on what would be needed first to save the single currency and then to make it work effectively. An investigation into the profound depths of Europe's crisis helps to explain why it was little closer to meaningful resolution in the mid-2010s than it had been in 2007.

A second argument was that, even though the practical and ideological limits to a market-based European integration project appeared to have been reached, this did not mean that the time had come for the EU to retreat from free markets. Rather the conclusion to be drawn was broader: market-based integration by itself is not enough. In economic terms, in the mid-2010s there were choices to be made about the correction of Europe-wide market failures, such as how best to support low-yield, long-term investments in research, power generation, infrastructure, industry and training, to give a few examples. So long as Europe remained mainly concerned with free market competition and the lifting of barriers to accommodate this, economic decisions that required less of the free market and more strategic decision making through a Europe-wide industrial policy were not taken. The EU should not be afraid to learn from the economic models of its global competitors with more economically activist governments. In other words, a concern for ideological purity should not get in the way of good policy.

Thirdly, and following on from the path-dependent ideological underpinnings of the European integration project, is the point that whilst in theory the EU is about values and sees its peoples as citizens, in practice the EU is about markets and primarily sees its peoples as consumers. There is nothing intrinsically wrong in this approach, because extending consumer choice and protection are worthy aims. Yet its limits are increasingly obvious since the political affairs of a major polity-in-the-making extend beyond the protection of consumer rights. Here again, an exclusively market-based model will simply not suffice any longer, not least because it means that the European integration project has always tended, in technocratic fashion, to put the economics before the politics. Political integration, in other words, was driven by economic necessity. This was the heart of the 'Monnet method', but it is a way of doing business that had probably run its course by the mid-2010s. The reasons for this are legion. To begin with, many of the positivist assumptions that were made about the management of the economy between the eclipse of the Keynesian consensus in the aftermath of the 1973 Oil Crisis and the Great Recession were wrong-footed, as the financial crisis showed. Those who were responsible for managing the European and world economy (of which Europe is a big part) made a serious set of miscalculations. Their assumptions, as it turned out, were flawed. Humans are not simply rational actors capable of rapidly calculating costs and benefits. Even the chairman of the US Federal Reserve from 1987–2006, Alan Greenspan, admitted this in retirement (quoted in Tett, 2013). A similar and more human-centred trend had begun to emerge in the discipline of economics by the mid-2010s (Carlin, 2013). Moreover, even if integration through markets delivered benefits to consumers as a whole, many of the gains were not shared across European society, and inequalities have been on a steadily upward trend since at least the mid-1980s across the EU-15. An exclusive emphasis on the free market creates market failures that need to be addressed by government. An exclusively ideological focus on free markets by governments in turn creates what could be termed government failure. In the mid-2010s, the EU appeared to be suffering from both, which explains in some part the intractability of its existential crisis.

A fourth argument, that follows on from the way in which the EU has consistently put economics before politics, is that after more than half a century of European integration not one, but two, Europes had come into being. There are two, distinct European societies which transcend national barriers: the broad 'elite', which comprised 17–20% of Europeans by the mid-2010s, and everyone else. The elite community shared a common European identity, believed that it benefited directly from European integration and had a greater propensity to be politically Europhile in orientation (Fligstein, 2008; Risse, 2010). The other section of the 'two Europes' consisted of everyone else. This much larger group had either a very weak or non-existent bond to European identity and was not interested in either European politics or the EU. Unless this seemingly disenfranchised group could be persuaded to take more of an interest in the affairs of Europe's polity-in-the-making, the situation of drift and decline looked likely to continue.

Fifth, this volume has pointed to the deeper structural weaknesses that had been building up in Europe since the beginnings of the 1980s: widening inequalities, declining competitiveness, inadequate institutions and high levels of unemployment. A lasting solution to Europe's economic woes would need to address the European-level government of the Eurozone, the vulnerabilities that stem from the creation of free markets for capital and the harder-to-address deeper challenges that are connected to the regulation of labour markets and the sustainability of the welfare state. Such problems have to be tackled at both the European level and the national level. Urgent reform and action were needed in the mid-2010s to address problems of insecurity resulting from Europe's large financial sectors, to reform the institutions that govern the Eurozone, to ensure a sustainable yet equitable balance in the provision of welfare, and to restore and maintain competitiveness across the whole Single Market area. Without such action, in the medium to long term, the sustainability of the European model of capitalism and the relatively high living standards that it supports appeared endangered.

Yet, as is argued in a sixth point, the balance of opinion across much of the EU in the mid-2010s, and especially in France (which could be described as Europe's 'swing state'), seemed to have inadequate regard for the future. Public opinion in Europe still had not reached the point where it had begun to embrace the need for change. France in the 2000s and 2010s was by far the most illustrative and fascinating case study of this wider European trend. Here, as elsewhere, the need for change was understood at a theoretical, intellectual and, above all, elite level (Baverez, 2004, 2012; Goulard, 2013; Goulard and Monti, 2012; Heisbourg, 2013; Herzog, 2013), yet the preference of the French majority was for stasis and decline. Social and economic systems require periodical renewal and redesign, which may create short-term losses to be traded off against long-term gains. Resistance to the notion of such short-term losses runs very deep in 21st century Western Europe, as is best summed up by the concepts of social 'rights' or social '*acquis*' (Herzog, 2013). There is an implication that what has once been acquired can never be modified, let alone surrendered. After all, for many in France as in the rest of Europe, life remained too comfortable to accept the need for reform, particularly on the part of the labour market insiders with access to protected jobs, generous welfare payments, housing, education and so on who could not see the need for greater flexibility to promote the creation of jobs. In France, social peace between the insiders and the outsiders was bought by transferring 46% of what was produced by its extraordinarily productive labour market insiders to labour market outsiders (Le Boucher, 2013). In turn, this created a growing strain on the state budget, which in France, as elsewhere in Europe was seldom ever balanced (at the time of writing in 2014 the last budget surplus in France was for the fiscal year 1974 – some 40 years previously).

Few Europeans appeared to understand the significance of Tancredi's remark to Don Fabrizio in Lampedusa's *The Leopard*, 'If we want things to stay as they are, things will have to change'. In common with Don Fabrizio, many Europeans thought decline was preferable to change. There is a wider importance to the choice of France as a case study. France and French opinion mattered a great deal because, if the French position could be moved closer to that of Germany, Europe's 'reluctant hegemon' (Paterson, 2011), a Europe-wide consensus on serious reform would have appeared to be far easier to reach. Collective action at the European level could also make the short-term bitter effects of reform easier to stomach. The Eurozone crisis bears this argument out. It has only been in those states that were forced, either through participation in the 'programme' as a bailout recipient (Greece, Cyprus, Portugal, Ireland), or through the threat of having to join the bailout countries (Italy and Spain), that with the greatest reluctance reform efforts have been made. Yet such reforms were seen as an imposition coming from the outside. This could be overcome if France were to undergo a conversion to the cause of positive reform in the Nixon-going-to-China mould. If all of Europe was to be mobilized to reform at the same moment, the perception of unfairness and imposition would be lessened. In short, whilst some Europeans could see the need for reform, their commitment to it for the most part was theoretical or hypothetical. Most importantly, reform should not affect them. This is why it tended only to be kick-started when the metaphorical bailiff is hammering on the front door. When taken as a whole, this amounted to a government failure that matched the market failures in Europe's banking system which had led to the Great Recession.

The seventh point is that, if the governments of member states were failing and in denial about the need to carry out painful reforms to put their own houses in order, they were also in denial about what the substance of European integration meant for their own states and, at times, about its very existence. National politicians, civil servants and judges – even at a senior level – all too often displayed a wilful ignorance of Brussels and its workings. At times, they gave the impression of hoping that if they buried their heads, the whole European integration project would simply go away. This was demonstrated in, for example, their stubborn refusal to gain an understanding of the basic principles and workings of the EU system and how the game had changed since the Lisbon Treaty, or insisting on reworking old ground on issues long since settled (such as contesting the supremacy of EU law), or unpicking long-standing Europe-wide agreements. Such attitudes were anachronistic by the mid-2010s. In the 21st century, to be interested in your own nation's politics, but not EU politics, is akin to a farmer who feigns a lack of interest in the weather. Like the weather, the EU is simply present as a part of the political life of Europe and will impact on our lives and experiences whether we want it to or not. Unlike the weather, it may at least be influenced and engaged with in such a way that its future direction can change. A linked tendency is the way in which national parliaments, courts and governments persist in expressing preferences for contradictory objectives. They resent perceived EU encroachments on sovereignty but they want a strong and unified EU – albeit one with weak institutions. They want the fruits of reform without painful sacrifices. They want to take the full credit for the achievements of the EU and to blame it when things do not run according to plan. In short, they want to have their cake and eat it. Such cognitive dissonance was not limited to the government of semi-detached member states such as the United Kingdom. It could also be seen in the ruling of the German Federal Constitutional Court on the Lisbon Treaty, which (whilst it acquiesced to the treaty) found the EU lacking in democracy, since seats in the European Parliament are apportioned in a way that prevents the complete domination of the legislature by the MEPs of the largest handful of countries (Wohlfahrt, 2009). After nearly 60 years of the European project, it was surely time for national institutions to catch up with Europe's political reality as a polity-in-the-making.

The eighth point returns to the overarching theme of understanding the existential crisis of the 2010s as one of incomplete transition at both the EU and member-state level. Whilst this is most readily seen in the incompleteness of prevailing policies, institutions and structures in place to manage the economic and monetary union, there was an equally important national dimension as well. The negative effects of the crisis were experienced across the whole Union yet some states were hit far worse than others. Some economies proved more resilient and capable of bouncing back after the slump, and some member states were more effective than others in beginning to reform their welfare states to make them sustainable. I argued in the Introduction that this points to a necessarily crude, stylized dichotomy between three kinds of member states in the EU-28. First, there were the north-western European states (such as Sweden or Germany) with relatively strong, neutral and independent national institutions (parliaments, governments, bureaucracies, courts, relationships with social partners and so on), a fairly high degree of social cohesion and a higher concentration of industries located towards the technological frontier. Second, there were the Central European, post-Communist countries of Central Europe (such as Poland or Slovakia) whose youthful institutions were shaped by the firm hand of EU conditionality in the 1990s and 2000s and whose economies continue to benefit from catch-up growth as they converge, gradually, on West European levels of GDP per capita. Third, there were the states of Southern Europe whose institutions did not have to pass the exacting tests of pre-accession conditionality (such as Italy or Greece) and where EU membership did not involve a shake-up of long-standing patterns of clientelism and patronage. The comparative economic advantage formerly enjoyed by this third group of member states had been eroded by globalization and the outsourcing of lower-value-added production both to the emerging economies of the Far East *and* to Central and Eastern Europe. In addition, the third group found it exceptionally challenging to cope with the need for rigour imposed by Eurozone membership which removed the possibility of periodic devaluation as a means of preserving competitiveness *vis-à-vis* their trading partners. In simple terms, the thinking that lay behind the politics and economics of rigour in the Eurozone was about attempting to transform the southern group of member states into copies of the north-western states, whilst simultaneously the Central and Eastern Europeans were snapping at their heels (at current trends, Slovenia, Estonia, the Czech Republic and Slovakia will overtake Portugal and Greece in per capita GDP in real terms by 2015 – in PPP terms, some Central European countries had already done so by 2013, *The Economist*, 2013). Yet what remained absent was a demand for reform by the southern European group of states to match its supply by the European institutions and their fellow member states. It seemed likely that there could be no meaningful recovery in the Union as a whole until there was a full understanding of the sheer scale of the institutional transformation that was required in southern Europe, and indeed at the popular level in the French Fifth Republic, and a demand for reform to match it.

The ninth argument that runs throughout the book is that the case for pessimism or optimism on the future of the European integration project is dependent on one's standpoint. The view in this book, for all of the preceding doom and gloom, is an optimistic one. Much has been created through 60 years of European integration. The EU's two achievements by the mid-2010s were a polity-in-the-making and, alongside it, a European identity-in-the-making – which was no mean feat. Moreover, the EU delivered valuable benefits and public goods that were much appreciated by Europeans as consumers, even if they took them for granted most of the time. Institutionally, 60 years' experience had shown that Europe could achieve great things when it acted unanimously in the pursuit of a clear set of objectives with adequate resources in place to reach them. The problem of the crisis of the 2010s was that neither of these conditions had been met and in consequence there was no sense of the direction in which the Union should be heading.

The tenth argument is that, if the EU wished to overcome its existential crisis successfully, it had a number of important choices lying ahead of it in the 2010s. There was an urgent need to concentrate on fixing the Union from within, both at the European and the national level. The impetus for such change had to come from the member states themselves, a process made all the harder by the fact that, in addition to the common challenges outlined previously, there, quite naturally, remained a high degree of variation between them to which it is appropriate to return to briefly.

As described in the Introduction, the differing degree of severity with which the Great Recession and Eurozone crisis struck each member state reflected the strength of their various national institutions and the level of institutional and structural transformation that had taken place since 1990s when globalization's effects began to be felt. To recap, a dichotomy between three broad groups of member states was discernible: the North-Western member states, the Central European member states and the Southern member states. Globalization had put the same fundamental choice before all three: reform or decline. Their responses to this challenge varied hugely. Globalization was met with greater or lesser enthusiasm but also action in North-Western and Central Europe. However, the response of the Southern Europeans until the eruption of the crisis was inertia, born in part of political culture and in part of the credit boom from 1999–2007 that followed the introduction of the single currency. The imposition of harsh austerity policies on Southern Europe states in isolation did little to improve their long-term economic prospects and in the short term, its effects were ruinous. Southern Europe was kept afloat, and not permitted to default on what looked to be unsustainable levels of debt, less through a sense of pan-European solidarity, as more through the fear of the catastrophic repercussions that default would have on the integrated European (and world) banking sector. The crippling weakness of the EU as an incomplete polity-in-the-making was most obvious here: it could act in unison to treat the acute symptoms of disease, but the EU system as it was designed in the 2010s could not cure the patient. Merely keeping Southern Europe afloat also had profoundly damaging consequences for the North-Western and Central European member states. Until the economies of Southern Europe could be restored to health, there could be no wider return of full confidence (Hanke and Walters, 1991; Keynes, 1936) to the EU economy as a whole, confidence that was essential both for trade and the business investment that would be needed to drive economic growth. Thus for all of the variations between the detail of the member states' particular economic position and the narcissism of small differences that they inspired, by the 2010s their economies were so intertwined that they had to escape from the crisis together – or not at all.

In the absence of reform, it seemed quite probable in the 2010s that the Union could muddle through for many more years to come, although many observers had begun to question whether the treatment for the Eurozone crisis was worse than the disease itself (Heisbourg, 2013). The sense of frustration was palpable. Yet another symptom of the crisis was that, for the first time ever, a member state was contemplating the idea of leaving should reform prove impossible. The decision would be made by the UK government following a referendum and would be subject, not only to an attempted renegotiation of the terms of British membership, but also to the Conservative Party forming a majority government after the 2015 general election. David Cameron's speech was met domestically and within the EU as an announcement of an intention to quit the EU. However, when taken at face value, this was not the main thrust of the message which instead spoke of 'a positive vision for the future of the EU ... in which Britain wants ... to play a committed and active part'. He declared that he wanted 'the EU to be a success ... [and] a relationship between Britain and the EU that keeps us in it' (Cameron, 2013). The five principles on which reform of the Union should be based – competitiveness, flexibility, subsidiarity, accountability and fairness – chimed with the themes and challenges that underlie the choices for Europe in the 2010s and have been outlined in this book. Although some continental observers (Goulard, 2013; Heisbourg, 2013) generously suggested that David Cameron should be taken at his word, what was conspicuously lacking from his intervention on the future of Europe was credibility. The UK is not a member of the Eurozone, does not take part in the Schengen area of free movement, refused to take part in both the fiscal compact and Banking Union and, moreover, had played the role of an awkward partner within the EU (George, 1998) for more than 40 years. Just as would-be reformers of a socialist party need to wrap themselves in the red flag as they speak in favour of arms-length relations with trade unions and the benefits of the free market, it is only those who bear the most impeccable European credentials who are capable of making such an appeal for reform of the EU and radical change. The UK was emphatically not well-placed to lead the charge for reform in Europe. The appeals of the British Prime Minister seemed likely to fall on deaf ears.

In the Introduction, a parallel was drawn between the 2010s and what appeared to be a systemic crisis in the lost world of European Communism in the 1980s. Yet perhaps the momentous revolutions of 1989 were not the best point of comparison for the moment of decision that Europe faced in the 2010s. Reflecting on what was taking place in crisis-struck Europe in the 2010s, there may be clearer parallels with the twilight of European colonialism in the 1950s and early 1960s, following the disastrous Franco–British attempt to regain control of the Suez Canal in 1956. Then as now, the Europeans were experiencing the end of an era in world politics linked to transitions taking place beyond their borders and beyond their control (Goulard, 2013). Some of the actors of the day, such as Harold Macmillan and Charles de Gaulle, could see that both the idea and the practice of European authoritarian colonial rule were finished. Others could not. Where the comparison between the Europe of the 2010s and colonial society in Algeria (or Rhodesia) in 1960 becomes sharpest is that those resistant to change, when confronted with realistic choices, rejected all options in favour of what de Gaulle called '*L'Algérie de papa*'. Their preference was for a return to an agreeable, perhaps imagined, Arcadian past before all the bothersome and disagreeable troubles began – an option that was not on the table. Worryingly, this was the attitude of many Europeans to the crisis of the 2010s. The simple lesson that can be drawn from this little historical detour is that it is far better to make choices whilst choices remain. We now turn to the big picture of those choices.

The Choices for Europe

In essence, the new choices for Europe can be reduced to three interconnected elements: (1) a new project, narrative or vision for Europe in the 21st century on which everyone can agree; (2) the means to deliver this project effectively at the European and national level; and (3) a decision about how far this new project of European integration will extend.

Since the 1950s, two overarching public narratives have been put forward as a justification for the European integration project. The first was about promoting peace and prosperity in the aftermath of the Second World War against a background of a far smaller world economy that was far less open to trade than is the case in the 21st century. By the 2010s, war between European countries had become almost unimaginable and the EU was just one of many actors engaged in the promotion of free trade. Moreover, since the Great Recession (and arguably for some time before) the EU and many of its member states had demonstrably failed in their quest for prosperity. A second narrative of European integration was about 'reuniting Europe' following the revolutions of 1989. The process of drawing into the fold as many European countries as wanted to join the Union had been more or less completed by the 2010s, with only the small states of the Western Balkans in the queue for accession. Neither of the two West European refuseniks of Norway and Switzerland had convincing popular majorities in favour of joining the EU. With the process of reuniting Europe drawing to a conclusion, its power as a narrative for the EU waned. As the attractive power of these two narratives declined, the EU struggled to find a new message or rationale. It appealed to, and even appropriated as 'European', the values of democracy, human rights and the rule of law, but although they may be worthy aims, they did not seem to have much purchase with the peoples of Europe. The claim that 'unity is strength' rang true but was too vague to underpin the European integration project. Complementing these two public narratives that dealt essentially with the strategy of European integration was the tactic by which they were both to be achieved: removing the barriers to free trade between member states. By the time of the Eurozone crisis, the boundaries of this market-based European integration project had been reached.

What the European integration project needs in the 2010s is a common purpose; a project on which everyone can agree; a new vision. Bluntly, there is a need to decide what the EU is actually for. The goals of a re-launched European integration project must necessarily be broad and consensual enough to appeal directly to the peoples of Europe. The goals must also appeal to all three groups of member states: the North-Western European states; the relative newcomers of Central and Eastern Europe; and the southern member states that struggled so much in the Eurozone crisis. This is of particular importance given that the member states will always be the primary means by which shared European objectives are delivered. The cornerstone of the European integration project must be about sustainable and equitable prosperity, a point of even greater importance in the aftermath of the economic disasters following the 2007 financial crisis. Given the distance that exists between the preferences of Europeans for their social and economic model on the one hand and reality on the other, a significant part of this challenge must be about sharing the fruits of European integration more widely by reducing the social, economic and cultural gap that exists between the 'two Europes'.

In terms of diagnosis this amounts to a collective need to take market failure and government failure in Europe much more seriously. These twin failures stem from the same short-termist roots. In the private sector, short-termism results from the need to placate shareholders and banks. In the public realm, short-termism is dictated by the demands of the electoral cycle. The effects of both are equally pernicious. The most obvious long-term challenge that the EU faced in the mid-2010s was rebuilding Europe's economy, society and government to cope with the dramatic effects of a rapidly ageing population. This seemed likely to require a significant recalibration of the welfare state that would go beyond even the most ambitious plans in some member states (Finland or the UK, for example) to increase the retirement age to 68, extending perhaps as far as 75 if life expectancy continues to climb. A second element related to this was about increasing the productivity of the European economy. Here the most obvious gains were to be made in the service sectors of many member states. A third element was about increasing labour market participation levels significantly and finding ways to tackle the excessive unemployment that has affected Europe since the 1970s. These are just a few of the measures that needed to be undertaken, and to this list might also be added long-term investment in energy and power generation, research and development, education, training and particularly languages, especially if we wish to maximize the potential of free movement across the EU. What all of these areas for action shared was that they required significant, costly, steady and certain, long-term investment, the returns on which would be relatively small, distant and prone to problems of free-riding. Yet the risk involved in not making these investments was at best more of the same (which, as discussed, would be both intolerable for many and unsustainable) or, at worst, a further and increasingly vertiginous decline. For that reason what Loukas Tsoukalis (2014) termed a new 'grand bargain' needs to be struck. This process of reform goes well beyond Europe's current model of freeing markets wherever possible, important as that is, and is about taking market and government failure far more seriously. Rebuilding Europe's economy and society will be painful, but it would be far better to do this in partnership with all the member states of the Union than on the basis of one country acting alone.

What was also striking about the crisis of the 2010s was the relative lack of discussion about wider questions of system design in the model of free markets operating in liberal democracies. During the Great Depression of the 1930s, there had been much discussion about the ideal economic system: socialism or capitalism (Herzog, 2013). Since the fall of Communism and the demise of any serious challengers to the Western model of liberal democracy and the free market economy after 1989, there was much less debate about *system design*, even though in the aftermath of the Eurozone crisis Europeans were living through a period of what amounted to market failure and government failure. This is not to suggest a return to the follies of the planned economy – far from it – merely that more debate is needed about the big picture of the relationship between the long-term needs of economy and society, and what the role of the government should be in ensuring that they are met. Here there seemed most definitely a role for the EU in compensating for, and overcoming, the pressures of short-termism on the part of both markets and national governments.

Yet deciding what the EU is for must go beyond the economic or the instrumental. The fruits of European integration are not limited to purely material benefits, even if these are what we measure most frequently. In other words we need to return to the question posed by Tsoukalis (2003) about what kind of Europe we want. Sharing the gains of European integration also means spreading more widely the broad benefits of a European identity alongside a national, regional or local one and is about extending access to European culture and civilization to anyone who wants to take part. The most fundamental means by which that culture can be accessed is through language learning. Learning the languages that are spoken in other member states helps people to identify more closely with them and to better understand their perspective. It is also perhaps the best means of extending the proportion of Europe's peoples who identify with the integration project. Pragmatically, greater linguistic facility would also serve to promote the proper functioning of the Single Market and bring Europe a step closer to the mobility and efficiency of the US labour market. Finally, making multiple language learning a core part of the curriculum follows the same logic that we apply in insisting that all schoolchildren acquire a grasp of, say, physics or mathematics – not because we believe that most of them will have any use for simultaneous equations in their lives, but because it develops advanced cognitive function.

The second choice for Europe in the 2010s was about equipping this new European project with the means to deliver its objectives effectively at the European and national level. What is required here is (1) political will; that is a unity of purpose between the political and societal actors, combined with the appropriate powers to intervene and support in the case of government failure in one of the member states. This in turn necessitates (2) robust, modernized institutions equipped with (3) the resources, both financial in the form of a decent-sized budget, and human in terms of the scale and scope of the European civil service. Whilst money is only one element of this, the EU's common budget for managing its currency union and the largest economy in the world between 2014 and 2020 seemed deeply inadequate at around 1% of the total GDP of the EU-28 (a reduction on the period 2007–13). Compared with federal states on a (broadly) similar scale to Europe's 500 million people, the federal budget in India is 14% of GDP; 21% in Brazil and 24% in the US. Even the member states redistribute within themselves much more than the EU, with French disbursements between regions, departments and communes amounting to 4% of GDP (Heisbourg, 2013). It was observed in the Introduction that one of the perplexing features of the EU's member states in the 2010s was their cognitive dissonance in desiring to meet contradictory objectives – nowhere was this better illustrated than in the EU budget. Both the institutions and budget of the Union were insufficient for its purposes in the 2010s.

The third and final choice for Europe relates to the delineation of the final borders of the European integration project. By the mid-2010s, the EU appeared to be very close to reaching its geographical limits with a process of 'filling-in' to be completed as the six Western Balkan states of Albania, Bosnia-Herzegovina, Kosovo, Macedonia, Montenegro and Serbia join over the next 15–20 years. Ukraine, Turkey, Moldova and Georgia appeared much less likely to join what seemed to be a EU more closely focused on putting its own house in order than extending its borders. It also appeared unlikely at the time of writing (2014) that the EU presages a deeper, worldwide integration project. Indeed after the Eurozone crisis began, planned currency unions in east and west Africa, the monarchies of the Gulf States and the ASEAN countries were put on hold. Moreover, given the lacklustre performance of the ENP during its first decade, the idea of a Europe integration project spreading wider and wider appeared far-fetched. Responding to the short-term needs of the Eurozone crisis derailed the structural reform agenda spelt out in the Lisbon and EU 2020 Strategies and indicated that the EU was only capable of concentrating its attention on a limited number of projects at one time. The crisis proved the impossibility of extending the EU's competences, deepening integration and widening the membership of the Union at the same time (Heisbourg, 2013). Since there must be a trade-off, deepening integration and, where necessary, extending competences, or rather fixing the Union, took the front seat to enlargement.

Europe in the 2010s is standing on the threshold of a number of important choices. Making these choices is all the harder because, despite the backdrop of the Eurozone crisis, for many, life in Europe remains as good as it has ever been – and perhaps as good as it will ever be. Yet this sense of peacefulness is illusionary and Europe's decline will not remain gentle if matters continue as they have been. The mere fact that the choices for Europe are present and beginning to be understood does not mean that they will be taken. Many of the hardest choices are made not at times of extreme difficulty, when the opportunity cost is low, but at times of relative prosperity when the short-term opportunity cost appears high. At such moments there is a responsibility to make clear what the choices and their alternatives might be. It is to be hoped that this book has made a contribution to this process by providing a greater understanding of how the Great Recession and Eurozone crisis have radically changed the EU and why the case for reform is more pressing than ever before.

References

Aghion, M., Bertola, G., Hellwig, M, Pisani-Ferry, J., Sapir, A., Vinals, J. and Wallace, H. (2003) *An Agenda for a Growing Europe: the Sapir Report* (Oxford: Oxford University Press).

Aghion, M., Burgess, R., Redding, S. and F. Zilibotti (2008) 'The unequal effects of liberalization: evidence from dismantling the license raj in India', *American Economic Review*, 94(4), 1397–1412.

Aglietta, M. and Brand, T. (2013) *Un New Deal pour l'Europe* (Paris: Odile Jacobs).

Albert, M. (1993) *Capitalisme Contre Capitalisme* (New York: Four Walls Eight Windows).

Alderman, L. (2012) 'Greek government and public at odds over new cuts', *International New York Times*, www.nytimes.com/2012/09/06/business/global/greek-government-and-public-at-odds-over-new-cuts.html?_r=0, date accessed 21 November 2013.

Allen, D. (2012) 'The Common Foreign and Security Policy' in A. Menon, E. Jones and S. Weatherall (eds) *The Oxford Handbook of European Integration* (Oxford: Oxford University Press).

Allen, D. and Smith, M. (1990) 'Western Europe's presence in the contemporary international arena', *Review of International Studies*, 16(1), 19–37.

Allen, D. and M. Smith (2010) 'Relations with the rest of the world', *Journal of Common Market Studies*, 48 (annual review), 183–204.

Almond, G.A. (1960) 'Introduction: a functional approach to comparative politics' in G.A. Almond and J.S. Coleman (eds) *The Politics of Developing Areas* (Princeton: Princeton University Press).

Amable, B. (2003) *The Diversity of Modern Capitalisms* (Oxford: Oxford University Press).

Anderson, B. (1983) *Imagined Communities* (London: Verso).

Archives of the French Government (2008) 'Le Président de la République veut refonder le capitalisme', *Portail du Gouvernement*, www.archives. gouvernement. fr/fillon_version2/gouvernement/le-president-de-la-republique-veut-refonder-le-capitalisme.html, date accessed 8 November 2013.

Baily, M.N. and Kirkegaard, J.F. (2004) 'Transforming the European economy', *Peterson Institute for International Economics*, 353.

Baldwin, R. (2006) 'The Euro's trade effects', *European Central Bank Working Paper Series*, 594.

Baldwin, R. and Wyplosz, C. (2012) *Economics of European Integration* (Maidenhead: McGraw-Hill Higher Education).

Balfour, R. and Missiroli, A. (2007) 'Reassessing the European neighbourhood Policy', *EPC Issue Paper,* 54.

Bandow, D. (2013) 'The continent without a military', *The National Interest*, www.nationalinterest.org/commentary/the-continent-without-military-8152?page=1, date accessed 1 December 2013.

Bank of International Settlements (2013) *Consolidated Foreign Claims and Other Potential Exposures*, www.bis.org/statistics/r_qa1312_hanx9e_u.pdf, date accessed 9 May 2014.

Barber, T. (2010) 'The appointments of Herman van Rompuy and Catherine Ashton', *Journal of Common Market Studies*, 48 (annual review), 55–67.

Barth, F. (1969) *Ethnic Groups and Boundaries* (Long Grove: Waveland).

Bassin, M. and Kelly, C. (2012) *Soviet and Post-Soviet Identities* (Cambridge, Cambridge University Press).

Baverez, N. (2004) *La France qui Tombe* (Paris: Perrin).

Baverez, N. (2012) *Réveillez-vous!* (Paris: Fayard).

BBC (2007) 'The downturn in facts and figures', www.news.bbc.co.uk/1/hi/7073131.stm, date accessed 22 November 2013.

BBC (2011a), 'Eurozone debt web: Who owes what to whom?', www.bbc.co.uk/news/business-15748696, date accessed 22 November 2013.

BBC (2011b) 'Q&A: The Lisbon Treaty', www.news.bbc.co.uk/2/hi/europe/ 6901353.stm, date accessed 3 December 2013.

BBC (2014a) 'EU Election: France's Hollande calls for reform of "remote" EU', available at: www.bbc.co.uk/news/world-europe-27579235

BBC (2014b) 'Brussels too big and too bossy, Cameron tells EU leaders', 27 May 2014, available at: www.bbc.co.uk/news/uk-politics-27583545

Bechev, D. (2012) 'The periphery of the periphery: the Western Balkans and the Euro crisis', *ECFR Policy Brief*, 60.

Bechtel, M.M., Hainmueller, J. and Margalit, Y.M. (2012) 'Preferences for international redistribution: the divide over the Eurozone bailouts', *MIT Political Science Department Research Paper*, 2012–5.

Beck, U. (2013) *Non à l'Europe allemande: vers un printemps européen?* (Paris: Editions Autrement).

Beck, U. and Grande, E. (2004) *Der kosmopolitische Europa* (Frankfurt: Suhrkamp), Trans. 2007 *Cosmopolitan Europe* (Cambridge: Polity).

Beetham, D. and Lord, C. (1998) *Legitimacy and the European Union* (London: Longman).

Bellamy, R. and Castiglione, D. (2013) 'Three models of democracy, political community and representation in the EU', *Journal of European Public Policy*, 20(2), 206–23.

Bellamy, R. and Warleigh, A. (2001) 'Introduction: the puzzle of EU citizenship' in R. Bellamy and A. Warleigh (eds) *Citizenship and Governance in the European Union* (London: Continuum).

Benn, T. and Worcester, K. (1991) 'Europe's democratic deficit', *World Policy Journal*, 8(4), 739–53.

Bindi F. and Angelescu, I. (eds) (2012) *The Foreign Policy of the European Union* (Washington, DC: Brookings).

Biscop, S. (2013) 'Military power: what will Europe do?', *Ideas on Europe*, www.europeangeostrategy.ideasoneurope.eu/2013/05/26/military-power-what-will-europe-do/, date accessed 1 December 2013.

Biscop, S. and Whitman, R.G. (2013) *The Routledge Handbook of European Security* (London: Routledge).

Blair, T. (2005) *Press Conference at EU Informal Summit Hampton Court.*

Blitz, J. (2011) 'Hague says euro "burning building" claim correct', *The Financial Times*, www.ft.com/cms/s/0/5481e860-e9fb-11e0-b997-00144feab49a.html#axz-z2lIgw0f73, date accessed 21 November 2013.

Bloomberg Market (2013) 'Greece Govt Bond 10 year acting as benchmark', www.bloomberg.com/quote/GGGB10YR:IND/chart, date accessed 11 December 2013.

Bolleyer, N. and Reh, C. (2011) 'EU legitimacy revisited: the normative foundations of a multilevel polity', *Journal of European Public Policy*, 19(4), 472–90.

Bonesmo Fredriksen, K. (2012) 'Income inequality in the European Union', *OECD Economics Department Working Papers*, 952.

Börzel, T., Risse, T. and Levi-Faur, D. (forthcoming) *The Oxford Handbook of Comparative Regionalism* (Oxford: Oxford University Press).

Bowman, A. (2013) 'UK trails in march of the robots', *Financial Times*, www.ft.com/cms/s/0/a5220492-a838-11e2-b031-00144feabdc0.html?siteedition=uk#axzz2n-CoFYUD1, date accessed 11 December 2013.

Brada, J.C., Radlo, M.-J. and Bienkowski, W. (2008) *Growth versus Security: Old and new EU members' quests for a new economic and social model* (Basingstoke: Palgrave Macmillan).

Bradley, R.L. (2003), 'A letter to President George W. Bush' in J.M. Griffin (ed.) *Global Climate Change: The science, economics and politics* (Cheltenham: Edward Elgar).

Bretherton, C. and Vogler, J. (2006) *The European Union as a Global Actor* (Oxford: Routledge).

Briscoe, S. and Fray, K. (2010) 'Bubble, trouble, boom and bust', *Financial Times*, www.ft.com/cms/s/0/8d50c070-377e-11df-88c6-00144feabdc0.html#axzz2lIgw0f73, date accessed 21 November 2013.

Brittan, S. (1996) *Capitalism with a Human Face* (Cambridge, MA: Harvard University Press).

Broz, J.L (1998) 'The origins of central banking: Solutions to the free-rider problem', *International Organization*, 52(2), 231–68.

Brubaker, R. and Cooper, F. (2000) 'Beyond identity', *Theory and Society*, 29(1), 1–47.

Bruter, M. (2005) *Citizens of Europe? The emergence of a mass European identity* (Basingstoke: Palgrave Macmillan).

Burke, E. (1790/1951) *Reflections on the Revolution in France* (London: J.M. Dent).

Burnett, A. (2010) 'Brazil: sustained flight?', BBC, www.bbc.co.uk/blogs/theeditors/2010/03/brazil_sustained_flight.html, date accessed 30 November 2013.

Buti, M., Turrini, A., Van den Noord, P. and Biroli, P. (2008) 'Defying the "Juncker curse": can reformist governments be reelected?', *European Economy – Economic Papers*, 324.

Cameron, D. (2013) *The danger is that Europe will fail [speech]*, www.spiegel.de/international/europe/the-full-text-of-the-david-cameron-speech-on-the-future-of-europe-a-879165.html, date accessed 9 May 2014.

Carlin, W. (2013) 'Economics explains our world but economics degrees don't', *Financial Times*.

Castles, F. (2004) *The Future of the Welfare State: Crisis myths and crisis realities* (Oxford: Oxford University Press).

Charlemagne (2010) 'What makes Germans so very cross about Greece', *The Economist*, www.economist.com/blogs/charlemagne/2010/02/greeces_generous_pensions, date accessed 18 November 2013.

Chastand, J.-B. (2014) 'Fin des cotisations patronales pour des familles', *Le Monde*, www.lemonde.fr/emploi/article/2014/01/14/la-fin-des-cotisations-patronales-pour-les-familles-une-victoire-pour-le-medef_4348036_1698637.html, date accessed 9 May 2014.

Checkel, J.T. (2005) 'International institutions and socialization in Europe: introduction and framework', *International Organization*, 59(4), 801–26.

Checkel, J.T. and Katzenstein, P.J. (2009) *European Identity* (Cambridge: Cambridge University Press).

Churchill, W.S. (1950–1954) *The Second World War* (London: Casell & Co).

Cienski, J. (2013) 'Poland sees uptick in economy as spectre of recession fades', *Financial Times*, www.ft.com/cms/s/0/f06c0acc-1eb4-11e3-b80b-00144feab7de.html#axzz2lIgw0f73, date accessed 22 November 2013.

Connolly, R. (2012) 'The determinants of the economic crisis in post-socialist Europe', *Europe-Asia Studies*, 64(1), 35–67.

Connolly, R. (2013) 'Developments in the economies of member states sutside the Eurozone', *Journal of Common Market Studies*, 51 (annual review), 201–18.

Copsey, N. and Haughton, T. (2009) 'The JCMS Annual Review of the European Union in 2008', *Journal of Common Market Studies*, 47(sI).

Copsey, N. and Haughton, T. (2014) 'The JCMS Annual Review of the European Union in 2013', *Journal of Common Market Studies*.

Copsey, N. and Pomorska, K. (2010) 'Poland's power and influence in the European Union: the case of its eastern policy', *Comparative European Politics*, 8(3), 304–26.

Copsey, N. and Pomorska, K. (2013) 'The influence of newer member states in the European Union: the case of Poland and the eastern partnership', *Europe-Asia Studies*, 66(3), 421–43.

Coudenhove-Kalergi, R. (1923) *Pan-Europa* (Vienna: Pan-Europa Verlag).

Council of the EU (2003) *Council Conclusions (14492/1/03 REV 1)*, Brussels.

Council of the EU (2011a) *Draft Regulation of the European Parliament and of the Council on the Prevention and Correction of Macroeconomic Imbalances (7839/11)*, Brussels.

Council of the EU (2011b) *Draft Regulation of the European Parliament and of the Council on Enforcement Measures to Correct Excessive Macroeconomic Imbalances in the Euro Area (7840/11)*, Brussels.

Council of the EU (2011c) *Draft Regulation of the European Parliament and of the Council amending Regulation (EC) No 1466/97 on the Strengthening of the Surveillance of Budgetary Positions and the Surveillance and Coordination of Economic Policies (7843/11)*, Brussels.

Council of the EU (2011d) *Draft Regulation of the European Parliament and of the Council on the Effective Enforcement of Budgetary Surveillance in the Euro Area (7846/11)*, Brussels.

Council of the EU (2011e) *Draft Council Directive on Requirements for Budgetary Frameworks of the Member States (7847/11)*, Brussels.

Council of the EU (2011f) *Draft Council regulation (EU) No.../... Amending Regulation (EC) No 1467/97 on Speeding up and Clarifying the Implementation of the Excessive Deficit Procedure (7848/11)*, Brussels.

Council on Foreign Relations (2011) *Preventive Priorities Survey: 2012* (Washington DC).

Crouch, C. (1993) 'The future of employment in Western Europe: reconciling demands for flexibility, quality and security', *Twelfth Hitachi Lecture*, Sussex European Institute.

Crouch, C. (1997) 'The terms of the neo-liberal consensus', *Political Quarterly*, 68(4), 352–60.

Crouch, C. (1999) *Social Change in Western Europe* (Oxford: Oxford University Press).

Crouch, C. (2008) 'Change in European societies since the 1970s', *West European Politics*, 31(1–2), 14–39.

Cutler, R.M. (1992) 'International relations theory and Soviet participation in multilateral global-economic regimes: GATT, IMF and the World Bank' in D.A. Palmieri (ed.) *The USSR and the World Economy* (New York: Praeger), www.robertcutler.org/download/html/ch92dap.html, date accessed 1 December 2013.

Dahl, R. (ed.) (1966) *Political Oppositions in Western Democracies* (New Haven, CT: Yale University Press).

Dahl, R. (1989) *Democracy and its Critics* (New Haven, CT: Yale University Press).

Damro, C. (2012) 'Market power Europe', *Journal of European Public Policy*, 19(5), 682–99.

Deacon, B. (2000) 'Eastern European welfare states: the impact of the politics of globalization', in G. Standing and A. Jens (eds) *Europe in a Comparative Global Context* (Essex: Longman).

De Grauwe, P. (2006) 'What have we learnt about monetary integration since the Maastricht treaty?', *JCMS*, 44(4), 711–30.

De Grauwe, P. (2013) 'The political economy of the Euro', *Annual Review of Political Science*, 16, 153–70.

De Grauwe, P. and Moesen, W. (2009) 'Gains for all: a proposal for a common Eurobond', *Intereconomics*, May–June.

Delanty, G. (2006) 'The idea of a post-Western Europe' in G. Delanty (ed.) *Europe and Asia Beyond East and West* (London: Routledge).

Delanty, G. and Rumford, C. (2005) *Rethinking Europe: Social theory and the implications of Europeanization* (London: Routledge).

Delors, J. (chairman), Committee for the Study of Economic and Monetary Union (1989) *Report on Economic and Monetary Union in the European Community (Delors Report)*.

Delors, J. (2013) 'Economic governance in the European Union: past, present and future', *Journal of Common Market Studies*, 51(2), 169–78.

Denison, E.F. (1967) *Why Growth Rates Differ* (Washington: The Brookings Institution).

de Tocqueville, A. (1856) *L'Ancien Régime et la Révolution* (Paris).

Deutsch, K.W. (1957) *Political Community and the North Atlantic Area: International organization in the light of historical experience* (Westport, CT: Greenwood Press).

Deutsch, K.W. (1966) *Nationalism and Social Communication* (Cambridge: MIT Press).

de Vasconselos, A. (2010) *Quelle Défense Européenne en 2020?* (Paris: ISS).

Dietl, R. (2006) 'Towards a European third force? Reflections on the European political and security cooperation, 1958–1964' in C. Nünlist and A. Locher (eds) *Transatlantic Relations at Stake: Aspects of NATO 1956-1972* (Zürich: ETH).

Dinan, D. (2005) *Ever Closer Union: An introduction to European integration* (Boulder: Lynne Rienner).

Duchêne, F. (1972) 'Europe's role in world peace' in R. Mayne (ed.) *Europe Tomorrow: Sixteen Europeans look ahead* (London: Fontana).

Duchêne, F. (2008) 'Europe's role in world peace' in W. Rees and M. Smith (eds) *International Relations of the European Union* (London: Sage).

Durand, C. (ed.) (2013) *En Finir avec l'Europe* (Paris: La Fabrique Editions).

Duval, G. (2006) 'Directive services: le retour de Bolkenstein', *Alternatives Economiques*, 243, www.alternatives-economiques.fr/directive-services-le-retour-de-bolkestein_fr_art_196_22582.html, date accessed 30 October 2013.

Dyson, K. (2000) *The Politics of the Euro-zone* (Oxford: Oxford University Press).

Easton, D. (1965) *A Systems Analysis of Political Life* (New York: Wiley & Sons).

Economist, The (2011) 'IMF influence: light-weight BRICS', www.economist.com/blogs/dailychart/2011/06/imf-influence, date accessed 1 December 2013.

Economist, The (2013) 'Channel deep and wide', www.economist.com/news/special-report/21589229-britains-leaders-do-not-want-it-leave-eu-it-could-happen-any-way-channel-deep, date accessed 24 November 2013.

Economist, The (2014) German foreign policy, no more shirking. www.economist.com/news/europe/21595956-germany-ready-have-foreign-policy-proportionate-its-weight-no-more-shirking.

Edwards, G. (2011) 'The pattern of the EU's global activity' in C. Hill and M. Smith (eds) *International Relations and the European Union* (Oxford: Oxford University Press).

Eichenberg, R.C. and Dalton, R.J. (2007) 'Post-Maastricht blues: the transformation of citizen support for European integration,1973–2004', *Acta Politica*, 42(2), 128–52.

Eichengreen, B. (2012) 'Escaping the middle-income trap', *Achieving Maximum Long-run Growth: A symposium sponsored by the Federal Reserve Bank of Kansas City*, pp. 409–19, www.kansascityfed.org/publicat/sympos/2011/Eichengreen_final.pdf, date accessed 30 November 2013.

Eichengreen, B., Park, D. and Shin, K. (2013) 'Growth slowdowns redux: new evidence on the middle-income trap', *NBER working paper*, 18673, www. papers.nber.org/tmp/73706-w18673.pdf, date accessed 30 November 2013.

Elitok, S.P. (2013) 'Estimating the potential migration from Turkey to the EU – a literature survey', *HWWI Policy Paper*, 3–11.

Elliott, L. (2011) 'Global financial crisis: five key stages 2007-2011', *Guardian*, www.guardian.co.uk/business/2011/aug/07/global-financial-crisis-key-stages, date accessed 22 November 2013.

Ellman, M. (2007) 'The rise and fall of socialist planning' in S. Estrin, G.W. Kolodko and M. Ovalic (eds) *Transition and Beyond* (Basingstoke: Palgrave Macmillan).

Emerson, M., Balfour, R., Corthaut, T., Wouters, J., Kaczynski, P.M. and Renard, T. (2011) *Upgrading the EU's Role as Global Actor: Institutions, law and the restructuring of European diplomacy* (Brussels: CEPS).

Emmott, B. (2012) *Good Italy, Bad Italy: Why Italy must conquer its demons to face the future* (New Haven and London: Yale University Press).

Enzensberger, H.M. (2011) *Brussels, The Gentle Monster: or the disenfranchisement of Europe* (Chicago: University of Chicago Press).

EPC (2011) 'The implementation of the Lisbon Treaty one year on', *EPC report*, S04/11, Brussels.

Erhard, L. (1959 – trans. 1965) *La Prospérité pour Tous*, trans. F. Brière and F. Ponthier (Meaux: Plon).

Erzan, R., Kuzubas, U. and Yildiz, N. (2006) 'Immigration scenarios: Turkey-EU', *Turkish Studies*, 7(1), 33–44.

Esping-Andersen, G. (1990) *The Three Worlds of Welfare Capitalism* (Cambridge: Polity).

Eucken W. (1952/2004) *Grundsätze der Wirkschaftspolitik*, ed. by E. Eucken and K.P. Hensel (Stuttgart: UTB).

EurActiv (2005) 'Will Wallström's "plan D" revive the European dream?', www.euractiv. com/priorities/wallstroems-plan-revive-european-news-214772, date accessed 7 November 2013.

Eurobarometer (1971–2013) – see European Commission

European Central Bank (2012) *Technical Features of Outright Monetary Transactions (press release)*, Frankfurt.

European Commission (1971–2013) *Eurobarometer*, No. 79, 78, 76, 73, 71, 70, 68, 66, 64, 62.

European Commission (2000) *An Internal Market Strategy for Services (COM(2000)888)*, Brussels.

European Commission (2002) *Commission Opinion on the Existence of an Excessive Deficit in Portugal (SEC(2002)1117 final)*, Brussels.

European Commission (2007) *Commission Staff Working Document – The Single Market: Review of achievements (SEC(2007)1521)*, Brussels.

European Commission (2010) *What are the Main Consequences of the Failure of the Procedure on Budget 2011? (MEMO/10/585)*, Brussels.

European Commission (2011) *Global Europe 2050*, Brussels.

European Commission (2013a) *EU Agricultural Economics Briefs, No. 8*, July, www. ec.europa.eu/agriculture/rural-area-economics/briefs/pdf/08_en.pdf, accessed 11 August 2014.

European Commission (2013b) *Communication from the Commission to the European Parliament and the Council – Enlargement Strategy and Main Challenges 2013-2014 (COM(2013)700 final)*, Brussels.

European Commission (2013c) *Digital Agenda for Europe: Roaming*, www.ec.europa. eu/digital-agenda/en/roaming, date accessed 22 November 2013.

European Commission (2013d) 'Living standards in Europe and the importance of social investment', *Speech by László Andor*, www.europa.eu/rapid/ press-release_ SPEECH-13-161_en.htm?locale=FR, date accessed 22 November 2013.

European Commission (2013e) *MFF in Figures*, www.ec.europa.eu/budget/mff/ index_en.cfm, date accessed 18 November 2013.

European Commission (2013f), *Your Voice in Europe*, www.ec.europa.eu/ yourvoice/ consultations/index_en.htm, date accessed 30 October 2013.

European Commission, Economic and Financial Affairs (2013a) 'Overview of SCPs and national reform programmes', *Multilateral Economic Coordination and Surveillance*, www.ec.europa.eu/economy_finance/economic_governance/sgp/ convergence/index_en.htm, date accessed 22 November 2013.

European Commission, Economic and Financial Affairs (2013b) *Quarterly Report on the Euro Area*, www.ec.europa.eu/economy_finance/publications/qr_euro_area/, date accessed 22 November 2013.

European Commission, DG Trade (2013a) *Consultations*, www.trade.ec.europa.eu/ consultations/, date accessed 30 October 2013.

European Commission, DG Trade (2013b) *DG Trade Statistical Pocket Guide*, (Luxembourg: Publications office of the EU), www.trade.ec.europa.eu/doclib/ docs/2013/may/tradoc_151348.pdf, date accessed 26 October 2013.

European Commission, Secretariat General (2011) *Vademecum on Working Relations with the EEAS (SEC(2011)1636)*, Brussels.

European Commission, Secretariat General (2012) *Working Arrangements between Commission Services and the EEAS in Relation to External Relations Issues (SEC(2012)48)*, Brussels.

European Convention (2002a) *Discussion Paper on External Action (CONV 161/02)*, Brussels.

European Convention (2002b) *Summary Report of the Plenary Session (CONV 200/02)*, Brussels.

European Council (1993) *Conclusions of the Presidency (SN 180/1/93 REV 1)*, Copenhagen.

European Defence Agency (2011) *2010 Defence Data*, Brussels, www.eda. europa.eu/ docs/eda-publications/defence_data_2010, date accessed 1 December 2013.

European External Action Service (2013a) *EEAS Review*, Brussels.

European External Action Service (2013b) *Policies*, www.eeas.europa.eu/ policies/ index_en.htm, date accessed 1 December 2013.

European External Action Service (2013c) 'HR/VP Statement on EEAS Review', *Speech 13/530*, www.europa.eu/rapid/press-release_SPEECH-13-530_en.htm, date accessed 1 December 2013.

European Parliament (2014) *Results of the 2014 European Elections*, www. results-elections2014.eu/en/election-results-2014.html

European Stability Mechanism (2013) *Financial Assistance*, www.esm. europa.eu/ assistance/index.htm, date accessed 5 November 2013.

Eurostat (2011a) *External and intra-EU trade: A statistical yearbook – Data 1958–2010* (Luxembourg: Publications Office of the European Union).

Eurostat (2011b) *Migrants in Europe – A statistical portrait of the first and second generation* (Luxemburg: EU Publications Office).

Eurostat (2011c) *Total Fertility Rate 1960–2011*, www.epp.eurostat.ec.europa.eu/ statistics_explained/index.php?title=File:Total_fertility_rate,_1960-2011_(live_ births_per_woman).png&filetimestamp=20130129121040, date accessed 26 November 2013.

Eurostat (2013a) *Median Age of the Population*, www.appsso.eurostat.ec.europa.eu/ nui/show.do?dataset=demo_pjanind&lang=en, date accessed 26 November 2013.

Eurostat (2013b) *Old Age Dependency*, www.epp.eurostat.ec.europa.eu/tgm/table. do?tab=table&init=1&plugin=1&language=en&pcode=tsdde510, date accessed 26 November 2013.

Eurostat (2013c) *Old-age Dependency Ratio*, www.epp.eurostat.ec.europa.eu/genericurl/ product?code=tsdde510&mode=view, date accessed 26 November 2013.

Eurostat (2013d) *Total Employment*, www.appsso.eurostat.ec.europa.eu/nui/show. do?dataset=lfsi_emp_a&lang=en and *Total Unemployment*, www. appsso.eurostat. ec.europa.eu/nui/show.do?dataset=lfsa_ugan&lang=en, date accessed 26 November 2013.

Eurostat (2013e) *Unemployment Statistics*, www.epp.eurostat.ec.europa.eu/statistics_ explained/index.php/Unemployment_statistics, date accessed 26 November 2013.

Eurostat (2013f) *Projected Old-age Dependency Ratio*, www.epp.eurostat.ec.europa. eu/tgm/table.do?tab=table&init=1&plugin=1&language=en&pcode=tsdde511, date accessed 26 November 2013.

Eurostat (2013g) *General Government Deficit/Surplus*, www.epp.eurostat.ec.europa.eu/ tgm/refreshTableAction.do?tab=table&plugin=1&pcode=tec00127&language=en, date accessed 22 November 2013.

Evans, P., Reuschemeyer, D. and Skocpol, T. (eds) (1985) *Bringing the State Back In* (Cambridge: Cambridge University Press).

Fabry, E. (2013) 'Think global – act European: thinking strategically about the EU's external action', *Notre Europe – Jacques Delors Institute Studies & Reports*, 96.

Falkner, G. (2013) 'The JCMS Annual Review Lecture: Is the European Union losing its credibility?', *Journal of Common Market Studies*, 51(s1), 13–30.

Feldstein, M. (1997) 'The political economy of the European Economic and Monetary Union: political sources of an economic liability', *Journal of Economic Perspectives*, 11(4), 23–42.

Fioramonti, L. (2012) 'Is the EU a "better" global player? An analysis of emerging powers' perceptions' in T. Renard and S. Biscop (eds) *The European Union and Emerging Powers in the 21st Century* (Farnham: Ashgate).

Flam, H. (2003) 'Turkey and the EU: politics and economics of accession', *CESIFO Working Paper*, 893.

Fligstein, N. (2008) *Euro-clash* (Oxford: Oxford University Press).

Follesdal, A. (2006) 'The legitimacy deficits of the European Union', *Journal of Political Philosophy*, 14(4), 441–68.

Follesdal, A. and Hix, S. (2006) 'Why there is a democratic deficit in the EU: a response to Majone and Moravcsik', *Journal of Common Market Studies*, 44(3), 533–62.

Freeman, R. (2006) 'Labour market imbalances: shortages, or surpluses, or fish stories?', *Paper prepared for Boston Federal Reserve Economics Conferences – Global Imbalance – As Giants Evolve*, June 14–16 (Chatham, MA).

Gaffney, J. (2005) 'Highly emotional states: French-US relations and the Iraq war' in K. Longhurst and M. Zaborowski (eds) *Old Europe, New Europe and the Transatlantic Security Agenda* (London: Routledge).

Galbraith, J.K. (1973) *The Great Crash* (London: Hamilton).

Galbraith, J.K. (2001) *The Affluent Society* (New York: Houghton Mifflin).

Gallup (2014) 'EU leadership at record low in Spain, Greece', www.gallup.com/ poll/166757/leadership-approval-record-low-spain-greece.aspx, date accessed 9 May 2014.

Ganesh, J. (2013) 'Living standards are too big a problem for politicians', *Financial Times*, www.ft.com/cms/s/0/6c865cea-0a8b-11e3-aeab-00144feabdc0.html, date accessed 29 November 2013.

Gates, R. (2011) 'Reflections on the status and future of the transatlantic alliance', *Security and Defence Agenda: Policy Speech Report*, www.securitydefenceagenda.org/Contentnavigation/Activities/Activitiesoverview/tabid/1292/EventType/EventView/EventId/1070/EventDateID/1087/PageID/5141/Reflectionsonthestatusandfutureofthetransatlanticalliance.aspx, date accessed 1 December 2013.

Geddes, A. (2013) *Britain and the European Union* (Basingstoke: Palgrave Macmillan).

George, S. (1998) *An Awkward Partner: Britain in the European Community* (Oxford: Oxford University Press).

Gerring, J. and Yesnowitz, J. (2006) 'A normative turn in political science?', *Polity*, 38(1), 101–33.

Giddens, A. (2014) *Turbulent and Mighty Continent: What future for Europe?* (Cambridge: Polity Press).

Giegerich, B. and Wallace, W. (2010) 'Foreign and security policy: civilian power Europe and American leadership' in H. Wallace, M.A. Pollack and A.R Young (eds) *Policy-making in the European Union* (Oxford: Oxford University Press).

Giersch, H. (1985) *Euroscelerosis* (Kiel: Inst. fur Weltwirtschaft).

Giusti, S. and T. Penkova (2012) 'Ukraine and Belarus: floating between the European Union and Russia' in F. Bindi and I. Angelescu (eds) *The Foreign Policy of the European Union: Assessing Europe's role in the world* (Washington, DC: Brookings Institution Press).

Glyn, A. (2006) *Capitalism Unleashed: Finance, globalization and welfare* (Oxford: Oxford University Press).

Gnesotto, N. (ed.) (2004) *EU Security and Defence Policy: The first five years (1999–2004)* (Paris: EU Institute for Security Studies).

Gordon, P.H. (1997/98) 'Europe's Uncommon Foreign Policy', *International Security*, 22(3), 74–100.

Goulard, S. (2013) *Europe: Amour ou chambre à part?* (Paris: Flammarion).

Goulard, S. and Monti, M. (2012) *De la Démocratie en Europe. Voir plus loin* (Paris: Flammarion).

Government of the Netherlands News (2013) 'European where necessary, national where possible', www.government.nl/news/2013/06/21/european-where-necessary-national-where-possible.html, date accessed 7 November 2013.

Graham, D. (2009) 'Study shows high cost of German reunification: report', *Reuters*, www.reuters.com/article/2009/11/07/us-germany-wall-idUSTRE-5A613B20091107, date accessed 18 November 2013.

Grevi, G., Helly, D., and Keohane, D. (2009) *European Security and Defence Policy: The first 10 years (1999–2009)* (Paris: ISS).

Grevi, G., Manca, D. and Quille, G. (2005) 'The EU foreign minister: beyond double-hatting', *The International Spectator*, 41(1), 59–75.

Gros, D. (2012) 'A simple model of multiple equilibria and default', *Mimeo*, CEPS.

Gros, D. and Mayer, T. (2012) 'Liquidity in times of crisis: even the ESM needs it', *CEPS Brief*, 265.

Guibernau, M. (2013) *Belonging: Solidarity and division in modern societies* (Cambridge: Polity).

Haas, E.B. (1958/2004) *The Uniting of Europe: Political, social and economic forces 1950–1957* (Notre Dame: Notre Dame University Press).

Haas, E.B. (1961) 'International integration: the European and the universal process', *International Organization*, 15(3), 366–92.

Haas, E.B. (1964) *Beyond the Nation-State. Functionalism and international organization* (Stanford: Stanford University Press).

Haas, E.B. (1967) 'The "uniting of Europe" and the "uniting of Latin America"', *Journal of Common Market Studies*, 5(4), 315–43.

Haas, E.B. (1970) 'The study of regional integration: reflections on the joy and anguish of pretheorizing', *International Organization*, 24(4), 606–46.

Haas, E.B. and Schmitter, P.C. (1964) 'Economics and differential patterns of political integration: projections about unity in Latin America', *International Organization*, 18(4), 705–37.

Habermas, J. (1996) *Between Facts and Norms: Contributions to a discourse theory of law and democracy* (Cambridge, MA: MIT Press).

Habermas, J. (2006) 'Religion in the public sphere', *European Journal of Philosophy*, 14(1), 1–25.

Habermas, J. (2009) *Europe, the Faltering Project* (Cambridge: Polity Press).

Habermas, J. (2012) *The Crisis of the European Union: A response* (Cambridge: Polity Press).

Hall, B. (2010) 'Lagarde criticises Berlin policy', *Financial Times*, www.ft.com/cms/s/0/225bbcc4-2f82-11df-9153-00144feabdc0.html#axzz2mOwA9Wwj, date accessed 3 December 2013.

Hall, P.A. and Gingerich, D.W. (2009) 'Varieties of capitalism and institutional complementarities in the political economy: an empirical analysis'. *BJPS*, 39(3), 449–82.

Hall, P.A. and Soskice, D. (eds) (2001) *Varieties of Capitalism: The institutional foundations of comparative advantage* (Oxford: Oxford University Press).

Hanke, S.H. and Walters, A.A. (1991) *Capital Markets and Economic Development* (San Francisco: Institute for Contemporary Studies Press).

Hay, C. and Wincott, D. (2012) *The Political Economy of European Welfare Capitalism* (Basingstoke: Palgrave Macmillan).

Hayes-Renshaw, F., Van Aken, W. and Wallace, H. (2006) 'When and why the EU Council of Ministers votes explicitly'. *JCMS*, 44(1), 161–94.

Heisbourg, F. (2013) *La Fin du Rêve Européen* (Paris: Editions Stock).

Held, D. (1995) *Democracy and the Global Order: From the modern state to cosmopolitan governance* (Cambridge: Polity).

Herzog, P. (2013) *Europe, Réveille-toi!* (Paris: Editions Le Manuscrit).

Heseltine, M. (1989) *The Challenge of Europe: Can Britain win?* (London: Weidenfeld & Nicolson).

Hill, C. (2006) 'The European powers in the Security Council: differing interests, differing arenas' in K.V. Laatikainen and K.E. Smith (eds) *The European Union at the United Nations: Intersecting multilateralisms* (Basingstoke: Palgrave Macmillan).

Hill, C. and Smith, M. (2011) 'International relations and the European Union: themes and issues' in C. Hill and M. Smith (eds) *International Relations and the European Union* (Oxford: Oxford University Press).

Hix, S. (1996) 'IR, CP and the EU: a rejoinder to Hurrell and Menon', *West European Politics*, 19(4), 802–4.

Hix, S. (2008) *What's Wrong with the European Union and How to Fix it* (Cambridge: Polity Press).

Hodges, M. (1972) *European Integration: Selected readings* (London: Penguin).

Hodson, D. (2011) 'The Eurozone in 2010: "Whatever it takes to preserve the Euro"?', *Journal of Common Market Studies*, 49 (Annual Review), 231–50.

Hodson, D. (2013) 'The Eurozone in 2012: "Whatever it takes to preserve the Euro"?', *Journal of Common Market Studies*, 53 (Annual Review), 183–200.

Hoffmann, S. (1966) 'Obstinate or obsolete? The fate of the nation-state and the case of Western Europe', *Daedalus*, 95(3), 862–915.

Hoffmann, S. (1995) *The European Sisyphus: Essays on Europe 1964–1994* (San Francisco and Oxford: Westview Press).

Hopkin, J. and Blyth, M. (2012) 'What can Okun teach Polanyi? Efficiency, regulation and equality in the OECD', *Review of International Political Economy*, 19(1), 1–33.

House of Commons (1999) 'The Resignation of the European Commission'. Research Paper 99/32, available at www.parliament.uk/documents/commons/lib/research/rp99/rp99-032.pdf

Howorth, J. (2007) *Security and Defence Policy in the European Union* (Basingstoke: Palgrave Macmillan).

Howorth, J. (2012) 'Developing a grand strategy for the EU' in T. Renard and S. Biscop (eds) *The European Union and Emerging Powers in the 21st Century* (Farnham: Ashgate).

Hurrelmann, A. (2007) 'European democracy, the permissive consensus and the collapse of the EU Constitution', *European Law Journal*, 13(3), 343–59.

Ikenberry, G.J. (2011) *Liberal Leviathan: The origins, crisis and transformation of the American World Order* (Princeton: Princeton University Press).

IMF (2013a) *World Economic Outlook* (Washington DC: IMF).

IMF (2013b) *Net International Investment Position*, www.principalglobalindicators.org/default.aspx, date accessed 20 November 2013.

IMF (2013c) *Government Finance Statistics*, www.principalglobalindicators.org/default.aspx, date accessed 20 November 2013.

Inglehart, R.F. (1970) *Modernization and Postmodernization* (Princeton: Princeton University Press).

Institute for Fiscal Studies (2012) *Living Standards, Poverty and Inequality in the UK, 2012*. Available at www:ifs.org.uk/comms/comm124.pdf, date accessed 20 August 2014.

Jones, E., Menon, A. and Weatherill, S. (eds) (2012) *The Oxford Handbook of the European Union* (Oxford: Oxford University Press).

Jones, J. (2013) "The truth about Ukip supporters', *The Spectator*, www.blogs.spectator.co.uk/coffeehouse/2013/03/the-truth-about-ukip-supporters/, date accessed 8 November 2013.

Jørgensen, K.E. (2013) 'Analysing the performance of the European Union', in K.E. Jørgensen and K.V. Laatikainen (eds) *Routledge Handbook on the European Union and International Institutions: Performance, policy, power* (Oxford: Routledge).

Jørgensen, K.E. and Laatikainen, K.V. (eds) (2013) *Routledge Handbook on the European Union and International Institutions: Performance, policy, power* (Oxford: Routledge).

Jørgensen, K.E. and Wessel, R.A. (2011) 'The position of the European Union in (other) international organizations: confronting legal and political approaches' in P. Koutrakos (ed.) *European Foreign Policy: Legal and political perspectives* (Cheltenham: Edward Elgar).

Jupille, K. and Caporaso, J.A. (1998) 'States, agency and rules: The European Union in global environmental politics' in C. Rhodes (ed.) *The European Union in the World Community* (Boulder, CO: Lynne Rienner).

Keeler, J. (2005) 'Mapping EU studies: the evolution from boutique to boom field 1960–2001', *Journal of Common Market Studies*, 43(3), 551–82.

Kenen, P. (1969) 'The theory of optimal currency areas: an eclectic view' in R. Mundell and A. Swoboda (eds) *Monetary Problems of the International Economy* (Chicago: Chicago University Press).

Keynes, J.M. (1924) *A Tract on Monetary Reform* (London: Macmillan).

Keynes, J.M. (1936) *The General Theory of Employment, Interest and Money* (Cambridge: Cambridge University Press).

Kharas, H. and Gertz, G. (2010) *The New Global Middle Class: A crossover from West to East* (Washington: Brookings Foundation), www.brookings.edu/~/media/research/files/papers/2010/3/china%20middle%20class%20kharas/03_china_middle_class_kharas.pdf, date accessed 22 November 2013.

King, G., Keohane, R.O. and Verba, S. (1994) *Designing Social Inquiry: Scientific inference in qualitative research* (Princeton: Princeton University Press).

Kirchheimer, O. (1966) 'The transformation of Western European party systems' in J. LaPalombara and M. Weiner (eds) *Political Parties and Political Development* (New Jersey: Princeton University Press).

Kohl, H. (1990) *Chancellor Kohl's television address on the day the currency union took effect*, www.germanhistorydocs.ghi-dc.org/sub_document.cfm?document_id=3101, date accessed 22 November 2013.

Koutrakos, P. (2013) *The EU Common Security and Defence Policy* (Oxford: Oxford University Press).

Krieger, H. (2004) 'Migration trends in an enlarged Europe', *European Foundation for the Improvement of Living and Working Conditions*.

Krieger, H. and Maitre, B. (2006) 'Migration trends in an enlarging European Union', *Turkish Studies*, 7(1), 45–66.

Kupchan, C.A. (2012) *No One's World: The West, the rest and the coming global turn* (Oxford: Oxford University Press).

Larsen, P.T. and Giles, C. (2007) 'Bank of England to bail out Northern Rock', *Financial Times*, www.ft.com/cms/s/0/c6de12c8-6258-11dc-bdf6-0000779fd2ac.html#axzz2IIgw0f73, date accessed 23 November 2013.

Lawson, N. (2009) *An Appeal to Reason: A cool look at global warming* (London: Duckworth).

Le Boucher, E. (2013) 'La préférence française pour le déclin', *Slate.fr*, www.slate.fr/story/79805/france-preference-declin, date accessed 19 November 2013.

Lehne, S. (2012) 'The Big Three in EU foreign policy', *Carnegie Endowment for international peace paper*, www.carnegieendowment.org/2012/07/05/big-three-in-eu-foreign-policy/ck4c, date accessed 30 November 2013.

Lejour, A.M., de Mooij, R.A. and Capel, C.H. (2004) 'Assessing the economic implications of Turkish accession to the EU', *CPB Netherlands Bureau for Economic Policy Analysis*, 56.

Le Monde (2005) 'La directive Bolkenstein', www.lemonde.fr/europe/visuel/2005/05/18/la-directive-bolkestein_651394_3214.html, date accessed 30 October 2013.

Lequesne, C. (2012) 'Old versus new' in E. Jones, A. Menon and S. Weatherill (eds) *The European Union* (Oxford: Oxford University Press).

Leuffen, D., Rittberger, B. and Schimmelfennig, F. (2013) *Differentiated Integration: Explaining variation in the European Union* (Basingstoke: Palgrave Macmillan).

Lijphart, A. (1977) *Democracy in Plural Societies: A comparative exploration* (New Haven, CT: Yale University Press).

Lincoln, A. (1863) *Gettysburg address.*

Lindberg, L.N. and Scheingold, S.A. (1970) *Europe's Would-be Polity: Patterns of change in the European Community* (Englewood Cliffs, NJ: Prentice-Hall).

Lindley-French, J. (2007) *A Chronology of Europe Security and Defence 1945–2007* (Oxford: Oxford University Press).

Linz, J.J. and Stepan, A.C. (1996) 'Towards consolidated democracies', *Journal of Democracy*, 7(2), 14–33.

Lippert, B. (2008) 'European Neighbourhood Policy: many reservations – some progress – uncertain prospects', *Friedrich Ebert Stiftung International Policy Analysis.*

Longhurst, K. and Zaborowski, M. (2007) 'The new Atlanticist: Poland's foreign and security policy priorities', *Chatham House Papers* (London: The Royal Institute of International Affairs).

Lord, C. (2004) *A Democratic Audit of the European Union* (Basingstoke: Palgrave Macmillan).

Lowi, T.J. (1972) 'Four systems of policy, politics and choice', *Public Administration Review*, 32(4), 298–310.

Luce, E. (2011) *In Spite of the Gods: The strange rise of modern India* (London: Abacus).

Lukes, S. (2005) *Power: A radical view* (Basingstoke: Palgrave Macmillan).

Mahony, H. (2009) 'EU chooses unknowns for new top jobs', www.*EUObserver.com*, www.euobserver.com/9/29151/?rk=1, date accessed 19 November 2009.

Mahony, H. (2010) 'Resignation rumours', *EUObserver.com*, www.blogs. euobserver. com/mahony/2010/04/30/a-resignation, date accessed 1 May 2010.

Mair, P. (2013) *Ruling the Void: The hollowing of Western democracy* (London: Verso).

Majone, G. (1998) 'Europe's democratic deficit', *European Law Journal*, 4(1), 5–28.

Majone, G. (2005, 2009) *Dilemmas of European Integration: The ambiguities and pitfalls of integration by stealth* (Oxford: Oxford University Press).

Manners, I. (2002) 'Normative power Europe: a contradiction in terms?', *Journal of Common Market Studies*, 40(2), 235–58.

Marangoni, A.-C. (2008) 'Le financement des opérations militaires de l'UE: des choix nationaux pour une politique européenne de sécurité et de défense?', *College of Europe EU Diplomacy Paper*, 6.

Marangoni, A.-C. (2012) 'Personification of diplomacy? The faces of EU foreign policy' in D. Mahncke and S. Gstöhl (eds) *European Union Diplomacy: Coherence, unity and effectiveness* (Brussels: PIE Peter Lang).

Marangoni, A.-C. (2013) 'Coordination of external policies: feudal fiefdoms to coordinate' in A. Boening, J.-F. Kremer and A. van Loon (eds) *Global Power Europe, vol. I* (Heidelberg: Springer).

March, J.G. and Olsen, J. (1989) *Rediscovering Institutions: The organizational basis of politics* (New York: Free Press).

Marks, G., Hooghe, L. and Blank, K. (1996) 'European integration since the 1980s: state-centric versus multi-level governance', *Journal of Common Market Studies*, 34(4), 341–78.

Marks, G., Scharpf, F., Schmitter, P. and Streeck, W. (1996) *Governance in the European Union* (London: Sage).

Marquand, D. (2011) *The End of the West: The once and future Europe* (Princeton and Oxford: Princeton University Press).

Marsh, D. (1992) *The Bundesbank: The bank that rules Europe* (London: Heinemann).

Marsh, D. (2009) *The Euro – The politics of the new global currency* (New Haven and London: Yale University Press).

Marsh, D. (2013) *Europe's Deadlock* (New Haven and London: Yale University Press).

Marsh, S. and Rees, W. (2012) *The European Union in the Security of Europe: From Cold War to Terror War* (London: Routledge).

Marshall, T.H. (1950) 'Citizenship and social class', *Citizenship and Social Class and Other Essays* (Cambridge: Cambridge University Press).

Martinelli, A. *et al.* (eds) (2007) *Transatlantic Divide: Comparing American and European society* (Oxford: Oxford University Press).

Marx, K. (1875/1970) *Critique of the Gotha Programme* (Moscow: Progress Publishers).

Mau, S. and Burkhardt, C. (2009) 'Migration and welfare state solidarity in Western Europe', *Journal of European Social Policy*, 19(3), 213–29.

Mayer, F. and Palmowski, J. (2004) 'European identities and the EU – the ties that bind the peoples of Europe', *Journal of Common Market Studies*, 42(3), 573–98.

Mayhew, A. (1998) *Recreating Europe: The European Union's policy towards Central and Eastern Europe* (Cambridge: Cambridge University Press).

Mazower, M. (1998) *Dark Continent: Europe's twentieth century* (London: Penguin).

Mazzucelli, C. (2007) 'The French rejection of the European Constitutional Treaty: Implications of a national debate for Europe's Union', *EUMA Papers*, 7(13).

McCormick, J. (2008) *The European Union: Politics and policies* (Boulder, CO: Westview).

McCormick, J. (2013) *Why Europe Matters: The case for the European Union* (Basingstoke: Palgrave Macmillan).

McKinnon, R. (1963) 'Optimal currency areas', *American Economic Review*, 53(4), 717–25.

McNamara, K.R. (2002) 'Rational fictions: central bank independence and the social logic of delegation', *West European Politics*, 25(1), 47–76.

Menon, A. (2008) *Europe: The state of the Union* (London: Atlantic Books).

Menon, A. (2014) 'Divided and declining: Europe in a changing world' in N. Copsey and T. Haughton (eds) *The Journal of Common Market Studies Annual Review of the European Union in 2013* (Oxford: Wiley).

Merkel, A. (2009) *Humboldt-Rede zu Europa*, www.grahnlaw.blogspot.co.uk/2009/05/merkels-germany-european-union.html, date accessed 18 November 2013.

Merlingen, M. and Ostrauskaité, R. (eds) (2008) *European Security and Defence Policy: An implementation perspective* (London: Routledge).

Merritt, G. (2009) 'Le Royaume-Uni et la France doivent s'impliquer dans le service diplomatique, sinon c'est mort', *Bruxelles2*, www.bruxelles2.over-blog.com/article-gilles-merritt-britanniques-et-fran-ais-doivent-s-impliquer-dans-le-service-diplomatique-40361686.html, date accessed 18 November 2013.

Meunier, S. and Nicolaïdis, K. (2006) 'The European Union as a conflicted trade power', *Journal of European Public Policy*, 13(6), 906–25.

Milward, A. (1992) *The European Rescue of the Nation-State* (London: Routledge).

Mitrany, D. (1944) *A Working Peace System: An argument for the functional development of international organisation* (Oxford: Oxford University Press).

Monnet, J. (1978) *Memoirs* (New York: Doubleday).

Moravcsik, A. (1991) 'Negotiating the single European Act: national interests and conventional statecraft in the European community', *International Organization*, 45(1), 19–56.

Moravcsik, A. (1993) 'Preferences and power in the European community: a liberal intergovernmentalist approach', *JCMS*, 31(4), 473–523.

Moravcsik, A. (1998) *The Choice for Europe: Social purpose and state power from Messina to Maastricht* (Ithaca, NY: Cornell UP).

Moravcsik, A. (2002) 'Reassessing legitimacy in the European Union', *Journal of Common Market Studies*, 40(4), 603–24.

Moravcsik, A. (2008) 'The myth of Europe's democratic deficit', *Intereconomics*, 43(6), 331–40.

Mundell, R.A. (1961) 'A theory of optimal currency areas', *American Economic Review*, 51(4), 657–65.

Myrdal, S. and Rhinard, M. (2010) 'The European Union's solidarity clause: empty letter or effective tool?', *UI Occasional Papers*, no.2, www.sipri.org/research/security/old-pages/euroatlantic/eu-seminar/documentation/2010_Myrdal%20Rhinard_EU%20Solidarity%20Clause_UIOP.pdf, date accessed 18 November 2013.

NatCen (2011) *Support for Scottish independence at six year high, but economic concerns still to be overcome*, www.nuffieldfoundation.org/news/support-scottish-independence-six-year-high-economic-concerns-still-be-overcome, date accessed 21 November 2011.

Neunreither, K. (2000) 'Political representation in the European Union: a common whole, various wholes or just a whole?' in K. Neunreither and A. Wiener (eds) *European Integration after Amsterdam* (Oxford: Oxford University Press).

Newport, F. (2013) 'Majority in US want wealth more evenly distributed', *Gallup politics*, www.gallup.com/poll/161927/majority-wealth-evenly-distributed.aspx, date accessed 22 November 2013.

Newton, I. (1676) *Letter to Robert Hooke.*

Nicolaïdis, K.A. and Whitman, R.G. (eds) (2013) 'European Union and normative power: assessing the decade', *Cooperation and Conflict*, 47(2), special issue.

Niemann, A. (2012) 'The Common Commercial Policy: from Nice to Lisbon' in F. Laursen (ed.) *The EU's Lisbon Treaty: Institutional choices and implementation*, (Farnham: Ashgate).

North, D.C. (1990) *Institutions, Institutional Change and Economic Performance* (Cambridge: Cambridge University Press).

Noutcheva, G., Pomorska, K. and Bosse, G. (2013) *The EU and its Neighbours: Values versus security in European foreign policy* (Manchester: Manchester University Press).

Nye, J.S. (2004) *Soft Power: The means to succeed in world politics* (New York: Public Affairs).

Nye, J.S. (2008) *The Powers to Lead* (Oxford: Oxford University Press).

Nye, J.S. (2011) *The Future of Power* (New York: Public Affairs).

OECD (2011) *OECD Economic Outlook*, vol. 2011/2 (OECD Publishing).

OECD (2012a) 'Household disposable income' in *OECD Factbook 2011-2012: Economic, environmental and social statistics*, www.oecd-ilibrary.org/sites/factbook-2011-en/03/02/02/index.html;jsessionid=f7npbascf7ks.delta?ontentType=/ns/StatisticalPublication%2C/ns/Chapter&itemId=/content/chapter/factbook-2011-21-en&containerItemId=/content/serial/18147364&accessItemIds=&mimeType=text/html, date accessed 21 November 2013.

OECD (2012b) *Europe: Health at a glance*, www.oecd-ilibrary.org/sites/9789264183896-en/02/06/g2-06-02.html?contentType=/ns/StatisticalPublication,/ns/Chapter&itemId=/content/chapter/9789264183896-25-en&containerItemId=/content/serial/23056088& accessItemIds=&mimeType=text/html, date accessed 21 November 2013.

OECD (2013a) *Background Document on public consultation*, www.oecd.org/mena/governance/36785341.pdf, date accessed 30 October 2013.

OECD (2013b) 'Producer support estimates (subsidies)', *Agriculture and Food: Key tables from OECD*, No.1, www.oecd-ilibrary.org/content/table/20755104-table1, date accessed 30 October 2013.

Offe, C. and Preuss, U. (2006) 'The problem of legitimacy in the European polity: is democratization the answer?' in C. Crouch and W. Streeck (eds) *The Diversity of Democracy: Corporatism, social order and political conflict* (Cheltenham: Edward Elgar).

Olsen, J.P. (2007) *Europe in Search of Political Order: An institutional perspective on unity/diversity, citizens/their helpers, democratic design/historical drift, and the co-existence of orders* (Oxford: OUP).

Olson, M. (1965) *The Logic of Collective Action: Public goods and the theory of groups* (Cambridge, MA: Harvard University Press).

Olson, M. (1982) *The Rise and Decline of Nations: Economic growth, stagflation and social rigidities* (New Haven, CT: Yale University Press).

Ortega y Gasset, J. (1929) *The Revolt of the Masses* (pub. 1994 by W.W. Norton).

Outhwaite, W. (2008) *European Society* (Cambridge: Polity Press).

Parsons, C. (2002) 'Showing ideas as causes: the origins of the European Union', *International Organization*, 56(1), 47–84.

Paterson, W.E. (2011) 'The reluctant hegemon? Germany moves centre stage in the European Union', *Journal of Common Market Studies*, 49(AR), 59–77.

Pawlak, J. (2013) 'EU revives membership talks with Turkey after three-year hiatus', *Reuters*, www.reuters.com/article/2013/10/22/us-eu-turkey-idUSBRE99L0L720131022, date accessed 29 November 2013.

Peel, Q. (2012) 'Merkel warns on cost of welfare', *Financial Times*, 16 December 2012, www.ft.com/cms/s/0/8cc0f584-45fa-11e2-b7ba-00144feabdc0.html#axzz33PPrLEhS.

Pettit, P. (2001) 'Political democracy and the case for depoliticizing government'. *University of NSW Law Journal*, 58.

Pew Research Centre (2013a) www.pewresearch.org, date accessed 5 November 2013.

Pew Research Centre (2013b) 'Chapter 4: Regional breakdowns' in *Global Attitudes Project*, www.pewglobal.org/2013/05/23/chapter-4-regional-breakdowns/, date accessed 21 November 2013.

Pierson, P. (1995) 'Fragmented welfare states: federal institutions and the development of social policy'. *Governance*, 8(4), 449–78.

Pierson, P. (1996) 'The path to European integration: a historical institutionalist analysis', *Comparative Political Studies*, 29(2), 123–63.

Pierson, P. (2001) *The New Politics of the Welfare State* (Oxford: Oxford University Press).

Piketty, T. (2014) *Capital in the Twenty-first Century* (Cambridge, MA: Harvard University Press).

Pinker, S. (2012) 'Violence: clarified', *Science*, 338(6105), 327.

Piodi, F. (2012) 'Le long chemin vers l'Euro', *Les Cahiers du CARDOC* (Luxembourg: EUR-OP).

Piris, J.-C. (2011) *The Future of Europe: Towards a two-speed EU?* (Cambridge, Cambridge University Press).

Pisani-Ferry, J. (2009) 'The accidental player: the European Union and the global economy', in K.E. Jørgensen (ed.) *The European Union and International Organizations* (London: Routledge).

Popper, K. (1957) *The Poverty of Historicism* (London: Routledge).

Przeworski, A. and Teune, H. (1982) *The Logic of Comparative Social Inquiry* (Malabar: Krieger).

Rachman, G. (2008) 'Irrelevance, Europe's logical choice', *Financial Times*, www.ft.com/cms/s/0/ae49f83a-25a3-11dd-b510-000077b07658.html#axzz2eIu8PS8z, date accessed 3 December 2013.

Rees, W. and Aldrich, R.J. (2008) 'Contending cultures of counterterrorism: Transatlantic divergence or convergence?' in W. Rees and M. Smith (eds) *International Relations of the European Union* (London: Sage).

Rees, W. and Smith, M. (eds) (2008) *International Relations of the European Union* (London: Sage).

Reif, K. and Schmitt, H. (1980) 'Nine second-order national elections: a conceptual framework for the analysis of European election results', *European Journal of Political Research*, 8(1), 3–44.

Rehn, O. (2011) 'EU's new "six-pack" shows just how tough Europe will be on national governments', *Telegraph*, www.telegraph.co.uk/finance/ comment/8839697/EUs-new-six-pack-shows-just-how-tough-Europe-will-be-on-national-governments.html, date accessed 21 November 2013.

Renan, E. (1882) *Qu'est ce qu'une Nation?* (Paris: Lévy).

Renard, T. and Biscop, S. (2012a) 'Conclusion: from global disorder to an effective multilateral order – an agenda for the EU' in T. Renard and S. Biscop (eds) *The European Union and Emerging Powers in the 21st Century* (Farnham: Ashgate).

Renard, T. and Biscop, S. (eds) (2012b) *The European Union and Emerging Powers in the 21st Century* (Farnham: Ashgate).

Rettman, A. (2010a) 'US welcomes EU's new foreign policy powers', www. *EUObserver.com*, www.euobserver.com/9/29322/?rk=1, date accessed 22 January 2010.

Rettman, A. (2010b) 'Game, set and match to Ashton on diplomatic hearings', www. *EUObserver.com*, www.euobserver.com/9/31120/?rk=1, date accessed 20 November 2011.

Rhodes, M. (2010) 'Employment policy: between efficacy and experimentation' in H. Wallace, M.A. Pollack and A.R. Young (eds) *Policy-making in the European Union* (Oxford: Oxford University Press).

Risse, T. (2005) 'Neo-functionalism, European identity, and the puzzles of European integration', *Journal of European Public Policy*, 12(2), 291–309.

Risse, T. (2010) *A Community of Europeans? Transnational identities and public spheres* (Ithaca and London: Cornell University Press).

Risse-Kappen, T. (2008) 'Exploring the nature of the beast: international relations theory and comparative policy analysis meet the European Union', *Journal of Common Market Studies*, 34(1), 53–80.

Rosamond, B. (1995) 'Mapping the European condition: the theory of integration and the integration of theory', *European Journal of international Relations*, 1(3), 391–405.

Rosamond, B. (2000) *Theories of European Integration* (Basingstoke: Palgrave).

Rosamond, B. (2007) 'European integration and the social science of EU studies: the disciplinary politics of a sub-field', *International Affairs*, 83(2), 231–52.

Rosamond, B. (2008) 'Open political science, methodological nationalism and European Union studies', *Government and Opposition*, 43(4), 599–612.

Rosenau, J. (1995) *Thinking Theory Thoroughly: Coherent approaches to an incoherent world* (Boulder, CO: Westview).

Ruiz Jiménez, A.M. *et al.* (2004) 'European and national identities in EU's old and new member states: ethnic, civic, instrumental and symbolic components', *European Integration Online Papers (EIoP)*, 8/11, www.eiop.or.at/eiop/texte/2004-011a. htm, date accessed 20 November 2013.

Sachs, J. (1990) 'Eastern Europe's economies – What is to be done?', *The Economist*, www.economist.com/node/13002085, date accessed 22 November 2013.

Sachs, J. (1994) *Poland's Jump to the Market Economy* (Cambridge: MIT Press).

Sandholtz, W. and Stone Sweet, A. (2012) 'Neo-functionalism and supranational governance' in E. Jones, A. Menon and S. Weatherill (eds) *The Oxford Handbook of the European Union* (Oxford: Oxford University Press).

Sandholtz, W. and Zysman, J. (1989) '1992: recasting the European bargain', *World Politics*, 42(1), 95–128.

Saxer, M. (2012) 'Multilateralism in crisis? Global governance in the 21st century' in T. Renard and S. Biscop (eds) *The European Union and Emerging Powers in the 21st Century* (Farnham: Ashgate).

Scharpf, F.W. (1988) 'The joint decision trap: lessons from German federalism and European integration', *Public Administration*, 66, 239–78.

Scharpf, F.W. (1991) *Crisis and Choice in European Social Democracy* (Ithaca: Cornell University Press).

Scharpf, F.W. (1994) 'Community and autonomy. Multilevel policy-making in the European Union', *Journal of European Public Policy*, 1, 219–42.

References 249

Scharpf, F.W. (1999) *Governing in Europe: Effective and democratic?* (Oxford: Oxford University Press).

Scharpf, F.W. (2001) 'Democratic legitimacy under conditions of regulatory competition. Why Europe differs from the United States' in K. Nicolaïdis and R. Howse (eds) *The Federal Vision: Legitimacy and levels of governance in the United States and the European Union* (New York: Oxford University Press).

Scharpf, F.W. (2002) 'The European social model: coping with the challenges of diversity', *Journal of Common Market Studies* 40(4), 645–70.

Shaw, J. (2000) 'Constitutional settlements and the citizen after the Treaty of Amsterdam' in K. Neunreither and A. Wiener (eds) *European Integration After Amsterdam* (Oxford: Oxford University Press).

Schimmelfenning, F. and Sedelmeier, U. (eds) (2005), *The Politics of European Union Enlargement: Theoretical approaches* (London: Routledge).

Schmidt, V.A. (2002) *The Futures of European Capitalism* (Oxford: Oxford University Press).

Schmidt, V.A. (2004) 'The European Union: democratic legitimacy in a regional state?', *Journal of Common Market Studies*, 42(5), 975–97.

Schmidt, V.A. (2006, 2009) *Democracy in Europe: The EU and national polities* (Oxford: Oxford University Press).

Schmidt, V.A. (2013) 'Democracy and legitimacy in the European Union revisited: input, output *and* 'throughput'', *Political Studies*, 61(1), 2–22.

Schmitter, P.C. (1996) 'Examining the present Euro-polity with the help of past theories' in G. Marks, F. Scharpf, P.C. Schmitter and W. Streeck (eds) *Governance in the European Union* (London: Sage).

Schuman, R. (1950) *La Déclaration Schuman du 9 Mai 1950*, www.europa.eu/about-eu/basic-information/symbols/europe-day/schuman-declaration/index_fr.htm, date accessed 1 December 2013.

Schweller, R. (2006) *Unanswered Threats: Political constraints on the balance of power* (Princeton, NJ: Princeton University Press).

Sedivy, J. and Zaborowski, M. (2005) 'Old Europe, new Europe and transatlantic relations' in K. Longhurst and M. Zaborowski (eds) *Old Europe, New Europe and the Transatlantic Security Agenda* (London: Routledge).

Serrano de Haro, P.A. (2012) 'Participation of the EU in the work of the UN: General Assembly resolution 65/276', *CLEER Working Papers*, 4.

Shafer, B. (2002) 'The US elections, November 2000', *Electoral Studies*, 21(3), 511–19.

Shore, C. (2000) *Building Europe: The cultural politics of European integration* (London: Routledge).

SIPRI (2013) *Military Expenditure Database*, www.sipri.org/research/armaments/milex/milex_database/milex_database, date accessed 1 December 2013.

Skinner, Q. (1978) *The Foundations of Modern Political Thought* (Cambridge: Cambridge University Press).

Smith, A. (1776) *The Wealth of Nations – An inquiry into the nature and causes of the wealth of nations* (London: W. Strahan & T. Cadell).

Smith, K.E. (2011) 'Enlargement, the neighbourhood and European order' in C. Hill and M. Smith (eds) *International Relations and the European Union* (Oxford: Oxford University Press).

Smith, M.L. and Stirk, P.M.R. (eds) (1990) *Making the New Europe: European unity and the Second World War* (London: Pinter).

Solana, J. (2004) 'Preface' in N. Gnesotto (ed.) *EU Security and Defence Policy: The first five years (1999–2004)* (Paris: EU Institute for Security Studies).

Spiegel (2011) 'If the Euro fails, Europe fails: Merkel says EU must be bound closer together', www.spiegel.de/international/germany/if-the-euro-fails-europe-fails-merkel-says-eu-must-be-bound-closer-together-a-784953.html, date accessed 9 May 2014.

Staar, R.F. (ed.) (1991) *East-Central Europe and the USSR* (Basingstoke: Macmillan).

Stiglitz, J.E. (2009) 'The anatomy of a murder: who killed America's economy?' *Critical Review*, 21(2), 329–39.

Stjernø, S. (2005) *Solidarity in Europe: The history of an idea* (Cambridge: Cambridge University Press).

Stoker, G. (1995) 'Introduction' in D. Marsh and G. Stoker (eds) *Theory and Methods in Political Science* (Basingstoke: Palgrave).

Stone Sweet, A., Sandholtz, W. and Fligstein, N. (2001) *The Institutionalization of Europe* (Oxford: Oxford University Press).

Streeck, W. (2013) 'Les marchés et les peuples: capitalisme démocratique et intégration Européenne' in C. Durand (ed.) *En Finir avec l'Europe* (Paris: La Fabrique Editions).

Szczerbiak, A. (2008) 'The birth of a bipolar party system or a referendum on a polarizing government? The October 2007 Polish parliamentary election', *Journal of Communist Studies and Transition Politics*, 24(3), 415–43.

Tallberg, J. (2008) 'Bargaining power in the European Council', *Journal of Common Market Studies*, 46(3), 685–708.

Taggart, P. (2013) *Questions of Europe: The domestic politics of the 2005 French and Dutch referendums and their challenge for the study of European integration*, www.web.clas.ufl.edu/users/kreppel/jmwkshp2006/Taggart.pdf, date accessed 3 December 2013.

Taggart, P. and Szczerbiak, A. (2004) 'Contemporary euroscepticism in the party systems of the European Union candidate states of Central and Eastern Europe', *European Journal of Political Research*, 43(1), 1–27.

Taggart, P. and Szczerbiak, A. (2008) *Opposing Europe: The comparative party politics of Euroscepticism* (2 vols) (Oxford: Oxford University Press).

Temin, P. (2002) 'The golden age of European growth reconsidered', *European Review of Economic History*, 6(1), 3–22.

Tett, G. (2013) 'An interview with Alan Greenspan', *Financial Times*.

Thatcher, M. (1984) 'Europe – the future', *Journal of Common Market Studies*, 84(1), 73–81.

Therborn, G. (1995) *European Modernity and Beyond* (London: Sage).

Togan, S. (2002) 'Turkey: towards EU accession', *Working Papers Economic Research Forum*, 0202.

Tsoukalis, L. (2003) *What Kind of Europe?* (Oxford: Oxford University Press).

Tsoukalis, L. (2011) 'The shattering of illusions – and what next?', *Journal of Common Market Studies*, 46 (Annual Review), 19–44.

Tsoukalis, L. (2014) 'The unhappy state of the Union: Europe needs a new grand bargain', *Policy pamphlet for Policy Network*.

UCL (2012) *The Impact of the Economic Downturn and Policy Changes on Health Inequalities in London*, www.instituteofhealthequity.org/projects/ demographics-finance-and-policy-london-2011-15-effects-on-housing-employment-and-income-and-strategies-to-reduce-health-inequalities, date accessed 21 November 2013.

United Nations, Department of Economic and Social Affairs, Population Division (2013) "Median age" and "Dependency ratio", *World Population Prospects: The 2012 Revision*, www.esa.un.org/wpp/unpp/panel_indicators.htm, date accessed 11 December 2013.

UNCTAD (2012) 'Chapter III: Evolution of income inequality: different time perspectives and dimensions', *Trade and development report, 2012 (UNCTAD/TDR/2012)*, Geneva.

UNCTAD (2013) *Inward and outward FDI stock total*, www.unctadstat. unctad. org/ReportFolders/reportFolders.aspx?sRF_ActivePath=P,5,27&sRF_Expanded=,P,5,27, date accessed 1 November 2013.

Uras, U. (2013) 'EU starts talking Turkey – again', *Aljazeera*, www.aljazeera.com/indepth/features/2013/10/eu-starts-talking-turkey-again-20131025105212119512.html, date accessed 29 November 2013.

Vachudova, M.A. (2009) 'Corruption and compliance in the EU's post-communist members and candidates', *Journal of Common Market Studies*, 47(s1), 43–62.

Van Rompuy, H. (2012) *Towards a Genuine Economic and Monetary Union*, www. ec.europa.eu/economy_finance/crisis/documents/131201_en.pdf.

Vargas-Silva, C. (2013) 'Migration flows of A8 and other EU migrants to and from the UK', *Oxford Migration Observatory – Briefing*, www.migration observatory.ox.ac. uk/sites/files/migobs/Migration%20Flows%20of%20A8%20and%20other%20 EU%20Migrants%20to%20and%20from%20the%20UK.pdf, date accessed 29 November 2013.

Vogler, J. (2011) 'The challenge of the environment, energy and climate change' in C. Hill and M. Smith (eds) *International Relations and the European Union* (Oxford: Oxford University Press).

Wagener, H.-J. (2002) 'The welfare state in transition economies and accession to the EU' in P. Mair and J. Zielonka (eds) *The Enlarged European Union: Diversity and adaptation* (London: Frank Cass).

Wallace, H., Wallace, W. and Pollack, M. (eds) (2005) *Policy-making in the European Union* (Oxford: Oxford University Press).

Wallace, W. (1983) 'Less than a federation, more than a regime: the community as a political system' in H. Wallace, *et al.* (eds) *Policy-Making in the European Community* (Chichester: John Wiley).

Wallace, W. (2005) 'Foreign and security policy: the painful path from shadow to substance' in H. Wallace, W. Wallace and M. Pollack (eds) *Policy-making in the European Union* (Oxford: Oxford University Press).

Warrell, H. (2013) 'Influx of EU workers sparks surprise rise in migration', *Financial Times*, www.ft.com/cms/s/0/c7301c46-581d-11e3-a2ed-00144 feabdc0.html?siteedition=uk#axzz2lpTfceIt, date accessed 29 November 2013.

Waterfield, B. (2009a) 'Anger at plans for 'official' European history', *The Telegraph*, http:www.telegraph.co.uk/news/worldnews/Europe/4077245/Anger-at-plans-for-official-European-history.html, date accessed 9 May 2014.

Waterfield, B. (2009b) 'Profile: Baroness Ashton, EU's new foreign minister', *The Telegraph*, www.telegraph.co.uk/news/worldnews/europe/eu/6609910/Profile-Baroness-Ashton-EUs-new-foreign-minister.html, date accessed 20 November 2010.

Watkins, S. (2013) 'Vanity and venality', *London Review of Books*, 35(16), 17–21.

Weber, M. (1976) *Peasants into Frenchmen* (Stanford: Stanford University Press).

Weiler, J.H.H. (1999) *The Constitution of Europe* (Cambridge: Harvard University Press).

Weingast, B.R. (1995) 'The economic role of political institutions: market-preserving federalism and economic development', *Journal of Law, Economics and Organization*, 11(1), 1–31.

Wells, H.G. (1930) *The Way to World Peace* (London: Benn).

Weschler, L. (1984) 'The twenty-one demands', *The Passion of Poland* (New York: Pantheon).

White, S., Korosteleva, J. and McAllister, I. (2008) 'A wider Europe? The view from Russia, Belarus and Ukraine', *Journal of Common Market Studies*, 46(2), 219–41.

Whitman, R.G. and Juncos, A.E. (2012) 'The Arab Spring, the Eurozone crisis and the neighbourhood: a region in flux', *Journal of Common Market Studies*, 50 (Annual Review), 147–61.

Wiener, A. and Diez, T. (2009) *European Integration Theory* (Oxford: Oxford University Press).

Wiesmann, G. (2012) 'Germany approves new Greek bailout', *Financial Times*, www.ft.com/cms/s/0/b0349fbe-3adf-11e2-b3f0-00144feabdc0.html#axzz2lIgw0f73, date accessed 21 November 2013.

Wilde, O. (1892/1995) *Lady Windermere's Fan* (London: Penguin).

Willetts, D. (2010) *The Pinch – How the baby boomers took their children's future and why they should give it back* (London: Atlantic Books).

Wincott, D. (2003) 'The idea of the European social model: limits and paradoxes of Europeanization' in K. Featherston and C. Radaelli (eds) *The Politics of Europeanization* (Oxford: Oxford University Press).

Wohlfahrt, C. (2009) 'The Lisbon Case: a critical summary', *German Law Journal*, 10, 1277–86.

World Bank (2013a) *Estimates of Migrants Stocks 2010*, available at www.econ.worldbank.org/WBSITE/EXTERNAL/EXTDEC/EXTDECPROSPECTS/0,,contentMDK:22803131~pagePK:64165401~piPK:64165026~theSitePK:476883,00.html, date accessed 30 October 2013.

World Bank (2013b) *Unemployment Total (% of total labor force)*, available at www.data.worldbank.org/indicator/SL.UEM.TOTL.ZS/countries?display= default, date accessed 1 November 2013.

World Bank (2013c) *GDP per capita (current US$), GNI per capita (current US$) & GNI per capita/PPP (current international $)*, www.data.worldbank.org/topic/economic-policy-and-external-debt, date accessed 2 November 2013.

World Bank (2013d) *Current Account Balance (current US$)*, www.data.worldbank.org/indicator/BN.CAB.XOKA.CD/countries, date accessed 18 November 2013.

World Bank (2013e) *Indice de Gini*, www.donnees.banquemondiale.org/indicateur/SI.POV.GINI, date accessed 26 November 2013.

World Bank (2013f) *High Technology Exports* www.data.worldbank.org/indicator/TX.VAL.TECH.CD, date accessed 26 November 2013.

World Bank (2014a) *GDP per capita (current US$)*, http://data.worldbank.org/indicator/NY.GDP.PCAP.CD, date accessed 25 September 2014.

World Bank (2014b), *GDP growth (annual %)*, http://data.worldbank.org/indicator/NY.GDP.MKTP.KD.ZG, date accessed 25 September 2014.

World Bank (2014c), *GDP (current US$)*, http://data.worldbank.org/indicator/NY.GDP.MKTP.CD, date accessed 3 October 2014

World Economics (2013) *Maddison Historical GDP Data*, www.worldeconomics.com/Data/MadisonHistoricalGDP/Madison%20Historical%20GDP%20Data.efp, date accessed 26 November 2013.

WTO (2013) *EU Trade Profile*, www.stat.wto.org/CountryProfile/WSDBCountryPFView.aspx?Language=E&Country=E27, date accessed 30 October 2013.

Xiaoping, D. (1984) *Build Socialism with Chinese Characteristics*, www.academics.wellesley.edu/Polisci/wj/China/Deng/Building.htm, date accessed 29 November 2013.

Youngs, R. (2010) *The EU's Role in World Politics: A retreat from liberal internationalism* (London: Routledge).

Your Europe (2012) *Passenger Rights*, www.europa.eu/youreurope/citizens/ travel/passenger-rights/air/, date accessed 22 November 2013.

Zakaria, F. (1997) 'The rise of illiberal democracy', *Foreign Affairs*, 76(6), 22–43.

Index